A HISTORY OF THE MEDIA
IN IRELAND

From the first book printed in Ireland in the sixteenth century, to the globalised digital media culture of today, Christopher Morash traces the history of forms of communication in Ireland over the past four centuries: the vigorous newspaper and pamphlet culture of the eighteenth century, the spread of popular literacy in the nineteenth century, and the impact of the telegraph, telephone, phonograph, cinema and radio, which arrived in Ireland just as the Irish Free State came into being. Morash picks out specific events for detailed analysis, such as the first radio broadcast, during the 1916 Rising, or the Live Aid concert in 1985. Outlining new ways to think about Irish culture, this important book breaks new ground within Irish studies. Its accessible narrative explains how Ireland developed into the modern, globally interconnected economy of today. This is an essential and hugely informative read for anyone interested in Irish cultural history.

CHRISTOPHER MORASH is Professor of English at the National University of Ireland, Maynooth. He is the author of *A History of Irish Theatre 1601–2000* (Cambridge, 2002; paperback edition, 2004).

A HISTORY OF THE MEDIA
IN IRELAND

CHRISTOPHER MORASH

CAMBRIDGE
UNIVERSITY PRESS

CAMBRIDGE UNIVERSITY PRESS
Cambridge, New York, Melbourne, Madrid, Cape Town, Singapore,
São Paulo, Delhi, Dubai, Tokyo

Cambridge University Press
The Edinburgh Building, Cambridge CB2 8RU, UK

Published in the United States of America by Cambridge University Press, New York

www.cambridge.org
Information on this title: www.cambridge.org/9780521843928

First published 2010

Printed in the United Kingdom at the University Press, Cambridge

A catalogue record for this publication is available from the British Library

Library of Congress Cataloging-in-Publication Data
Morash, Chris, 1963–
A history of the media in Ireland / Christopher Morash.
p.   cm.
Includes bibliographical references and index.
ISBN 978-0-521-84392-8 (hardback)
1. Mass media–Ireland–History. I. Title.
P92.I76M67 2009
302.2309417–dc22

2009035297

ISBN 978-0-521-84392-8 Hardback

Contents

Illustrations

Figures

Acknowledgements

This book makes forays into so many discrete disciplines that I wrote it with an acute sense of standing on the shoulders of a great many diverse scholars, from early print specialists, to railway and postal historians, to commentators on contemporary broadcasting legislation. In recompense, I hope that these scholars in turn will find here, at the very least, something that will connect their own fields to others in ways that might be new or unexpected. More specifically, I would like to thank the numerous librarians and archivists who were so generous with their time, with particular thanks to the staff of the National Library of Ireland, the Royal Irish Academy, the British Library, RTÉ, the Linenhall Library and the National Archives of Ireland (who are owed particular thanks for permission to quote from unpublished materials contained here). Charles Benson of Early Printed Books in Trinity College Dublin, was a particular source of wisdom, as were Nicholas Carolan in the Irish Traditional Music Archive and the staff of the library at the National University of Ireland, Maynooth (especially Penny Woods in the Russell Library). I also found (perhaps ironically for a book that is about everything other than face-to-face conversation) that ideas for the project as often as not arose from talking with colleagues too numerous to name in the NUI Maynooth, where a genuine collegiality makes it possible to have enthusiastic discussions with friends in many fields, including Diarmuid O'Donoghue in the Department of Computer Science, who generously provided me with his work on internet visualisation. I owe particular thanks to colleagues in the School of English, Media and Theatre Studies, for their conversation, ideas and friendship. Three former students, Denis Condon, Deirdre Quinn and Tom Richards, particularly helped me to shape my ideas. Further afield, Peter Hart was especially helpful. The nature of this project was such that I picked up ideas from good friends outside of academia, especially Dave Selkirk and Woytek Kosinski, an engineer and an internet entrepreneur respectively. The organisers of the

2008 International Association for the Study of Irish Literature (IASIL) conference in Porto gave me the opportunity to give some of the work here a public airing at a crucial stage, in a way that valuably sharpened the argument for me. I was also fortunate in the final stages in having a keen research assistant, Shane Creevy, funded under NUI Maynooth's SPUR initiative to encourage young researchers.

From the beginning, my editor at Cambridge, Ray Ryan, believed in this project; for bringing into the medium of print so many important contributions to Irish studies he has earned his own place in this history. Throughout the writing of this book, I have had a sense that it has all really been an attempt to explain the intensely mediated world of my children, Christopher, Dara and Aoife, who will know better than most why I dedicate it to the person to whom we all owe most, my wife Ann.

Chronology

1800	Act of Union
1801	Copyright Act (41 Geo. III cap. 107)
1803	Abortive rising led by Robert Emmet
1813	Irish Endowed Schools Act (53 Geo. III, cap. 107)
	Paddle steamer *Thames* makes first crossing from Dublin to London
	Bianconi cars begin running from Clonmel to Cahir
1818	*Rob Roy* makes first steam crossing between Clyde and Belfast
1824	*Morning Register* (Dublin)
1828	*Pilot* (Dublin)
1829	Catholic Emancipation
1831	Postmaster General Act (1 Will. IV, cap. 8)
	Act Authorising Dublin–Kingstown Railway (1 and 2 Will. IV, cap. 69)
1832	*Dublin Penny Journal*
1833	*Dublin University Magazine*
	First steam-powered press in Ireland
1834	Dublin–Kingstown Railway; first in Ireland
1837	First commercial telegraph line, London
1838	Steamer *Sirius* makes first trans-Atlantic crossing without sail, Cork to New York
1839	Daguerre makes public technique for daguerrotypes
1841	*Cork Examiner*
	First photographic studio opens in Dublin
1842	*The Nation* (Dublin; suppressed 1848)
1844	Samuel Morse invents Morse Code
	First Irish telegraph line, Dalkey
1845	Great telescope at Birr Castle completed
	Potato crop fails; first year of Famine
1848	*United Irishman* (suppressed May, 1848)
	Abortive Young Ireland rebellion
	Regular mail service by rail between London and Dublin
1851	Julius Reuter founds telegraph news agency
1852	Submarine telegraph cable, Holyhead to Howth
1853	Dublin–Belfast rail line
1858	First trans-Atlantic telegraph cable
1859	*Irish Times* (Dublin)
1863	*The Irish People* (Dublin; suppressed 1865)
1866	First regular trans-Atlantic telegraph service

1867   Fenian disturbances in England and Ireland
        Clan na Gael founded in New York
1870   *Irish World* (New York)
        Belfast Telegraph
1873   *Irish Monthly Magazine*
1874   650,000 miles of telegraph cable worldwide
1875   *Southern Cross* (Buenos Aires)
1876   Alexander Graham Bell patents telephone
1878   Thomas Edison patents phonograph
1879   University Education (Ireland) Act (42 & 43 Vict. cap. 65)
1880   First Irish telephone exchange opens, Dublin
1881   *United Ireland* (Dublin)
1882   *Irisleabhar na Gaedhilge: the Gaelic Journal*
1884   Gaelic Athletic Association formed
1890   Eaweard Muybridge displays zoopraxiscope, Dublin
1891   *Irish Daily Independent* (Dublin)
        Death of Parnell
1892   Irish Education Act (55 and 56 Vict. cap. 42); compulsory
        education
1893   Electric railways from Haddington Road to Dalkey
        Gaelic League founded
1895   *Irish Homestead*
        Edison kinetoscope on display in Dublin
1896   First Irish cinematograph show, at Olympia Theatre
        First phonographs for home use
1897   First Lumière films made in Ireland
        Marconi patents wireless telegraphy
1898   First use of wireless telegraph for news reporting, Dublin
1899   First production of Irish Literary Theatre
1903   John McCormack; first recording
        Wyndham Land Act, allows tenants to buy land
1905   *Sunday Independent* (Dublin)
1907   Wireless trans-Atlantic telegraph begins
1910   *The Lad from Old Ireland* (dir. Sidney Olcott); first feature
        film shot in Ireland
1913   Irish Transport and General Workers' Strike
1916   Easter Rising; rebels attempt radio transmission
1919   First meeting of Dáil Éireann
1920   KDKA begins broadcasting in Philadelphia

1921	Anglo-Irish Treaty ends War of Independence
1922	Beginning of Civil War
	Marconi Company makes first English radio broadcast
	BBC begins broadcasting
1923	White Paper on Wireless Broadcasting
	De Valera orders suspension of Anti-Treaty Campaign
	Irish Statesman (Dublin)
	Dublin Magazine
	Censorship of Films Act
1924	BBC Belfast first broadcast as 2BE
1925	Boundary Commission defines border between Free State and Northern Ireland
1926	First broadcast of 2RN
	John Logie Baird demonstrates 'televisor' in Dublin
1929	Censorship of Publications Act
1931	*Irish Press* (Dublin)
1934	*Man of Aran* (dir. Robert Flaherty)
1936	*Vigilanti Cura*; Papal Encyclical on cinema
	BBC begin first regular television broadcasts
1937	EMI open first Dublin recording studio
	Irish Constitution
1940	*The Bell* (Dublin)
1948	33 rpm LP and 45 rpm single replace 78 rpm disc
1949	Republic of Ireland Act
1952	BBC television begins broadcasting from Belfast
1954	Television Act lays basis for commercial television in UK
1958	Ardmore Studios (cinema) opens, Bray
1959	UTV begins broadcasting, Belfast
1960	Broadcasting Authority Act
1961	Telefís Éireann; first broadcast (New Year's Eve)
1962	First broadcast of *The Late Late Show*
	Telstar satellite launched
1964	Radio Caroline begins broadcasting in North Sea
1968	Television coverage of disturbances in Northern Ireland
	Satellite coverage of Mexico City Olympics; first major live global television event
1969	First email sent; UCLA to Stanford University
	Riots in Derry and Belfast; British troops enter Northern Ireland

1970	*Fortnight* (Belfast)
1971	First colour broadcast by RTÉ
	Directive under Section 31 of Broadcasting Act bans interviews with members of organisations linked to political violence
1972	'Bloody Sunday'; British Army kill thirteen people in Derry
1973	*Sunday World* (Dublin)
1974	First use of word 'internet' to describe linked computers
1976	*In Dublin* (Dublin)
1977	*Hot Press* (Dublin)
	Magill (Dublin)
1978	RTÉ2 (television)
1979	RTÉ launches Radio 2
1980	*Sunday Tribune* (Dublin)
1982	*Angel* (dir. Neil Jordan); first film funded by Irish Film Board
1986	Anglo-Irish Agreement
1988	Broadcasting and Wireless Telegraphy Act
	Section 35 of Finance Bill facilitates film production
	Independent Radio and Television Commission (IRTC)
1989	First licensed commercial station in Republic: Capital Radio
	Sky begins satellite broadcasting
	EU Television without Frontiers Directive
	My Left Foot (dir. Jim Sheridan) wins two Oscars, 1990
1990	Tim Berners-Lee and Robert Cailliau develop World Wide Web
1994	IRA announces ceasefire; Loyalist paramilitaries follow
	Netscape Navigator launched
	Irish Times launches online edition: Ireland.com
1995	First computer operating system with web browser: Windows 95
	Green Paper on Broadcasting
	Referendum legalises divorce in Republic
1996	Telefís na Gaeilge begins broadcasting (TG4 as of 1999)
1998	First commercial broadcaster in Republic: TV3
	Michael Collins (dir. Neil Jordan)
	Good Friday Agreement
1999	Exchequer surplus in Republic exceeds €1 billion
2000	*Metro Éireann*, multi-ethnic newspaper (Dublin)
2002	*Foreign Policy* ranks Ireland as world's most globalised society

2003   BBC begins Digital Audio Broadcasting (DAB) in Northern
        Ireland
2008   Broadcasting Bill
        RTÉ begins DAB broadcasting; announces Digital Terrestrial
        Television (DTT) for 2009
        Economy enters recession

Introduction: Ireland and the world

There is a map, originally prepared for Lucien Febvre and Henri-Jean Martin's *L'Apparition du livre* in 1958, but reprinted frequently since, which shows the spread of printing in Europe before 1500. Little clusters of dots, densely packed around centres such as Venice and Strasbourg, more sparsely scattered elsewhere, indicate the first appearance of printed books in the half century after Gutenberg's introduction to Europe of moveable type in the 1450s. It is one of those clear, useful maps that unfolds for its reader an entire history at a glance, tracing the footprints of the new technology along trade routes and over the Alps, as it defines a new geography of knowledge.

For the Irish reader, however, this map tells a different story – although perhaps not the one its authors intended. The map's legend, explaining the meaning of the variously shaped dots, is placed squarely in the upper left-hand corner, completely blotting out the entire island of Ireland. In the early history of the printed word, Ireland simply does not exist.

If we move forward to the year 2004, the journal *Foreign Policy* published a bar graph, like a silhouetted cityscape, showing what it considered to be the sixty-two most globalised countries in the world, based on four criteria: economic integration, personal contact, techno-logical connectivity and political engagement. For the third year in a row, towering over the rest of the world, as 'the most globalized country in the world', was Ireland, ahead of Singapore and Switzerland in second and third place, well clear both of the United States in seventh place and of the United Kingdom in twelfth. Ireland's new status as the world's most globalised nation was buoyed not only by massive amounts of foreign inward investment, but also by being among the most connected coun-tries on the planet, ranking seventh, for instance, in the number of secure internet servers per capita.

In a sense, this book is about the territory between these two points; it is the story of how a particular culture, with a particular history, interacted with a succession of new media – of which print is the earliest – all of which have a distinctive history in Ireland, but none of which originated in Ireland. When a German goldsmith, Johann Gutenberg, cut the first moveable type in Europe, he was changing Irish history. So too was Tim Berners-Lee when he wrote the code that would form the basis of the World Wide Web; but neither technological development would have an immediate impact on Ireland, and neither would have exactly the same impact on Ireland that they would have in other parts of the world.

Turning back to Febvre and Martin's map, the spine of early print-works from Mainz, where Gutenberg printed his Bible in the months just before August, 1456, to Lausanne and Grenoble, is, of course, the cradle of the Reformation; and, indeed, it has long been argued that the development of print made possible the Reformation, just as the string of early printers along the Italian coast, from Urbino, through Florence to Venice, map on to the centres we associate with the Renaissance. This equation of print with the Reformation and the Renaissance is so familiar that it is worth conjuring up, as Elizabeth L. Eisenstein does in *The Printing Press as an Agent of Change*, a 'counter-factual' past, in which the invention of the printing press might have been 'welcomed and put to entirely different uses – monopolized by priests and rulers, for example, and withheld from free-wheeling urban entrepreneurs.'[1] In a sense, Ireland in the sixteenth century was that 'counter-factual' land. A late adopter of print culture – the first book was not published in Ireland until 1551 – in Ireland print was not so much the cause of a Reformation, as the product of the Reformation in England.

That this kind of reversal of cause and effect is possible in an Irish context should warn us against any simple kind of technological determinism, one that would retrospectively see the effects of any given new media as inevitable. Certainly, innovations in media technology can have social and cultural effects. There is little doubt, for instance, that had moveable type (or something like it) not been developed in the middle of the fifteenth century, European history would have taken a different course. At the same time, there is no guarantee that any given society will adopt a new technology simply because it is new or better; nor is there any guarantee that, if it is introduced, it will have a predictable effect; or, indeed, if we can be reasonably sure of anything in this regard, it is that the effect of a given media technology has as much to do with the culture in which it arrives as it does with the nature of the technology itself. So, if

[1] Elizabeth L. Eisenstein, *The Printing Press as an Agent of Change*, Vol. II (Cambridge, 1979), 703.

we consider the history of the mediated world from the perspective of a country such as Ireland, which is both part of Europe and yet has had a particular experience of colonisation, we get a very different perspective on the effects of the printing press, for instance, than we would if we looked at the same history from the perspective of Florence, Paris or London; and the same is true of the telegraph, or cinema, radio, television or the internet.

If an Irish perspective on the media allows us to see the history of the media differently, the opposite is also true: a media-history perspective on Irish history helps us to trace, over time, some of the ways life in Ireland has been shaped by, and has shaped, media technologies. If, for instance, we take it that geography has been a determining factor in Irish life, then it is worth thinking about the Irish sense of peripherality, of being on the balcony of Europe, and the ways in which this sense can ebb or flow with forms of media that are more or less constrained by geography. 'Oh, she is as mad', the character of Murrogh O'Dogherty complains of his wife in Charles Macklin's play *The True-Born Irishman* in 1762. 'The devil a thing in this poor country but what gives her the spleen, and the vapours – then such a phrenzy of admiration for every thing in England.'[2] To a large extent in the Dublin of the eighteenth century, that 'phrenzy' was the product of a thriving print culture, both in London and in Dublin, that carried accounts of London social, cultural and political life to avid Irish readers, for whom the very fact that such accounts could only be experienced in mediated form was a mark of their coloniality, their peripherality. In some ways, a similar moment occurred again, although in a different form, when cinema came to Ireland in the early decades of the twentieth century, and again when television arrived in the late 1950s and early 1960s, and the experience of watching American Westerns, for instance, helped contribute to a distinctive sense of being part of a cultural formation whose centre was elsewhere. By contrast, other media created something quite different, in the form of a simultaneous field with no centre and no periphery; there was a hint of this possibility in 1858, when the first trans-Atlantic telegraph cable ran from Valentia, in County Kerry, and suddenly made Mallow a suburb of New York, and Ireland a hub of a new telecommunications geography. That geography was reshaped again in the 1920s, during the early days of radio, when voices suddenly began flooding into Ireland from all over the world. And it would be transformed most fully and most radically in the final decade of

[2] Charles Macklin, *The True-Born Irishman* (Dublin, 1783), 8.

the twentieth century, with digital media that not only create a new spaceless geography, but are increasingly subsuming all earlier media within them.

This book attempts to trace this fluctuating world of mediated experience from an Irish perspective; of feeling both connected to, and at times distant from, a world that is outside of Ireland – and thereby demarcating the imagined space that is Ireland in the process. It is in this sense a history of the way in which Irish people have presented themselves to one another. From this point of view, it is a materialist history, a history of things: of books, railroads, canals, telegraph lines, cinema screens, phonograph cylinders, radio transmitters, fibre-optic cables and the ways in which they are produced, regulated and traded. What it is not is a history of oral culture. Words spoken from one person to another, unmediated by print or a radio microphone or a camera, are a kind of wild zone, falling outside of such a history. So, this book comes with a *caveat*: any claims that it makes must be qualified by the recognition that in parallel to the mediated Irish world, there is another world, a world of talk, of face-to-face conversation. Its importance in Irish culture is proverbial – but that in itself may well be, at least in part, a product of the history traced here.

CHAPTER I

'Stumpeworne letters': 1551–1660

BEGINNINGS

By the year 1500, more than fifty printing presses had been established in Germany; in Italy, seventy-two; in France, forty-one.

In Ireland, there were none.

It would not be until almost a century after Johann Gutenberg published his Bible in 1456 that the first book was printed in Ireland. In 1541, Henry VIII declared himself King of Ireland, signalling a new seriousness in the English project of governing Ireland that had been pursued in fits and starts since the twelfth century. As part of this initiative, under the Lord Deputy-ship of Sir Anthony St Leger in 1550, a London bookseller, Humphrey Powell, was granted £20 by an Act of the Privy Council in London to set up a printworks in Dublin. A year later, in 1551, he printed the earliest known Irish book, *The Boke of Common Praier* of the Anglican communion.

While this might seem superficially similar to the first moments of European print culture elsewhere (at least in that the first book printed was a religious book), the differences between Mainz and Dublin were profound. Gutenberg was a goldsmith by profession, who developed moveable type with the help of an investment from a Mainz lawyer; hence, from what little documentation exists, it would seem that their choice of the Bible as the first book to print was, to a some extent, a prescient piece of market calculation. Powell's Dublin press, on the other hand, did not arise out of an indigenous culture, nor did it respond to a need in the marketplace. In any case, Powell certainly did not see his Irish monopoly as much of a business opportunity, for in the following seventeen years he appears to have printed only three other sheets of paper: *A Proclamacyon set fourth ... Against Shane O'Neil* (1561); a similar proclamation against the 'rebels of the O'Conors' (1564), and *A Brefe Declaration of Certein Principall Articles of Religion* (1567) – after which he retired, presumably not unduly exhausted by his labours.

It would be wrong, however, to blame Humphrey Powell for Ireland's less than spectacular entry into the world of print. A contrast with the situation in England is useful here. In 1557, shortly after Powell was given his Irish patent, Queen Mary established the Stationers' Company, and gave them control over nearly all the printers in England. While this had the effect of maintaining a measure of state control, it also permitted competition among licensed printers within a regulated marketplace. As a result, printing thrived. In Ireland, restricting the function of print to religious works and proclamations assigned to print a very limited, and (for the vast majority of the population) oppositional role in the culture. Printing a proclamation rather than having it copied by hand was not done out of necessity, given that most were only a single sheet, and they do not appear to have been distributed in great numbers in any case. The point in printing a proclamation or ordinance was a public display of the technological prowess of the administration. In a society in which the press was tightly controlled, a printed proclamation, whatever else it said, always made one clear statement on behalf of the colonial administration to the population as a whole: we have the technology to do this (and you do not).

The initial impact of print in Ireland, then, was to draw yet another line of division in a culture that was already riven with fissures of linguistic, religious, political, familial and ethnic allegiances. That print was to be an instrument in the Crown's efforts to reassert control in Ireland, and to push forward the parallel project of extending the English Reformation to Ireland, was further underlined in 1571, when, under the Lord Deputyship of Sir Henry Sidney, Queen Elizabeth paid for the first set of Irish type to be cut. From this set of letters, an anonymous printer (possibly John Kearney, the Treasurer of St Patrick's Cathedral), produced the first printed book in Irish in Ireland, *Aibidil Gaoidheilge agus Caiticiosma* (illustration 1). Along with the very first book printed in Irish, *Foirm na nUrrnuidheadh* (which was produced by an Edinburgh press in 1567), *Aibidil* would be the first of many attempts to use print to provide a reformed catechism for an Irish-language readership, 'for the glory of God and the queen of this realm'. However, *Aibidil* is more than simply a catechism. Near the front of the book, it presents its reader with a three-column table, beginning (on the left, where the eye would fall first) with a letter from the new Irish type; followed by its phonetic equivalent, which is followed in turn by the roman equivalent. As a book, *Aibidil* thus shows an excited, self-conscious awareness that it is performing an act of translation – or perhaps, more precisely, an act of conversion – in

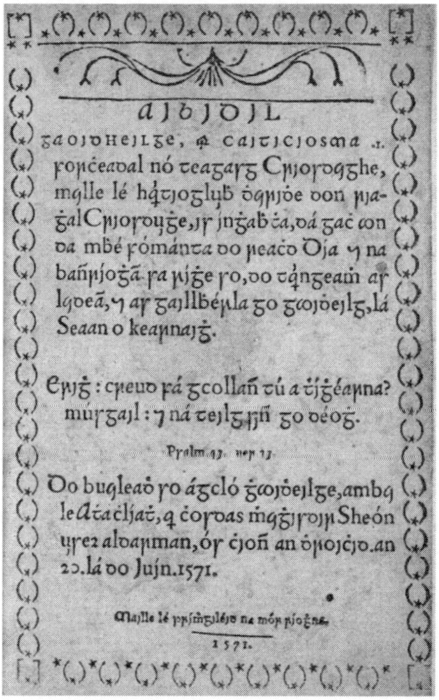
AIBIDIL
GAOIDHEILGE, & CAITICIOSMA .i.
forcheadal nó teagasg Criosdaighe,
maille lé hairtioglaibh áirighe don ria-
ghail Chriosdaighe, is inghabhtha, dá gach aon
da mbé fómánta do reacht Dia ⁊ na
banríoghna fa ríghe so, do tairngeamh as
laidean, ⁊ as gallbhéarla go gaoidheilg, lá
Seaan o Kearnaigh.

Eirigh: creud fá gcolladh tú a thighearna?
múscail: ⁊ ná teilg inn go deóigh.

Psalm 43. vers 23.

Do buaileadh so a gcló gaoidheilge, a mbaile
Athacliath, ar chostas maighistir Sheón
Uiser aldarman, os cionn an droichid an
20. lá do Iuin. 1571.

Maille lé priuiléid na mór ríoghna.

1571.

Illustration 1. *Aibidil Gaoidheilge agus Caiticiosma*, the first book printed in Irish in Ireland, was produced with specially cut type in 1571. It would be the first of many attempts to provide an Irish-language readership with a reformed catechism.

bringing the Irish language into print, mediating between manuscript, print and the sounds of language.

The existence of an Irish typeface as early as 1571 raises an obvious question: why did the first printed book in Irish not appear under the patronage of a Gaelic, or an Old English nobleman? While it is always slightly suspect from an historical point of view to ask why something did *not* happen, it is worth speculating why sixteenth-century Gaelic Ireland never developed its own print culture (just as it never developed its own theatre). While the Lords Deputy kept tight control of the Dublin printworks, their control of anything outside of Dublin was far from complete. At the very least, it could be said that there have certainly been other times and other places in which illegal hand presses operated under much more watchful eyes than those that looked out over large stretches of Connaught and Ulster in the sixteenth century.

In the first instance, to say that Gaelic Ireland had no printing presses is not to say that it had no books. Ireland had been producing manuscript books for a very long time prior to the arrival of print in the 1550s. The earliest surviving Irish manuscripts date from the seventh century, but in some cases appear to have been based on even earlier written texts, now lost. Still, an astounding amount of material survives; and, even more remarkably, much of it is not in Latin, but in the vernacular, Irish. The arrival of print – at least initially – had little impact on the practice of copying books by hand in Ireland, which would continue for certain texts well into the nineteenth century. To understand the culture in which these manuscripts were produced and circulated, however, it is worth remembering that they were part of a complex and highly formalised oral tradition. 'The *seanchas* [law] of the men of Ireland, what has sustained it?' asks the author of an eighth-century legal document, *An Seanchas Mór*. 'The joint memory of the old men, transmission from one ear to another, the chanting of the *filid*, supplementation from the law of the letter.'[1] In the case of legal texts, as with other forms of knowledge in Gaelic culture, manuscripts would often appear to have achieved fullness of meaning only when read in conjunction with knowledge that had been transmitted orally.

It could well have been the case that sixteenth-century Gaelic Ireland was a classic instance of a culture in which one kind of information technology was so tightly entangled with other kinds of social networks that innovation offended powerful vested interests – in this case, the families of hereditary scholars, bards and *filid*, whose guardianship of both manuscripts and orature provided them with access to knowledge and to power. There is certainly at least one document from the period that suggests members of traditional bardic families felt that that their hereditary craft was incompatible with the new world of print. 'I have decided on another profession, to abandon Gaelic poetry,' wrote Giolla Brighde Ó hEoghusa to a friend, explaining his decision to become a Franciscan friar in Leuven.

It is not hatred of my forefather's art that has unsettled my mind; nor the fact that the honour which was once bestowed on it by the Irish race has disappeared.

---

[1] Cited in Jane Stevenson, 'Literacy and Orality in Early Modern Ireland', in *Cultural Identity and Cultural Integration: Ireland and Europe in the Early Middle Ages*, ed. Doris Edel (Dublin, 1995), 11–22, 13.

Though our knowledge of them is small, it is the study of learned books – the most noble profession known to me – that has enticed me away from you.[2]

For those not 'enticed away', it may have been that the fundamentally local nature of extended family ties within Gaelic society meant that there was no pressing need for new instruments of mass communication, at least within Ireland,

At the same time, any need to spread ideas further afield could be better met through Continental printing presses. The centrality of the Catholic Church to Gaelic culture meant that many Irish scholar-clerics had access to a Europe-wide network of Catholic printers, from Paris to Leuven (where the Franciscans opened their own printshop) to Rheims. Indeed, as early as the 1490s, Maurice O'Fihely – born in Baltimore, County Cork, and later Archbishop of Tuam – was principal corrector at Octavian Schott's press in Venice, which published his *Enchiridion fidei* in 1500.[3] More than a century later, Thomas Messingham published his *Florilegium sanctorum, sue vitae et acta sanctorum Hiberniae* in Paris in 1624, and other Irish writers published works with the press established in 1611 by the Franciscans in St Anthony's College, Leuven.

Indeed, it has been argued that the Franciscan press in Leuven was to have a profound effect on the development of modern Irish. The Franciscans realised that if they were to counter the effect of Protestant works such as the *Aibidil*, they would need to use a written form of Irish that was more direct, and less ornate than that which had evolved in bardic culture, particularly with work that they were translating from other European languages. 'Our aim in writing is not to teach Irish but repentance,' wrote Aodh Mac Aingil, in his devotional work, *Scáthán Shacramuinte na hAithridhe*, published in Leuven in 1618. 'The trauma of the seventeenth century had, in a one sense, a curiously liberatory effect,' observes one historian of translation. 'The emphasis on greater simplicity and communicative effectiveness that guided the translation work in Leuven and elsewhere would embolden others in their rejection of strict adherence to bardic conventions.'[4] In other words, one lineage of modern Irish leads

[2] Cited in Katharine Simms, 'Literacy and the Irish Bards', in *Literacy in Medieval Celtic Societies*, ed. Huw Pryce (Cambridge, 1998), 238–58, 253.

[3] Robert Welch, 'The Book in Ireland from the Tudor Re-conquest to the Battle of the Boyne', in *The Cambridge History of the Book in Britain*, Vol. IV, ed. John Barnard and D.F. McKenzie (Cambridge, 2002), 701–18, 704.

[4] Cited in (and translated by) Michael Cronin, *Translating Ireland: Translation, Languages, Cultures* (Cork, 1996), 63.

back to the printing press in Leuven, and an attempt to adapt the language to the new medium of print.

Insofar as the press in Leuven was a Counter-Reformation response to the Dublin press, it could be said that the publication of the *Aibidil* did have an important, if largely unintended, indirect effect. And yet, in other ways, it now appears almost like a book existing in a vacuum, produced only because there was a powerful ideological logic that it should exist. Nonetheless, this same emerging evangelical imperative to see the word of God in every possible language was enough to carry the project of printing in Irish forward, and in 1587 the Irish type cut for the *Aibidil* was passed on to William Kearney (a nephew of John Kearney, who had died in 1581), who was given the right to print the New Testament in Irish. Kearney arrived in Ireland in 1592, the same year that Trinity College Dublin, was founded, and by 1595 he was based in the College, where he printed a partial New Testament. As Queen's Printer, he also picked up Powell's old business of printing proclamations, with the innovation that his proclamation against Hugh O'Neill, for instance, was printed bilingually, in both English and Irish. In the end, the fact that the first printed Bible in Irish, and a proclamation outlawing one of the leaders of Gaelic Ireland should both have been produced with different combinations of the same pieces of moveable type can stand as an icon of the place of Irish in the attenuated print culture of sixteenth-century Ireland.

'UTTERLY LOST, AND BURIED IN OBLIVION'

The trickle of print in any language in the Ireland of the sixteenth century – eight items in fifty years – does not mean, however, that there were no printed books in Ireland in the early seventeenth century; quite the contrary. A catalogue of the library of the ninth Earl of Kildare, Gerald Fitzgerald, from 1526, for instance, lists ninety-two items, many of which were printed, including a copy of Sir Thomas More's *Utopia*, first published in 1516.[5] As early as 1545, a Dublin stationer, James Dartas, was selling books in Dublin, and there is some evidence to suggest that there were books printed in London prior to 1550 specifically for the Dublin market.[6] Gradually, then, books were creeping into the country,

---

[5] Elizabeth Boran, 'Libraries and Collecting, 1550–1700', in *The Oxford History of the Irish Book*, Vol. III: *The Book in English 1550–1800*, ed. Raymond Gillespie and Andrew Hadfield (Oxford, 2006), 91–110, 97.

[6] Raymond Gillespie, 'Print Culture 1550–1700', in *The Oxford History of the Irish Book*, Vol. III: *The Book in English 1550–1800*, ed. Gillespie and Hadfield, 17–33, 18.

where they were sold, often by general merchants, ranged along the shelves with soap, socks and candles. For instance, Raymond Gillespie's analysis of port records from the city of Bristol shows a steady increase in the number of books being shipped into southern Ireland from the late sixteenth century onwards, from 553 in 1592, to 2,675 in 1612. These books found their way into shops in Cork, Limerick, Waterford and Kilkenny, where customers could buy titles including *The Right and Variable Tradigall history of Fortuanus*, Francis Seager's *School of Virtue* (a didactic religious work for children), as well as classical works by Ovid, Virgil, Catullus, Cicero and Peter Ramus's *Dialectica*. What is more, Catholic books were entering the country. Although it is difficult to track this illegal trade, a ship seized in Cork in 1617, for instance, was found to be carrying Latin Bibles, the *Rituale Romanum, Summae doctrinaie Christianae* and a *Malleus maleficarum*, while an Irishman, Patrick Dones, based in Rouen, earned at least part of his living by shipping Catholic books from Newhaven to Ireland.[7]

This steady growth in the book trade in the years before and after 1601 forms an unexpected counterpoint to some of the most traumatic and chaotic years in Irish history. As Hugh O'Neill made his way from Ulster to Kinsale, through an Ireland 'harried and wasted', books were trickling into the ports. In the wake of the Battle of Kinsale, as the new Lord Deputy, Sir George Carey, set about establishing a centralised administration, it must have become clear that if left to its own devices, the market would produce a print culture in Ireland of its own accord. So, in 1604 a patent – in manuscript – was issued to John Franckton, giving him the sole right to 'imprint, bynde, setforth, offer to sale, or sell … within this Kingdome of Ireland, any bookes, volumes, Statutes, proclamations, Almanackes, or other bookes',[8] and thus making him the first King's Printer in Ireland.

While Franckton's output was not great – he averaged about two items per year – his time as King's Printer, until 1618, sees a slightly more nuanced understanding of the possible role of print in Irish culture. For instance, John Davies, Ireland's Attorney General from 1606 to 1619, argued in his influential polemic, *A Discoverie of the True Causes Why Ireland Was Never Entirely Subdued* (1612), that earlier conquests of Ireland had never taken root because 'the Kings of England … did not

---

[7] Raymond Gillespie, 'The Book Trade in Southern Ireland, 1590–1640', in *Books Beyond the Pale: Aspects of the Provincial Book Trade in Ireland before 1850* (Dublin, 1996), 1–17.
[8] Cited in Robert Munter, *A Dictionary of the Print Trade in Ireland, 1550–1775* (New York, 1988), 107.

upon the submissions of the Irish, communicate their Lawes unto them, nor admit them to the state and condition of Free-subjectes.'[9] For Davies, then, the 'true causes why Ireland was never entirely subdued' could be traced, at least in part, to poor communications hindering the functioning of a centralised administration – for which print provided an obvious remedy. The common law of England, he writes later, 'is nothing else but the Common custome of the Realme: … it can be recorded and registered no where, but in the memory of the people.' In Ireland, however, where the 'Common custome' was not common for historical reasons, it was necessary to have published records of legal case histories. Accordingly, in 1615 Davies published *Le Primer report des Cases & Matters en Ley resolues & adiudges en les Courts del Roy en Ireland*:

During all the time that the lawes of England have had theire course in Ireland, which is nowe full foure hundred years, there hath not beene any Report made & published of any Case in lawe, argued and adjudged in this Kingdome; but all the arguments & reasons of the judgements & resolutions given in the Courts of Ireland, have hitherto beene utterly lost, & buried in oblivion.[10]

For Davies, it was a matter of policy that Irish case law be given the permanence and authority of print. What is more, he published this first book of Irish case law in 'Lawe French', a version of Norman French that had been used for English case law for centuries, thus removing even linguistic jurisdiction from the Gaelic families who had been the guardians of a legal culture enshrined in manuscripts and orature.

Davies' impression that the Ireland that existed outside of the tiny circle of print culture was 'utterly lost, & buried in oblivion' in some ways captures the shape of the informational world of Ireland in the early seventeenth century. Within the small and tightly controlled sphere in which print circulated legally there was a kind of visibility, in which anyone who could afford to buy *Primer report des Cases & Matters*, for instance, had access to the law. Beyond it was a much larger Ireland that was predominantly Irish-speaking and Catholic, in which information was handed on by word of mouth, through smuggled print or in manuscript, all of which circulated through networks of kinship and affiliation,

[9] John Davies, *A Discoverie of the True Causes Why Ireland Was Never Entirely Subdued, nor Brought under Obedience of the Crowne of England, untill the Beginning of His Maisties Happie Raigne* (London, 1612), 131.

[10] John Davies, *Le Primer report des Cases & Matters en Ley resolues & adiudges en les Courts del Roy en Ireland* (Dublin, 1615), ii.

which, to those not part of them, seemed secretive, exclusive and ultimately threatening.

'A PROTESTANT PRESSE'

The print culture of early seventeenth-century Ireland, then, has a curious internal asymmetry, locked in conflict with a cultural formation that was, almost by definition, outside of the world of print (or at least outside of legally circulating print). For instance, in 1603, John Rider, the Dean of St Patrick's Cathedral in Dublin, published a pamphlet *A Friendly Caveat to Ireland's Cathoickes*, in which he entered into a controversy with a Catholic, Henry Fitzsimon. The debate centred around the question as to whether the Catholic or the Anglican Church was the true apostolic heir of the primitive church (a theological dispute that would run and run, stoked in the early seventeenth century by James Ussher, but continuing to heat tempers for four centuries). As the title suggests, Rider is ostensibly addressing a Catholic readership in what purports to be a series of letters, written by the Catholic Fitzsimon, and now being exposed by Rider through print; however, it is equally clear that Fitzsimon himself has no access to print, so his views must be mediated by Rider, who – not surprisingly – takes the opportunity to discredit them in the process of transmission.

In one fascinating passage, Rider's attack on Fitzsimon moves into a complex and extended metaphor drawn from the language of the print culture in which he is exposing and attacking Fitzsimon. 'If the Irish Testament (a godly laborious and profitable worke to Gods Church) had not imbusied the Printers Presse,' he tells his adversary, he would have made Fitzsimon's letters public sooner; but, he writes:

I could go no further … till the Printers returne from London with new letters and whereas there be some faults escaped, impute them not to the skilfull Printer, but to the stumpeworne letter; so as weapons unsteeled cut not, so letters overworne print not. I have laid downe your prooffes and speeches. … not adding diminishing, or altring one sillable or letter.[11]

The metaphorical conceit here assumes a readership familiar with the language of the print shop: 'letters', 'proofs', 'print' etc. The meaning of the word 'letter' in this paragraph slides from referring to an individual

---

[11] John Rider, *A Friendly Caveat to Ireland's Cathoickes Concerning the Dangerous Dreame of Christs Corporall (yet Invisible) Presence in the Sacrament of the Lords Supper* (Dublin, 1603), A4.

letter of type, to Fitzsimon's letters (as in epistles), to the more general 'letters' as characters of writing (whether printed or handwritten). Hence, the 'stumpeworne letters' are, on a literal level, the type worn smooth by the 'godly laborious' work of printing the New Testament in Irish, the existence of which has rendered 'stumpeworne' the archaic, tired and obsolete theological arguments put forward by Catholic theologians, such as Fitzsimon. Such 'overworne print', Rider intimates, will not stand up to 'proof' (with the obvious play on the word 'proof', as in 'proof copy').

A Friendly Caveat to Ireland's Cathoickes, like Davies' *True Causes of Why Ireland Was Never Entirely Subdued*, suggests the extent to which print had the potential to become central to the project of creating a centrally administered Protestant state. At the same time, we also glimpse the impediments to creating a print culture when struggling to do battle with 'stumpeworne letters'. Moreover, by 1615, there would appear to have been a growing sense that one of those impediments was the monopoly that had been granted to John Franckton in 1604. From the perspective of their thriving business, the Stationers' Company in London must have seen Franckton's domain as being ripe for a take-over. Accordingly, in 1618 the Privy Council urged the Lord Deputy in Ireland, to 'deal with him [Franckton] there for the surrender of his Patent'.[12] Franckton duly sold his patent to the Stationers' Company, who set about assembling what became known as their 'Irish stock', to be kept distinct (at least in theory) from their English (and Latin) stocks. The immediate effect was to make more books available in Ireland; while Franckton averaged two publications a year, over the next couple of decades the Stationers would average ten. At the same time, increasing the flow of print was a way of stepping up the cultural war between print culture and its occluded rival.

We can see this clearly in the work of Christopher Sibthorp, a Justice of the King's Bench, who in 1622 printed *A Friendly Advertisement to the Pretended Catholics of Ireland*, arguing (like Rider before him) that the Church of Ireland was the true heir of the early Christian church. However, Sibthorp's tone is much more aggressive than Rider's, and it is even more conscious of the radical asymmetry of debate in a culture in which access to print was the exclusive domain of one part of a bifurcated culture. When after publishing one pamphlet, an 'adversary' does (allegedly) produce a manuscript contesting some of his views, and requesting that Sibthorp help publish it, Sibthorp fumes indignantly in a follow-up pamphlet of 1627: 'Doe you desire of mee, that I would bee

---

[12] BL, Sloan MS 4756, fol. 153, in Munter, *Print Trade in Ireland*, 107.

a mean to procure it to bee Printed, by the Protestant Presse here in *Dublin*. A verie bold, unbecoming, and strange request, to be demanded.'[13] And yet, if a Catholic allegedly requesting the use of a 'Protestant Presse' was 'unbecoming', circulating an argument in manuscript was equally suspect. 'Why did he rather choose to divulge it in a Manuscript?' asks Sibthorp, claiming that his opponent might have found a Catholic publisher 'unto Doway, or to Rhemes.' 'Did he thinke, that by that course used, he might the more freely speake and write what he listed, and that no man would answere or reply unto it, … what reason is there for any man, to clayme, expect, or to be allowed such a priviledge?'[14]

This little skirmish gives us a good sense of the heated climate in which the 'Protestant Presse' operated following the entry of the Stationers into Ireland. With extensive London stocks of books to draw on, the Stationers were able to make more readily available many of the books (although obviously not the Catholic theological works) that had been imported illegally for the previous half-century. For instance, a list of books offered for sale by Thomas Downes, 'Printer Generall within this his Majesties Realm of Ireland', acting for the Stationers' Company in Dublin in the 1620s, shows that he relied heavily on sales of Bibles (seven different editions), 'Communion books' (three different editions), and devotional works such as Alexander Nowell's *Catechismus*. In every case, a surviving price list also shows that the Stationers were charging their Irish customers more than their London counterparts: a folio 'Church bible', for instance, bound with clasps, sold in London for £1 12s.; in Dublin, it was marked up to £2.

Whenever a medium expands, however, the effects of that expansion can be in excess of what is intended, and there are indications of this starting to happen in Ireland in the early seventeenth century. For instance, Downes was also finding a market for standard classical works (Ovid and Cicero), and 'other small schoolbooks', which suggests that growing numbers were learning to read. Raymond Gillespie notes that when forty-seven Cavan people sent a petition to the Lord Deputy in 1629, only three could not sign their names.[15] That the 'middling sort of people' were reading is further suggested by the publication in 1612 (while Franckton still held the patent) of William Farmer's *Prognosticall Almanacke*. The *Almanacke* is a record of fairs, markets, tides and phases

---

[13] Christopher Sibthorp, *A Surreplication to the Rejoynder of a Popish Adversarie* (Dublin, 1627), n.p.
[14] Christopher Sibthorp, *A Reply to an Answer Made by a Popish Adversarie* (Dublin, 1625), n.p.
[15] Gillespie, 'Print Culture 1550–1700', 22–3.

of the moon, 'referred particularly to the latetude and meridan of the auncient cititie of Dublin'. It also contains a potted history of 'things done since the first inhabitation of this kingdome' as well as 'a briefe register of all the principall highways of Ireland, with the distance and number of styles from Dublin to any principal remote place of the kingdome.' In short, it is one of the first indications in Ireland of print becoming part of the fabric of everyday life. 'I have taken great paynes and charges in venturing the printing of this Almanacke', Franckton writes in his capacity as printer at the beginning of the volume, 'in the hope it will be accepted of: It falleth out to be much bigger than the common Kallendar, by reason of many necessities in this Kingdome worthy of remembrance, more than hath beene hitherto ever printed.'[16]

In the 1620s we also see the beginnings of an Irish literary culture mediated through print. It was, admittedly, a slow beginning; by the middle of that decade literary books made up only around eight per cent of the Stationers' Irish stock, according to one estimate.[17] Most were imported from London. However, there was an early attempt to establish an English-language literary sphere in Dublin when, in 1624, the Dublin Stationers published Richard Bellings' addition to Sir Philip Sidney's *Arcadia*, which had been originally published in five books in London in 1593. Adding to Sidney's mixture of prose romance and pastoral eclogues was more than simply a random choice on Bellings' part. Sidney's father, Sir Henry Sidney, had been an active and influential Lord Deputy of Ireland three times in the late sixteenth century. There is a sense, therefore, that by publishing his *Arcadia* in Dublin, Bellings is making an implicit claim for its Irishness. If so, this is one of the earliest instances of the tug of war of literary ownership that would so preoccupy Irish writers of the eighteenth and nineteenth centuries. As would happen so often in later centuries, Bellings was caught in an awkward, but familiar, posture, both claiming a common culture with Sidney, and defining his own difference from England, telling the reader that his 'mother tongue differs as much from this language [of Sidney's], as *Irish* from *English*'.[18]

Bellings continued to be involved in Dublin's literary life, writing a prologue for the Dublin edition of a play, *The Royal Master*, by James

---

[16] William Farmer, *His Prognostical Almanacke for this Bissextile Yeere* (Dublin, 1612), A2.
[17] Raymond Gillespie, 'Irish Printing in the Early Seventeenth Century', *Irish Economic and Social History* 15 (1988), 81–8, 85.
[18] Richard Bellings, *A Sixth Booke to the Countess of Pembrokes Arcadia* (Dublin, 1624), n.p.

Shirley in 1638. Shirley was an English playwright who was invited to Dublin in 1636 by the Lord Lieutenant, Thomas Wentworth, to write plays for Ireland's first theatre, on Dublin's Werburgh Street. Several of the plays that Shirley wrote for the Werburgh Street Theatre were first published in Dublin, as was the theatre's first play by an Irish author, Henry Burnell's *Landgartha,* performed in 1639, and published in 1641 (possibly by an unlicensed printer). Another play by Burnell (now lost), *The Irish Gentleman,* has a prologue by Shirley. In this little nest of connections, we begin to glimpse what is arguably Ireland's first literary coterie mediated through print and the public theatre. This in itself is less remarkable than the fact that the group who gathered around Bellings and Shirley were not only all staunch royalists (as their patronage by Wentworth would suggest); they were all Catholics.[19] In another place or time, this might not have mattered. In Dublin in the 1630s, it mattered intensely, and only a Catholic author with impeccable links to high literary culture and daunting political connections could hope to gain access to an Irish press.

BARE TRADITIONS AND REMEMBRANCES OF BARDS

For most Irish Catholic writers of the time having work printed within Ireland may not have been a possibility; however, this does not mean that they had no involvement in print culture, even if we leave aside Irish links to the press in Leuven. 'Printing, and the use of the printed book', David McKitterick argues, 'both depended on and influenced manuscripts long after the invention of movable type.'[20] Nowhere is this clearer than in one of the most important, and certainly one of the most influential, books to have been written in Ireland in the early seventeenth century: Geoffrey Keating's history of Ireland, *Foras Feasa ar Éirinn.* Born near Cahir, in County Tipperary, as a young man Keating was trained in the oral and manuscript tradition of a bardic school, was ordained, and then moved to Bourdeaux and Rheims, a centre for Catholic printing. By the time he began work on *Foras Feasa,* which he completed in 1634, Keating was working with three media – print, manuscript and orature – as fluently as he worked in at least three languages – Irish, Latin and English.

---

[19] While Shirley has not been shown definitively to have been Catholic, the evidence is strong, and he certainly had Catholic sympathies. See Sandra A. Burner, *James Shirley: A Study of Literary Coteries and Patronage in Seventeenth-Century England* (New York, 1988).

[20] David McKitterick, *Print, Manuscript and the Search for Order, 1450–1830* (Cambridge, 2003), 47.

In one sense, Keating was like generations of Irish scholars before him, working from manuscript sources, often many centuries old, supplemented by oral lore. In particular, we know that Keating drew heavily on *Leabhar gabhála Éireann* (*Book of the Taking of Ireland*), *Réim ríorgh-raidhe Éireann* (*Succession of Kings of Ireland*) and a composite work, now lost, known as the *Pslater of Cashel*, dating from *ca* AD 1000, which drew together a collection of even earlier material. For almost all of his sources, whatever the language, the major issue for Keating was not interpretation (*Foras Feasa* is the work of an author who has a very clear sense of his own purpose); it was access. As Bernadette Cunningham puts it, '*Foras Feasa* could not have been undertaken without the active support and encouragement of the scholarly families who were still the custodians of many Gaelic manuscripts.'[21] Equally, the same scholarly families who were keepers of the old manuscripts also provided patronage for the *filid*, the 'old men' who could recall generations of oral lore, and who consequently had privileged access to the Gaelic political elite, even as late as the early 1630s. However, unlike many of his predecessors – and here lies at least one of the innovations of *Foras Feasa* – Keating consciously and vigorously engages with the printed word, making reference to almost forty different published books, ranging from recently published books by New English historians, such as Davies' *Discoverie of the True Causes* (1612), to English works such as John Speed's *History of Great Britaine* (1623), back to Giraldus Cambrensis' *Topographia Hiberniae*, which had been published in an English translation in Holinshed's *Chronicles* in 1586.[22]

While Keating leaves little doubt that he is formulating a rejoinder to writers such as these, who had 'have not made a stoop for the virtues or good customs of the old Galls or of the Gaels',[23] it is not simply the case that Keating is writing on behalf of a culture whose primary media were manuscripts and orature, and which is opposed to a print culture. In many cases, the printed works against which Keating was directing his attack had also drawn on manuscript and oral sources. For instance, in his *Short View of the Present State of Ireland* (one of Keating's targets) Spenser (speaking through the character of Irenius) admits that 'I do herein rely upon those bards or Irish chronicles … but unto them besides I add my

[21] Bernadette Cunningham, *The World of Geoffrey Keating: History, Myth and Religion in Seventeenth-Century Ireland* (Dublin, 2000), 60.

[22] Ann Cronin, 'Sources of Keating's *Forus Feasa ar Éirinn*', *Éigse* 4:4 (1944), 235–79. See also, Cunningham, *World of Geoffrey Keating*, 83–104.

[23] Geoffrey Keating, *Vindication of the Sources of Irish History*, trans. David Comyn (Dublin, 1898), 54.

own reading, and out of them both together ... I do gather a likelihood of truth.'[24] What is more, Spenser's *Short View*, like Meredith Hanmer's *Chronicle of Ireland*, had circulated in manuscript for nearly half a century before Sir James Ware published them in 1633. Hence, if print seemed like the exclusive preserve of the Protestant New English, and manuscripts the territory of the Gaelic Irish and Old English, in the early decades of the seventeenth century there were areas of overlap in which the two worlds met.

There is, however, an important difference between Keating and his New English contemporaries: while their works found their way into print by the early seventeenth century as part of an administrative project 'to erect and polish a lasting structure of our Irish affaires' (as Sir James Ware puts it in the preface to his 1633 edition of Hanmer, Campion and Spenser),[25] the cultural schism that separated print from manuscript in early modern Ireland meant that even though Keating's work was quickly translated into English and Latin, the full Irish text would remain in manuscript, and would not be published in its original form until the twentieth century. Rather than creating a more unified culture, then, print in early seventeenth-century Ireland helped widen existing divides by giving them a media-specific form; however, this distinction could only exist with the kind of clarity we find in the 1630s in a print culture that was relatively small, and highly controlled. And that control was to slip, with shocking suddenness, in the opening years of the next decade.

'THIS SODAINE SENDING'

I have no time to write largely for this sodaine sending, for fear to lose the opportunity. By the next you shall heare further: I landed here upon Thursday.[26]

The tone is breathless, urgent, saturated with the awareness of time: the time of writing, the time of reading and the dizzying convergence of the two. On one level, the form of a pamphlet such as *A Perfect Copy of a Letter Sent from Dublin* (1642), from which the passage above is taken, is a direct transcription to print of the practice of professional letter-writers,

---

[24] Edmund Spenser, *A Short View of the Present State of Ireland*, ed. W.L. Renwick (Oxford, 1970), 39.

[25] James Ware, 'To the Right Honourable Thomas, Viscount Wentworth,' *The Historie of Ireland Collected by Three Learned Authors* (Dublin, 1633), 3.

[26] *Perfect Copy of a Letter Sent from Dublin Relating the True Condition of Ireland as it Now Stands* (Dublin, 1642), A2.

who sent manuscript digests of the latest news to their subscribers throughout the century. As late as the 1650s, indeed, one English letter-writer was earning '£500 a year by writing the news to several persons.'[27] At the same time, these timely dispatches bring a new tone to print; these are not the words of the compositor of a manuscript, aware that his work will be copied laboriously by hand, circulated among a limited number of associates, pondered and stored for centuries; these are words written by and for a new kind of print culture, quickly produced, distributed and then possibly discarded in an uncertain future.

The first violence of the Irish Rebellion – which would eventually spill over into the English Civil War, or War of the Three Kingdoms – took place on October 23, 1641; on November 29, *The Heads of Severall Proceedings in this Present Parliament* was published in London 'and with this', writes a recent historian, 'the first periodical newsbook to communicate domestic news in England had been born'.[28] What is more, the first news in what was effectively the first English newspaper was of Ireland: 'Monday, November the 29. there were Letters Read in the Lords House, which came from Ireland'.[29] Both in these first newsbooks, and in the pamphlets of the period, a radical change takes place in print culture, both in England and in Ireland: time becomes a factor in the media culture. In a situation that was changing almost by the day, the currency of news suddenly became an issue, and so publications of the 1640s become dense with references to time: 'Monday, November the 29', 'I landed here upon Thursday' and so on.

The newsbook (and eventually the newspaper) would flourish in England in the 1640s, with more than 250 titles appearing in the decade. Initially, at least, Ireland would be more a source of news than of newsbooks, as the under-developed print culture scrambled to keep up with events. Moreover, those pamphlets and letters that were published often re-directed the flow of rumour and counter-rumour in ways that were shaped by the historically embedded place of print in the culture wars of seventeenth-century Ireland. For instance, the Dublin printer (and former Sheriff) William Bladen published *Three Letters Sent from Rome to Some of*

---

[27] Sabrina A. Baron, 'The Guises of Dissemination in Early Seventeenth-Century England: News in Manuscript and Print', in *The Politics of Information in Early Modern Europe*, ed. Brendan Dooley and Sabrina Baron (London, 2001), 41–56, 41.

[28] David O'Hara, *English Newsbooks and Irish Rebellion 1641–1649* (Dublin, 2006), 13; see also Joad Raymond, *The Invention of the Newspaper: English Newsbooks 1641–1649* (Oxford, 1996), 109.

[29] *Dyurnall Occurants, or the Heads of Proceedings in Parliament from the 29 of November to the Sixth of December, 1641* (London, 1641), A2.

the *Principall Actors of the Rebellion in Ireland, Dated 4. of January 1642*,
which, as its title suggests, purports to be letters sent by leaders of the Irish
rebellion. 'The first two were written in Irish', readers are informed, 'and
now translated into English, and laid open to the view of the world.'
Drawing on more than half a century in which Irish had been treated by
print culture as something like a secret language, it takes only the smallest
nudge to suggest that it is effectively a conspiratorial code. Similarly,
Bladen is able to manipulate the suspicion attaching to a manuscript as
something that passes from hand to hand through ties of kinship, as
opposed to circulating openly – a suspicion that goes back to Sibthorp's
pamphlets of the 1620s, and before him to Rider in 1603. 'Deliver this to
Connor mac Guyre Lord of Iniskillin', concludes one of these letters, 'or
in his absence to his brother Roory Mac Guire in Ireland.'[30] If the original
letters could only be read by people with the right hereditary ties, the
pamphlet in which the letters were published could be bought in the
marketplace by anyone with a few shillings, thereby undermining
the secrecy, and hence the power, of those older networks of affiliation.
Once again, the medium of print itself is as important to a pamphlet's
meaning as its contents.

It is one of the ironies of the situation in Ireland in the early 1640s that,
while institutions built up over the previous decades collapsed one by one,
print thrived, with the number of works printed in Ireland doubling in
the 1640s. As the old, uneasy standoff between the Old English, Irish and
New English splintered and broke into open warfare in the early months
of 1642, there was an effective collapse of a single central administration to
license printing. With one of the major impediments to public debate in
Ireland gone, it is hardly surprising that when the Catholic Irish and
Old English allied as a Catholic Confederation in Kilkenny in October of
1642, they set about establishing presses in Kilkenny and Waterford. Here
they published pamphlets, declarations and a play by Henry Burkhead,
A Tragedy of Cola's Furie, or, Lirenda's Miserie (1646), which chronicles
(with thinly disguised pseudonyms) the war then taking place.

When the Catholic Confederation itself later split after 1646, so too did
its print culture, further spreading presses around the country and away
from Dublin. Up until 1646, most of the material printed under the
Confederation bears the imprint of Thomas Bourke, who worked in both
Kilkenny and Waterford (indeed, Walter Enos apologises in his *Second
Part of the Survey of the Articles of the Late Rejected Peace* that 'pages 36 and

---

[30] *Three Letters Sent from Rome* (Dublin, 1642), 4.

41 meete not together, because the worke was printed in severall places').[31]
However, after 1646, the tone of material coming from Bourke's presses
changes, as he appears to have sided with a faction supporting the Papal
Nuncio. The most immediate indication that this is the case is the
appearance of Church censors (no doubt confirming the worst fears of
any Protestants who may have chanced upon these publications), whose
endorsements make up two, three, sometimes four pages of prefatory
material. 'If lay men should take upon them to Censure this worke, which
hath been approved by the Clergie, they are excommunicated *bulla caena*',
warns Enos at the beginning of the *Second Part* of his *Survey*.

While it is true that the printed word might seem suited to conditions
of peace and stability, the chaos of war – particularly civil war – can
produce an urgent need to order the flow of information. In England,
where there was already a highly developed print culture, this need,
coupled with a breakdown of centralised control, produced a dizzying
number of diurnals, courants and news-sheets, which effectively laid the
ground for the newspaper. In Ireland, the effect was similar, but on a far
less extensive scale, and it was the Cromwellian army who produced
Ireland's first newspaper. *The Irish Monthly Mercury*, published in Cork,
first appeared in December of 1649, and survived until February of 1651.
'It is but just that the People should have News for their Money,' declares
the paper's first edition, 'and that they should hear, as well as feel the
effects of their Taxes.'[32]

The Irish Monthly Mercury appeared in more or less regular, dated
issues, but lacked the sense of breathless urgency of the one-off expresses
and short pamphlets that brought news of battles, fresh (or relatively
fresh) from the field. Indeed, the *Monthly Mercury* sometimes apologises
for the gap between events and their reporting. 'I will run over briefly
those principal Occurrences which happened before I could come to the
convenience of a Press', writes its anonymous editor. The *Mercury* did not
so much convey news; it imposed an order on the rumours and manuscript letters that would have been circulating in an unregulated form,
with its editor promising that he will 'henceforth Monthly, deduce you
all things in as set a Form, as the Common Prayer or Presbytery'. In
this regard, this first newspaper had a function not far removed from
the official proclamations that had been a staple of the Irish press since
its inception. Indeed, it was probably the same press that produced

---

[31] Walter Enos, *Second Part of the Survey of the Late Rejected Peace* (Kilkenny, 1646), n.p.
[32] *Irish Monthly Mercury* 1 (December 21, 1649), 1.

The Irish Monthly Mercury that was used in 1650 by Cromwell's second-in-command, Henry Ireton, to publish *A Declaration and Proclamation of the Deputy-General Concerning the Hand of God in the Visitation of the Plague*: 'for the better and speedier communication of what is herein required or desired, I do hereby Appoint the same to be Printed and Published'.[33]

When existing channels of communication unravel, there is a need for new sources of information. However, new media do not simply provide the same old types of information in a different format; they transform modes of perception, and do so in ways that carry culturally specific traces of the social, political and religious origins of the media itself. The advent of newsbooks, newspapers and pamphlets relaying the news introduces an awareness of contemporaneity, a fundamentally modern sense of the present, for which there is very little evidence in early seventeenth-century Ireland. It was thus out of the very forces that were devastating an earlier social order that we see the first faint signs of a modern print-mediated public sphere in Ireland.

---

[33] Henry Ireton, *A Declaration and Proclamation of the Deputy-General of Ireland Concerning the Present Hand of God in the Visitation of the Plague and for the Exercise of Fasting and Prayer in Relation Thereunto* (Cork and London, 1650), 15.

Media Event 1:
'Bloudy newes from Ireland', October 23, 1641

At first, rumours of what was happening in Ulster in October of 1641 (and would later spread elsewhere in Ireland) travelled by word of mouth, tales of horror that must have hardly seemed credible. Owen Franklin, who lived in Dublin, was told by a friend travelling from Ulster, Michael Garry, that Garry had heard of a Scotsman, living in Newry, who had been stripped naked, marched to the edge of town and forced to watch while his pregnant wife had her womb ripped open, before he too was 'cut to pieces'. Franklin told this story to John Wisdome, Parish Clerk of the Cathedral in Armagh, who in turn told him that another man, William Pitchfork, had seen 'eightscore persons' drowned at the bridge in Portadown, a fate Pitchfork himself escaped only after 'being begged by an Irish Rebell to be his servant'. Philip Taylor, a farmer from Portadown, also heard that 'the said Rebels drowned a great number of English Protestants, of men, women and children, … some with their hands tyed on their backs.' Upon being released, Taylor reported that he came upon a woman lying dead in a ditch, and had to 'drive a Sow away that was eating one of her children'.[1]

The Ireland in which these horrific rumours circulated was a place in which news travelled through erratic channels: travellers brought stories, which were spread in taverns and coffee houses; manuscript letters changed hands, carried by merchants, sea captains, soldiers and others.

---

[1] Henry Jones, *A Remonstrance of Divers Remarkable Passages Concerning the Church and Kingdome of Ireland Recommended by Letters from the Right Honorable the Lords Justices, and Counsell of Ireland, and Presented by Henry Jones Doctor of Divinity and Agent for the Ministers of the Gospel in that Kingdom to the Honourable House of Commons in England* (London, 1642), 62–3.

However, it was also a culture that was on the edge of a media revolution, for just over a month after the eruption of the rebellion in Ulster in October of 1641, the first English newsbook *The Heads of Severall Proceedings in this Present Parliament* appeared in London. For readers of *Heads of Severall Proceedings*, the weekly appearance of a digest of news would have produced the novel sensation of experiencing current events as a regulated procession of verifiable facts, following one another in a cause and effect sequence through time. However, the newsbooks were being read alongside pamphlets, whose register was often very different. In his study of news in the period, Ethan Shagan has argued that there is a clear distinction between pamphlets that draw their tone and imagery from John Foxe's *Acts and Monuments*, emphasising the torments and sufferings of Protestants at the hands of Catholics as iconic types of good and evil, and those pamphlets that are more concerned with the more immediate implications of events in Ireland in the context of the power struggle between Parliament and Charles I.[2]

In the longer term, the various registers were to have very different impacts. For instance, *A Coppy of a Letter Sent by the Rebells in Ireland to Lord Dillon, to Declare the Maiestie the Cause of Their Taking up Armes*, published in 1641, opens with what purports to be a letter, in which the leaders of the rebellion pledge allegiance to both the Catholic Church and to Charles I – a rumour with obvious political value in the struggle between Parliament and King. However, appended to it is an account, supposedly from a 'Master Georg Jackson', of witnessing rebels torturing Protestants by 'making holes in their bellies, cutting away the skine, so that their entrailes may be seene, and laid hold of, then they fasten a Lute or Violl string unto the umbelick or Navill gut',[3] thus disembowelling their captives. For a reader picking up this pamphlet in December of 1641, it may have seemed that the first section was the most serious, alleging royal involvement in the rebellion, while the gruesome account of disembowelling was simply a piece of sensationalist reinforcement. The former was part of the temporal world of the newsbook; the latter was a shadow from a dark place outside the world of 'newes'. In the longer term, however, it would be these unnerving vignettes of torture that would

---

[2] Ethan Howard Shagan, 'Constructing Discord: Ideology, Propaganda, and English Responses to the Irish Rebellion of 1641', *The Journal of British Studies* 36:1 (January 1997), 4–34.
[3] *A Coppy of a Letter Sent by the Rebells in Ireland to Lord Dillon, to Declare the Maiestie the Cause of Their Taking up Armes* (London, 1641), A2.

persist, like memories of trauma, long after the intricacies of political manoeuvrings had been forgotten.

The recording of these atrocities fell to a clergyman, Henry Jones, who in December 1641 was given a commission to take depositions from survivors and eye-witnesses of the attacks. His initial report, the innocuously titled *Remonstrance of Divers Remarkable Passages Concerning the Church and Kingdome of Ireland*, appeared in April of 1642. In these vividly gruesome accounts, the oral culture of rumour and counter-rumour made its way first to manuscript, and then into print, where it could multiply and spread in graphic accounts of torture and cruelty, all legally witnessed and dated. Initially, Jones's *Remonstrance* provided fodder for the pamphleteers; however, within a few years, it would form the basis for central sections of the book that would do most to create a place for the events of 1641 in Irish history: John Temple's *The Irish Rebellion*, first published in 1646 (illustration 2).

Like many who would later publish accounts of those years – including Edmund Borlase and Edward Hyde, the first Earl of Clarendon – Temple (who had been created Master of the Rolls of Ireland in January of 1641) was a leading public figure at the time of the rebellion. And, like many in those years, his fortunes rose and fell precipitously (he spent nearly a year in prison at one point), but by 1646 he was getting ready for re-entry into public life. He is credited with the authorship of a shorter work in dialogue form, *Ormonds Curtain Drawn* (1646), which linked the Duke of Ormond with the massacres, although in that book the author's fictional alter ego says he 'shall passe over those monstrous, unheard of cruelties which I saw with these eyes'.[4] In *The Irish Rebellion* there is no such restraint, and at its centre, disrupting the political narrative, is a chapter made up entirely of the depositions.

Temple may have written *The Irish Rebellion* for a very specific political purpose; however, the power of the deposition testimonies would be such that the book would have an impact long after his rivalry with Ormond had been forgotten. There would be twelve editions of Temple's book in the years leading up to 1800, and it would become apparent to later historians that these appeared at moments of perceived Catholic threat.[5] For instance, after four London editions, the first Dublin edition appeared in 1698, the year after Catholic clergy were banished by an Act

[4] John Temple [attrib.], *Ormonds Curtain Drawn* (London, 1646), 4.
[5] Nicholas Canny, 'What Really Happened in Ireland in 1641?', in *Ireland From Independence to Occupation 1641–1660*, ed. Jane H. Ohlmeyer (Cambridge, 1995), 24–42, 25.

Illustration 2. John Temple's account of the massacres of 1641, *The Irish Rebellion*, originally published in 1646, would be republished at moments of sectarian tensions for the next three centuries. This edition, produced by the Dublin printer Aaron Rhames in 1724, contains some impressively grisly woodcuts.

of Parliament. There were, however, other publications that kept the depositions alive in the intervening years: *An Abstract of Some Few of those Barbarous, Cruell Massacres and Murthers, of the Protestants, and English* appeared just after the Restoration of Charles II in 1662, and *An Abstract of the Unnatural Rebellion and Barbarous Massacre of the Protestants in the Kingdom of Ireland in the Year 1641* was printed at the time of the Siege of Derry in 1689. However, Temple's book continued to hold its authority. There were two further Dublin editions of *The Irish Rebellion* (1713 and 1716) book-ending the Scottish Jacobite rebellion of 1715; both editions were bound with a later work in similar vein, *The State of the Protestants under the Late King James's Government* (1691). In 1724, the Dublin publisher Aaron Rhames printed an edition with impressively grisly woodcuts (reminiscent of those which had adorned editions of Foxe's *Book of Marytrs* in the previous century), at a time when there was debate over removing the voting franchise from Catholics. There were two more London editions in 1746, coinciding with the 1745 Jacobite rising, and a

Dublin edition in 1751. A Cork edition appeared in 1766, in the wake of the formation of the Catholic Committee to lobby for improved rights for Catholics in 1760.

In 1812, at a time when there was concern about 'outrages' being committed by secret societies in the south-west (and the year before the first July Twelfth sectarian riots in Belfast), there was a new London edition, which contained the texts of several pamphlets from the 1640s, as well as extracts from Richard Musgrave's equally gore-laden account of the more recent 1798 Rebellion. The edition's subtitle – *Now Reprinted for the Perusal of all Protestants, as the Most Effectual Warning-Piece to Keep Them upon their Guard against the Encroachments of Popery* – left little doubt as to why Temple was still in print. 'The Petition of the Roman-Catholicks, or Papists, of both Great Britain and Ireland, to Parliament, for what they call *Catholick Emancipation*', warned the editor of the 1812 edition, 'ought to be examined and considered, with the greatest degree of care and attention.'[6] Later in the century, the issue would still be alive as the liberal historian J. E. H. Lecky attempted to defuse the version of history that had become associated with Temple, against the equally strong opposing views of J.A. Froude, who wrote an enthusiastic introduction to a major late-nineteenth-century transcription of the depositions, full of gory detail, edited by Mary Hickson in 1884.[7] As late as 1887, Quaker Home Rule campaigner Alfred Webb felt the need to launch a polemic against Temple, and 'those long and sickening catalogues of horrors which made a lasting impression on the English mind',[8] in a short book entitled *The Alleged Massacre of 1641*.

Whatever may really have happened in Ulster on those late October days in 1641, its lasting impact over more than two centuries was the product of a very specific collision between two kinds of media culture. The Ireland in which the rebellion arose was a place where news still travelled predominantly by word of mouth, or by manuscript. The larger context in which that rebellion took place was at the point of emerging into a new kind of print culture, the culture of the newspaper, where

---

[6] Francis Maseres, 'Preface', Sir John Temple, *The Irish Rebellion: Or, an History of the Attempts of the Irish Papists to Extirpate the Protestants in the Kingdom of Ireland; Together with the Barbarous Cruelties and Bloody Massacres Which Ensued Thereupon. Now Reprinted for the Perusal of all Protestants, as the Most Effectual Warning-Piece to Keep Them upon their Guard against the Encroachments of Popery* (London, 1812), v.

[7] Mary Hickson, *Ireland in the Seventeenth Century or the Irish Massacres of 1641–42: Their Causes and Results* (London, 1884).

[8] Alfred Webb, *The Alleged Massacre of 1641* (London, 1887), 17.

verifiable facts appeared at regulated intervals in chronological sequence. While other events of the time could be accommodated to this new sense of events in time, the massacres of 1641 seemed to arise out of nowhere, to belong in no context. Audley Mervin, a Member of Parliament from County Tyrone, told the House of Commons in June, 1642, that the Rebellion was 'conceived among us, and yet, never felt to kick in the wombe, nor struggle in the birth'.[9] As such, it could assume something of the character of a monstrous prodigy, appearing suddenly and without explanation, barely containable by the print culture that for more than two centuries would clutch it to memory as a fragment of a world just beyond the margins of the printed word.

[9] Mervin Audley, *A Relation of Such Occurences as have happened in the Severall Counties of Donegall, Tyrone, Fermanagh and London-derry since the Beginning of the Rebellion in Ireland, in October last* (London, 1642).

CHAPTER 2

Public spirits: 1660–1800

'IMPARTIAL OCCURRENCES'

If the cornerstone of a print-mediated public sphere is the newspaper, the long, slow trudge towards establishing a regular newspaper in Ireland gives us a measure of the fragility of the culture that was assembled after 1660. The first Irish newspaper, *The Irish Monthly Mercury*, was printed irregularly by Cromwell's army in Cork for less than two years, from 1649 to 1651, and with its reports of victories, and hymns of praise to 'Brave Cromwell (and his valiant blades)',[1] was a fairly unsubtle attempt to use print as an instrument of state policy, and lasted only a few issues. It would be almost a decade before it was to have a successor, when *An Account of the Chief Occurences in Ireland* began publication in 1660; however, it too folded after a few short issues. In spite of having support from the state, both of these early Irish newspapers collapsed for reasons that were not so much cultural or political as infrastructural.

The defining characteristic of a newspaper is its periodicity. Arguably the most important feature of any newspaper is the masthead, which contains two vital pieces of information: the name of the newspaper (which, in comparison with a book, for instance, is the same from edition to edition, even though the contents change); and the date, equidistant in time from both the previous edition and the next edition. Periodicity can only be achieved when there is a regular flow of information, and in the seventeenth century movement of information meant the movement of people. It was only when the ability to gather information with some degree of regularity and speed was combined with the ability to print and distribute the news (again with regularity and speed) that the printed word could become a part of the daily lives of its readers. In other words, production of a newspaper requires more than a press and some cases of

---

[1] *Irish Monthly Mercury* 1 (December 21, 1649).

font; it requires safe roads, navigable sea lanes, horses, riders, inns – the entire apparatus of a reliable postal system.

In the Ireland of 1660, this communications infrastructure simply did not exist. A letter office and post boat had been established as early as 1572, part of the same effort to assert state control that brought print to Ireland. A Deputy Postmaster, Evan Vaughan, was appointed in 1638, but by 1663 there were still only three main postroads in Ireland,[2] and *Chief Occurences in Ireland* fell by the wayside. It would be another quarter century or more until newspaper publication began in Ireland with any regularity. The first Irish newspaper from which we can really trace a lineage is probably the *The News Letter* (January 10 until December 29, 1685), followed by *Dublin Intelligence* (September 30, 1690 until May 1695), which in turn was followed by *The Flying Post*. First published on March 7, 1699, *The Flying Post* survived until the 1720s, and had progeny even later in the century. Like many of the newspapers that were to follow them in the eighteenth century, these little newspapers were (initially at least) only four pages in length; and, like their successors, they gathered news from three or four distinct sources.

Like similarly named publications throughout Europe, *The News Letter* was exactly what the title proclaimed: a digest of letters bearing news, provided by the professional letter-writers, 'correspondents' in the original meaning of the word, who continued to provide those who could afford their private services with a posted flow of handwritten 'advices'. *The News Letter*, like other newspapers of the period, used the press to make these epistles available to a wider readership at a more affordable price. For instance, typical articles from February 25, 1685, begin: 'Letters from Venice inform us'; 'Letters from Paris contain the following advices' and so on.[3] This form of presenting the news as a series of letters would continue for some time, even when the source of news was not a professional letter-writer, but another newspaper. This is not to say, however, that papers of the period took any great pains to disguise the source of stories copied from other newspapers, particularly the overseas press. Indeed, the printer Cornelius Carter offered a journal called *The Paris Gazette English'd* in 1703; it was originally published in Paris, translated and printed in London, and then reprinted in Dublin. In other cases, it was common practice to present items from English or Dutch newspapers as if they were eye-witness accounts fresh from the latest bundle of

---

[2] David Feldman and William Kane, *Handbook of Irish Postal History to 1840* (Dublin, 1975), 5.
[3] *The News Letter* (February 25, 1685).

correspondence, and both English and Irish newspapers maintained phantom networks of correspondents well into mid-century.[4]

In London, stories 'English'd' from the Continental press were supplemented by extracts from regional papers that were emerging around England; in Dublin, however, no comparable source of news was available, because in the late seventeenth century there were no newspapers outside of Dublin. This meant that Irish readers of the time had an informational map of the world that was strangely skewed. In the *News Letter* of the 1680s, for instance, reports from Venice, Vienna, Leiden and Paris were commonplace. However, reports from around Ireland are rarer, far more sporadic, and almost impossible to verify. 'We live now in this place in a great Melancholy and Distraction, having the apprehension of a bloody Warr before our eyes, and the certainly of a famine', pleads a single-sheet express from Donegal, dated February, 1689. 'I have not received any Letter from England, or the Countrey this three weeks.'[5] A Dublin newspaper-reader in the late seventeenth century would thus have had a context for events unfolding in Venice or Paris, as regular reports from Continental Europe built up a running narrative that became part of the daily chatter of the coffee houses: the news from Donegal or Kerry, by contrast, trickled in only as the occasional alarming dispatch, frequently only a whisper away from rumour.

It was not until after the Battle of the Boyne that we see an Irish administration stable enough to provide a continuous supply of what would become one of the main sources of news: government dispatches. *Dublin Intelligence*, the first such newspaper of any longevity, makes its political stance – and its main source of news – clear on its masthead: 'Published by Authority.' When it first appeared on September 30, 1690, in the aftermath of the Battle of the Boyne, William of Orange had just left Ireland, but would return the following year. The process of consolidating the victory at the Boyne was thus underway, and *Dublin Intelligence* was part of that process. Like *The Irish Monthly Mercury* before it, and like its successor, *The Dublin Gazette*, *Dublin Intelligence* was a vehicle for imposing a new administrative order through the medium of print. 'That the Publick may not be Imposed upon by any False Account of News, Their Excellencies the Lords Justices have Allowed the Paper, Intitled *The Dublin Gazette*, to be Published by Their Authority, and have

---

[4] James Sutherland, *The Restoration Newspaper and Its Development* (Cambridge, 1986), 126.
[5] *The Present Dangerous Condition of the Protestants in Ireland; with a New Order of Tyrconil's* (London, 1689), 1.

Appointed Their Secretary to Peruse the same constantly before it is to be Printed'.[6] Equally close to the administration was *Whalley's Flying Post*, which published the heads of bills before the Irish Parliament, thereby putting prospective legislation into the public domain.

The newspaper, however, was an unruly medium for state control. In the issue of *Dublin Intelligence* for 15–22 April, an advertisement appears informing readers that 'Sir Toby Butler, did cause a false and scandalous Advertisement to be put in the last Intelligence, insinuating Nicholas Fitz-Gerald Esq. … did endeavour to Assassinate him. … The said Mr. Fitz-Gerald doth hereby give publick Notice, that every particular in the said Advertisement is False, Malicious and Scandalous.'[7] Two issues later, the plot thickened further, when a second advertisement advised readers that it was not really Sir Toby Butler who had inserted the original notice, nor had the original notice been licensed by the Lord Lieutenant, who, the paper reported, had 'shown the Printer thereof such Mark of Displeasure as may further deter him from Committing the like Offence'.[8] This is an ephemeral skirmish, possibly a practical joke; but it gives us a glimpse into a world which is struggling towards an economy of information at a time when sources of information are limited, and rumour, counter-rumour and innuendo can easily spill over into a government newspaper.

Even after the wars of the early 1690s were over, then, the flow of information into Ireland, and within Ireland, continued to be problematic. News could only travel as quickly as a horse could travel along the road, or a ship could cross the Irish Sea. At the beginning of the eighteenth century, it took from three to five days for post to travel from London to Holyhead, and then, if the weather was reasonable, a further twenty-four hours to cross the Irish Sea. In 1710, the publisher Edwin Sandys (who also had the monopoly to print the *Dublin Gazette*) announced that he was going to reprint the London *Tatler* thrice-weekly, 'if the Packets come in'.[9] As it turned out, Sandys was slightly ahead of his time, and for the first half of the eighteenth century, it was customary to print newspapers twice a week – on Tuesdays and Saturdays – so as to fit in with the arrivals of the ships bearing letters and foreign newspapers. When the flow of news did quicken on occasion, twice-weekly publication meant that there was

[6] *That the Publick May Not Be Imposed upon by Any False Account of News* (Dublin, 1705), 1.
[7] *Dublin Intelligence* 128 (April 15–22, 1693).
[8] *Dublin Intelligence* 130 (April 29–May 11, 1693).
[9] Robert Munter, *The History of the Irish Newspaper: 1685–1760* (Cambridge, 1967), 70–2.

sometimes a build-up of incoming information: 'Since my last we had 4 packets, which brought 1 mail from France, and 3 from Holland, with the following Advices...' began a characteristic summary of the week's events in *Pue's Impartial Occurences* in 1718.[10] In either case, the simple geographical fact of the Irish Sea, combined with a smaller local population, meant that Dublin fell behind London, which had its first successful daily newspaper, the *Daily Courant*, in 1702.

Indeed, storms and the dangers of piracy meant that the post was often late, and even twice-weekly publication was difficult; or, conversely, an event might arise whose newsworthiness was such that it could not wait the three or four days until the next edition. In either case, printers would turn to earlier forms: the news-sheet (a single-sheet report, not published as part of a series), and the 'occasional' (a news-sheet published as an irregular series). For instance, a report on May 29, 1707, told readers of a Dublin packet ship, the *James*, taken in the Irish Sea by French privateers, leaving the Dublin papers that week with no foreign stories. However, when the captain of the *James* did make it ashore on May 31, valiantly clutching his manuscript letters and foreign newspapers, readers were belatedly offered a single-sheet occasional, entitled: *The James Packet Boat being taken by a Privateer on the 29th Instant, the following Letter was Preserved by the Master, which gives the following Advices of Two Holland and Two Flanders Mails from Great Britain.*[11] Similarly, a fascinatingly gruesome crime or a hanging that called out for the kind of detail the newspapers could not provide would bring out a string of news-sheets, such as (the self-explanatorily titled) *Full and True Account of the Surprizing and Apprehending of Capt. Fitz Garrald and four of his Rappareries near Tallow-Hill, in the House of one Mr. Ransford on the fifth of this Instant December in the Morning* (1717). And, every so often, a news-sheet took on a polemical role. For example, when the price of coal rose in 1711, John Whalley published an open letter *To the Right Honourable the Knights, Citizens and Burgesses in Parliament Assembled,* accusing a coal merchant of 'making use of short and false Measure'.[12]

---

[10] *Pue's Occurences Containing the Most Authentick and Frequent Transactions from All Parts, Carefully Collected and Impartially Translated* 16:1 (December 30 – January 3, 1718–19).

[11] *An Express from the Earl of Galway with Particulars of the late Bloody Battle fought with the Duke of Berwick in Spain, brought by a Ship in 18 days from Alican. As also the taking of a French Privateer by Capt. Saunders which is brought in here, together with News from Donaghadee and Dungarvan* (Dublin, 1707), n.p.

[12] *To the Right Honourable the Knights, Citizens and Burgesses in Parliament Assembled: A further and More Particular Account of the Several Publick Grievances committeed by John Mercer and those concern'd under him in the Coal-Trade, &c in the City of Dublin* (Dublin, 1711).

In addition to news-sheets, early eighteenth-century Irish journalists made allowance for late-breaking news in the layout of their regular newspapers. 'If any Pacquet or Pacquets shall happen to come in the same day soon after the Intelligence shall come forth,' *The Flying Post* informed its readers in 1702, 'the most material Matters of the same shall be Printed, by way of Postscript, on one side the blank half sheet and allowed to Subscribers (in the City and Suburbs) for Two Shillings and Six-pence per Quarter.'[13] It may have been a cumbersome way of produc-ing a newspaper; however, it testifies to the need to close, by whatever means possible, the time lapse between an event and its reporting in a journalistic world where the key word was 'fresh'. Thomas Toulmin's *Dublin Post*, for instance, advertised on its masthead 'the Freshest Advices, Foreign and Domestick', while the playful colophon for *The Flying Post* reads as follows:

Dublin: Printed by S. Powell and F. Dickson, next Door to the Post-Office ... where fresh and full News will always be Printed, without imparting old Trash on the Publick, 1708.

An Express from Lisbon, printed by Cornelius Carter (publisher of *The Flying Post*) on June 11, 1707 gives us a sense of the speed at which news travelled at its quickest in those years. Dated 'Cork, June 8th, 1707', the single-sheet occasional begins: 'A Ship just arrived here in 14 days from Lisbon, the Master says, the day before he came away his Portuguese Majesty had received an Express from the young Marquis das Minas, that according to his Majesty's Orders, he had repassed the River Tagus, ... and accordingly on the 22nd day of May, N.S., he attacked the enemy.' In other words, a battle was fought in the Portuguese countryside on May 22; on May 24, an 'Express' report of the battle reached Lisbon; fourteen days later, the report sailed into Cork harbour; and three days later it is printed in Dublin. In total, the elapsed time for news to travel from Portugal to Dublin in 1707 is twenty days. Twenty-five years later, in 1732, the regular post between Dublin and Cork still took three days, although it was delivered three times a week. Having said this, news sent in regular dispatches travelled more quickly, and a newspaper such as *Pue's Impartial Occurences* for July 24–27, 1714, for instance, contains stories with bylines dating from the previous week from London, Hamburg, The Hague and Paris, along with stories from two weeks previously from Vienna and Dresden.

---

[13] *The Flying Post* (June 29, 1702).

The printing of fresh news, whether from Lisbon or from Cork, was only the beginning of its circulation. The blank half-sheet found on so many Dublin newspapers of the period was not only for fast-breaking stories. As late as 1734, *Dalton's Impartial Newsletter* advised its readers that the paper was 'printed in a whole sheet, one half thereof being left blank, for the conveniency of any Gentleman or Dealers writing to his friend or correspondent therein',[14] and other papers continued this practice into the 1750s. This should remind us that reading an eighteenth-century newspaper was not exclusively a solitary activity. Certainly, 'gentlemen' had the newspapers delivered to their homes, and 'Dealers' to their businesses; but when that 'gentleman' wrote his own commentary on the printed news in the blank half-sheet, he was entering into dialogue with the printed word, producing, as it were, a personalised editorial, adding opinion and analysis to bare fact.

What is more, when Irish people were not reading newspapers at home, they were more often than not reading them in public places, such as coffee houses or taverns, where many of the major newspapers were based. For instance, Dick's Coffee House, in Dublin's Skinner's Lane, housed the press of Cornelius Carter, who published *The Flying Post*. Dick's later appears as the imprint for the work of Aaron Rhames, who published a series of short-lived newspapers, including *The Dublin Courant* (1705), the *Diverting Post* (1709), as well as a major edition of Temple's *The Irish Rebellion* (1724). 'I must say of this Dick,' wrote a visitor to the city in 1699, 'that he is a Witty and Ingenious man, makes the best Coffee in Dublin, and is very Civil and Obliging.'[15] Located only a short stroll from Dublin Castle, the Smock Alley Theatre and across the Liffey from the Courts, the citizens of Dublin would step into the rich atmosphere of coffee and pipe smoke, meet one another, read a newspaper, and perhaps add a few comments of their own on the blank half-sheet, before posting a copy to a friend (post offices were also associated with coffee houses). In the rear, Cornelius Carter would be sifting through the latest packet of letters, perhaps extracting a paragraph from the last week's *Hague Courant*, while his apprentice set up the type for the next issue of *The Flying Post*. A traveller who happened to drop in for a cup of coffee would be quizzed about events in Madrid or Bruges, or a boy from Ringsend might arrive with news of the ships docked in port that day.

[14] Munter, *History of the Irish Newspaper*, 75.
[15] John Dunton, *The Dublin Scuffle* (Dublin, 1699), 327.

The reader of *The Flying Post* was thus not by any means an isolated private individual. Indeed, if there is a single characteristic of the media world of Dublin in the eighteenth century, it is its vibrant intimacy. In coffee houses such as Dick's, debates took place not only among readers, but with the editor of the newspaper. If nothing else, this suggests that we must exercise judgement and imagination when reading news reports from the early decades of the eighteenth century which, to modern eyes, seem astonishingly laconic. 'On Wednesday last Mary Gaffany, born in Rabael in the County of Dublin, was Burned at the Common place of Execution near St. Stephen's Green, for the Murder of her Bastard Child', reports *The Dublin Gazette* during Christmas week, 1709.[16] An event which today would stir up a storm of analysis and commentary is baldly stated in 1709. But this does not mean there was no debate. Only the bare facts needed to be set down on paper; the kind of editorial opinion and commentary that would become so important later appears to have been provided in person, or on the blank half-sheet. In their own messy, personal way, places like Dick's – and newspapers like *The Flying Post* – were setting the conditions for what would become a vigorous public debate carried on through print in eighteenth-century Ireland.

THRIVING IN A LEGAL LOOPHOLE

Among the coffee cups and newspapers scattered over the tables in Dick's Coffee House were occasional advertisements for book auctions, which were also held on the premises. When the London bookseller, John Dunton, arrived in the city in 1699 with a consignment of books to sell, he was advised to go directly to Dick's, and to hold his auction there. Over the next quarter century notices regularly appear in the Dublin papers advertising book auctions, for which 'Catalogues may be had … at Luca's, Patts, Dicks and Pedrow's Coffee Houses.'[17] This in turn was part of a steady growth in the Dublin book trade, going back to 1672, when the Dublin booksellers organised themselves into a guild – the Guild of St Luke – and sidestepped the monopoly that had been given the King's Printer. When there was an attempt to re-appoint a King's Printer in 1685, Joseph Ray (who also produced *The News Letter*, and would later publish *Dublin Intelligence*) protested that such 'privileges were destructive to the

---

[16] *The Dublin Gazette*, (December 28 – January 1, 1708–9).
[17] *Pue's Impartial Occurences* (December 30 – January 3, 1718–19).

whole faculty of stationer members'.[18] Consequently, by the beginning of the seventeenth century, Irish printers and booksellers were prosperous enough, independent enough, and well enough organised to take advantage of a legislative change that would have a profound influence on Irish print culture for almost a century.

In the early years of the reign of Queen Anne, there was a brief period during which printers in England and Ireland both operated in an invigorating state of legal ambiguity. However, in 1709 this situation was brought to an end by the major piece of English copyright legislation of the period (8 Anne cap. 19), enacted 'for the encouragement of learned men to compose and write useful books'. As with the later Licensing Act of 1737 (10 Geo. II cap. 28), which regulated the theatre, this key piece of English law was never passed by the Irish Parliament, so that the rarefied air of a legislative vacuum that had existed in England prior to 1709 continued in Ireland until 1801. Instead of a code of law, Irish printers operated within the flexible framework of a series of gentlemen's agreements. As the book historian James Phillips puts it, 'the Dubliners' awareness of their extra-legal position, and of the advantages to be derived from it, was one of the basic factors in the growth of the Dublin trade'.[19]

Until this loophole opened up, it looked as if the Irish book trade was going to be limited by the size of the domestic market. In the late seventeenth century, the population of Dublin, while growing, was only going to support a limited number of booksellers. After 1709, it became possible for Irish printers to produce books more cheaply than their English counterparts, and to export them to England. On one hand, this did little to foster a literary culture in Ireland, insofar as just about every major Irish writer of the period packed their bags for London, where they had a reasonable chance of collecting some royalties. Thomas Southerne, George Farquhar and Richard Steele – to name just a few – were all born in Ireland, and based their careers in London. Jonathan Swift was something of an exception, but his residence in Dublin was enforced by his appointment as Dean of St Patrick's, so he had little choice in the matter. For Irish readers, on the other hand, the decades after 1709 were boom years. In the streets and alleys off of Dublin's Dame Street, with Trinity College at one end, Christchurch Cathedral at the other, there were

---

[18] Munter, *Dictionary of the Print Trade in Ireland*, 227.
[19] James W. Phillips, *Printing and Bookselling in Dublin, 1670–1800: A Bibliographic Enquiry* (Dublin, 1998), 107.

literally dozens of small printers and booksellers, jostling for attention amid the coffee houses and taverns.

We can take a rough measure of the rapid rise of printing in Ireland in the eighteenth century by counting the number of books with Dublin imprints for the period, as recorded by the *Eighteenth-Century Short Title Catalogue*. Admittedly, this is a crude measure: when exporting books to England, some Irish publishers were not above using a false London imprint, particularly after the Importation Act of 1739 made it illegal to import to Britain a copy of any book first published there. However, even as a rough guide, the upward curve is clear; from fewer than 1,000 items published in the first decade of the century, to a relatively constant figure of around 2,000 items per decade in the middle of the century, to the final, upward leap to more than 4,000 items per decade by the close of the century, boosted in part by the rapid growth of exports to North America after 1776.

We can measure the growth of Irish printing in the eighteenth century in another, perhaps cruder, but more striking manner. Robert Munter has shown that by 1737 there were about 32,000 reams of paper being imported into Ireland annually.[20] This tallies with figures contained in the *Commons Journal: Ireland*, which show that from 1749 to 1765, a total of 455,860 reams of paper were imported into Ireland, of which 130,628 were classified as 'writing paper', and the remainder, 325,232, was for printing. These numbers tell us two things. First of all, in terms of volume, the printed word surpassed the handwritten word as a means of communication by a factor of more than two to one by mid-century. Second, given that a ream of paper is 500 sheets, there were potentially as many as 160 million sheets (or 320 million pages) printed in Ireland in a 16-year period (or 20 million pages per annum).

Exactly how this paper was used must remain a matter of educated guesswork in the absence of any comprehensive distribution figures. We know, for instance, that the *Belfast Newsletter* was claiming distribution figures of between 2,000 and 3,000 copies per week by mid-century, but a lower figure probably pertains for the early part of the century. Taking a standard of four pages per newspaper, and an average of about ten strong newspapers in existence at any one time, by mid-century about ten per cent of the total (or 2 million sheets of paper) was being used for newspapers. The remainder, then, must have been used for other publications, ranging from proclamations and dispatches of a single sheet,

[20] Munter, *History of the Irish Newspaper*, 46.

to pamphlets, through to single and multi-volume works several hundred pages in length. By any measure, this is a substantial quantity of information.

As the volume of print began to increase, we find in Ireland a world that was not only increasingly ordered by print; we also find print being used to order print. Apart from booksellers' catalogues, there are publications such as *The Irish Historical Library* (1724), in which the Lord Bishop of Derry, William Nicholson, attempted to list all available historical sources, both print and manuscript, available at the time.[21] In 1751, theatre-goers who did not have time to attend the theatre could turn to *A Companion to the Theatre,* which summarised sixty-one popular plays, so that 'a very little Time employed in the perusal of any particular Play, gives the Reader that just and perfect Idea of it',[22] and this in turn was part of a burgeoning market in reference works of all kinds. In 1751, the Dublin printer George Faulkner, to take just one example, was selling *Chamber's Dictionary,* a seven-volume *Universal History* (an expensive purchase, at £9 20s. in folio), as well as a much more affordable volume, *The Compleat Family Piece: with Directions for Hunting, Hawking, Fishing, Fowling, Conserves, Confectionary, Cookery, Physick and Surgery,* selling at 3s. 3d.

One of the best ways of tracing the ways in which print came to order everyday life is through the fortunes of the almanacs. In the early seventeenth century, almanacs containing prophesies, astronomical information, travel directions and dates of fairs and markets, were among the first Irish books to have been printed for what might be called a general readership. In the later seventeenth century, Irish booksellers such as Andrew Crooke picked up where their predecessors had left off, publishing the first edition of *Whalley's Almanack* in 1685. However, by the 1720s, the old pronogostical almanacs had become a source of mockery, and in 1729 the Dublin bookseller and publisher John Watson decided to change the format, issuing the first *Gentlemen and Citizen's Almanack* in 1729, and then annually until 1766.[23] As the city expanded, Watson recognised that cryptic foreknowledge of the future was less important than being

[21] William Nicholson, *The Irish Historical Library, Pointing at Most of the Authors and Records in Print or Manuscript, Which May be Serviceable to the Compilers of a General History of Ireland* (Dublin, 1724).

[22] *A Companion to the Theatre: Or, A View of our Most Celebrated Dramatic Pieces: In which the Plan, Characters, and Incidents of each are Particularly Explained. Interspersed with Remarks Historical, Critical and Moral* (Dublin, 1751), n.p.

[23] Edward Evans, *Historical and Bibliographical Account of Almanacks, Directories, etc.* (Dublin, 1897), 20.

able to find a reputable solicitor or hosier, so he dropped most of the old prophecy in favour of a directory of business listings. Peter Wilson, a bookseller whose Dame Street premises were near those of Watson on Merchant's Quay, developed this idea further in 1751, when he offered the first *Dublin Directory* for sale – a publication that would continue into the nineteenth century, until it was replaced by *Thom's Directory*. Thus, in tiny stages, every time an Irish person consulted an almanac or a directory, Irish life took one more step towards being ordered by print – or at least life in those parts of the country that were within reach of print.

As well as expanding in volume, print in Ireland spread geographically in the middle years of the eighteenth century. The old-style almanac (which survived alongside the new directories of mid-century), and its chronicle of fairs and markets were staple goods in the packs of travelling pedlars. From 1746, travelling pedlars in Ireland were compelled to hold a licence, which cost £1 per year (plus £1 for every pack animal); by 1750, the annual revenue from this licence was £2,258, which represented some 1,800 pedlars. While the almanacs sold by travelling pedlars changed from year to year, most of the small, cheaply bound books (or 'chapbooks') that made up the stock of these itinerant booksellers changed little over the course of the century, composed mostly of popular histories, chivalric romances, pious miscellanies and tales of crime. Hugh Reily's *Impartial History of Ireland*, for instance, went through at least nineteen editions between 1690 and 1837, while an 1801 edition of *The Seven Champions of Christendom* claimed to be the '21st edition'. Indeed, there were some printers who seem to have specialised in chapbooks. For instance, *The Late Dreadful Plague, &c*, which gave practical advice on how to avoid infection (dispensed with the claim that it had sold 400,000 copies in England), was printed in Dublin by Catherine Hicks, 'at the Rein Deer in Montrath-Street, for the Good of the Publick. Where Chapmen may be furnish'd with Story-Books, and Ballads, &c., at Reasonable Rates'.[24] Similarly, Niall Ó Ciosáin notes that the Dublin Quaker bookseller Samuel Fuller had 700 bound and 26,000 unbound chapbooks in stock when he died in 1735.[25]

While the reading matter available to Irish people around the country who depended on the chapmen remained limited for many years, for those with access to the Dublin booksellers the variety of items published in Ireland mushroomed in the first half of the eighteenth century.

---

[24] *The Late Dreadful Plague, &c.* (Dublin, n.d.).
[25] Niall Ó Ciosáin, *Print and Popular Culture in Ireland, 1750–1850* (Basingstoke, 1997), 63, 54.

As might be expected, there was a rush to print new work by major English-language writers, with more than forty works by Alexander Pope published in the 1730s, for instance, and more than fifty by Jonathan Swift. In the cases of Pope, Swift, Joseph Addison, Farquhar and other major figures, it is also possible to see canonical literary reputations taking shape, as each of their new works appears initially in individual volumes, followed a decade or two later by a collected works. So, for instance, in the case of Pope the forty-two editions of the 1730s had shrunk to one edition of *The Rights of Man*, and twelve different editions of *The Works of Alex. Pope Esq.* by 1750. Equally, books began to be published in Dublin in languages other than English. For instance, in the decade from 1731 to 1740, there were twelve different books by Voltaire available with Irish imprints, including three different editions of his *Siècle de Louis XIV* in the original French and a Dublin French-language edition of the *Lettres philosophiques* in 1739.

On one hand, the existence of a small, but vigorous, French-language publishing industry in mid-eighteenth-century Dublin is a vivid rebuttal of the idea that Irish culture was isolated or inward-looking. On the other hand, it makes the position of the Irish language, which continued to be spoken by the vast majority of the Irish population, all the more anomalous. The habitués of the Dublin coffee houses lived in a world that was saturated with print: their opinions, beliefs and knowledge of the world were shaped by the printed word. They prayed with its aid, argued by means of pamphlets, regulated their society through printed laws and took part in a world beyond Irish shores through the growing number of books available from abroad. Meanwhile, for the more than one and a half million people whose first language was Irish, there were just over thirty books with Irish imprints published in the Irish language throughout the entire eighteenth century. Eight of these were Bibles, and most of the rest were various theological tracts, including *A Book of Common Prayer, to Which Are Prefixed Brief and Plain Rules for Reading the Irish Language*, published in Dublin in 1710, suggesting that the function of printed Irish had not changed substantially since *Aibidil Gaoidheilge agus Caiticiosma* in 1571. There were, of course, some exceptions. An *Almanack an gaoidheilg arson uliana an Tighnearna Croisda*, published at the instigation of the philosopher Francis Hutcheson in 1724, for instance, made a hesitant move towards making print part of everyday life for Irish-speakers, in the way that early almanacs had done for English-speakers in the 1620s. However, this was an isolated case, and for the most part the schisms etched between print culture and oral culture along linguistic lines continued throughout the eighteenth century.

Monoglot Irish-speakers (or, indeed, illiterate English-speakers) were thus increasingly cut off from a society upon which order was being imposed through the medium of print. The volume of proclamations issued by the Lords Justices, for instance, increased exponentially in the decade after 1710, and remained high throughout the century. And, even as pamphlets continued to tumble off the presses complaining about the lack of real legislative power accorded to the Irish Parliament, its proceedings were handsomely printed, and bound in what are considered some of the finest bindings ever produced. There are two ways of looking at this increase in the printing of legal documents; on one hand, it might be seen simply as an instrument of state control reaching further and further into the lives of its citizens. At the same time, as the laws became public, they became accessible, thereby empowering citizens in their exercise. *An Exact Abridgement of All the Publick Printed Statutes*, published in Dublin 1724, for instance, made it possible for any literate person to gain access to basic legislation that had previously been, at best, the exclusive domain of a professional legal class. Later, Giles Jacob took this idea a step further with his popular *Every Man His Own Lawyer* (1755), 'calculated for giving Country Gentlemen, Merchants, Tradesmen and others, a General Idea of our Common and Statute Laws: so that by the diligent Perusal of this instructive Treatise, they may, in a great Measure, be enabled to know what the Law is … without giving them the Trouble of turning over a great Number of Books.'[26] We get a sense of the politics of publishing *Every Man His Own Lawyer* when we recognise that the man who printed and sold it, Oliver Nelson, would be instrumental in leading the Guild of St Luke to take a stand on the freedom of the press in the late 1740s and early 1750s.

'MIXING TRUE NEWS WITH WHAT'S SPURIOUS'

The grounds for those print wars of mid-century were laid, at least in part, in the spring of 1725, when James Carson, publisher of the occasional *Dublin Intelligence*, was approached by Lord Molesworth and James Arbuckle with a view to producing a new kind of Irish periodical. When Dubliners picked up the first copies of the *Dublin Weekly Journal* on

---

[26] *Every Man His Own Lawyer; Or, A Summary of the Laws Now in Force in Ireland, in a New and Instructive Method* (Dublin, 1755), i.

April 3, 1725, it would have looked like a newspaper: it had a masthead, banner, would appear regularly, was dated and had continuous pagination. However, the content (written largely by Arbuckle, with later contributions from others, notably the philosopher Francis Hutcheson) went far beyond simple news, and it would go on to publish Hutcheson's influential 'Inquiry into the Original of our Ideas of Beauty and Virtue', essays on liberty, aesthetics, exploration, natural history and poetry, all framed by extracts from the *London Gazette*, letters from European capitals, some local news, a weekly 'Bill of Mortality for the City and Suburbs of Dublin', and the first column in an Irish newspaper directed at women readers (signed 'Martha Love-Rule'). Robert Munter has argued that the *Dublin Weekly Journal* is important as Ireland's first literary periodical,[27] but it is more than that. 'The Publick good [has been] the chief motive for my Writing,' announces Arbuckle on Christmas Eve, 1725, 'to recommend universal Benevolence, publick Spirit; and the Love of our Country'.[28] Interweaving the quotidian with philosophical speculation, the *Dublin Weekly Journal* set about creating print-mediated environment in which ideas were part of the fabric of daily life. Or, as a single-sheet poem of 1726 put it:

> Arbuckle writes in's *Wee[k]ly Journal*
> How Phoebus rose and set diurnal, ...
> And mixes true News with what's Spurious,
> To please the Ignorant, and Curious.
> Yet after all this Stir and Pother,
> The *Journal* soon becomes Bumfodder.[29]

When philosophy gets mixed with daily news, there is clearly something astir in a culture, and the *Dublin Weekly Journal* was part of a larger shift in Irish culture in the 1720s. In its first edition, Arbuckle makes clear his purpose in launching the journal:

If a good piece happens at any Time to be wrote among ourselves, there is scarce One in Ten will vouchsafe it a Reading, unless it be made Authentick by being Printed in London. Thus, our Brains are being Manufactured Abroad, become an Expence to the Nation; and we are forced to make a Purchase of our own Wit and Learning, which hereby are made hurtful to the Native Soil.[30]

---

[27] Munter, *History of the Irish Newspaper*, 160.
[28] *Dublin Weekly Journal* (December 24, 1725).
[29] *The Printers Petition to the Poetical Senate Assembled in Grub Street* (Dublin, 1726).
[30] *Dublin Weekly Journal* (April 3, 1725).

The political context for this new assertiveness is the Declaratory Act of 1720, which was intended as a step towards the further consolidation of the new terms under which Ireland was governed after the Treaty of Limerick. In practice, however, by proclaiming the right of the Westminster Parliament to legislate for Ireland, the Act gave focus to a percolating sense of resentment, solidarity and identity among descendents of the Anglo-Irish who had settled in the country in waves throughout the seventeenth century. 'To be born in Ireland is usually looked upon as a Misfortune', commented Arbuckle in 1725. 'Yet I once knew a Gentleman, who said, He had the Honour to be born in Ireland; a saying I have always reflected upon with a great deal of Pleasure.'[31] For the first time, this group – who were at the heart of print culture – began to claim for themselves a 'Native' culture (a word that had been used up until that point effectively as a synonym for Gaelic Ireland), and to write of themselves as a 'Nation' – both words that Arbuckle uses in his first essay in the *Weekly Journal*.

To put this in a wider context, the *Weekly Journal* began publication within a year of Jonathan's Swift's *Drapier's Letters*, which responded to a proposal to introduce a new Irish coinage by arguing for greater Irish self-determination. 'Am I a Free man in England,' demanded Swift's Drapier, in words that would be reprinted many times over the coming century, 'and do I become a Slave in six Hours by crossing the Channel?'[32] Swift's pamphlets were part of an upsurge in printing in the city: only sixteen new newspaper titles appeared in the first decade of the century, in the decade 1710–19 there were twenty-six new newspapers, and a further twenty-eight new titles in the 1720s. For the rest of the century, the average number of new titles per decade would be eleven. Few of the new newspapers launched in the 1720s lasted more than a few months. However, the willingness to go on launching new titles suggests a perception that there was an unsatisfied hunger for new sources of information, or for new angles on that information. Amidst all of this activity, there is a powerful new idea emerging: that there exists a 'Publick' whom the medium of print could address, improve and (with a logical sleight of hand) bring into being.

The *Dublin Weekly Journal* continued until 1752, and over the years the paper's mission to 'recommend … publick Spirit' led Carson to support

---

[31] *Dublin Weekly Journal* (November 6, 1725).
[32] Jonathan Swift, *The Drapier's Letters and Other Works, 1724–1725*, ed. Herbert Davis (Oxford, 1941), 31.

the campaigns of the Dublin apothecary and Councillor, Charles Lucas. Lucas was elected to the Common Council of the City of Dublin in 1741, and soon set about using public opinion to battle a corrupt system of patronage at municipal level, and ultimately to question the role of England in Irish government. 'Ireland,' he wrote in an open letter addressed to George II in 1749, 'by the frequent incursions of powerful, savage Invaders, ... was, at length, reduced to that blind Ignorance, that base Bigotry, and Barbarism, the fatal, the horrid, though Necessary, Consequence of the Deprivation of Liberty.'[33] For 1749, this was a step too far: Lucas was declared a public enemy, and banished from Dublin (although he returned in 1760, was elected to Parliament, and in 1763 founded the *Freeman's Journal* with Henry Brooks).

Both the *Drapier's Letters* affair, and Lucas's campaign of 1749 used the print media to bypass sanctioned (and tightly controlled) forms of public discourse, such as Parliamentary debate. Nonetheless, the paper war of 1749 marks a shift in Ireland's media culture. As well as speaking publicly, and publishing pamphlets, Lucas founded a newspaper, *The Censor Extraordinary*, which was a newspaper unlike any previous Irish newspaper:

Whosoever taketh a View of the State of this Nation from the first Dawnings of Government in it, will see a Scene, perhaps, the most melancholy that History affords, such a Succession of TYRANNY, handed down under the names of Kings, Priests, Lords, Lords Lieutenants, Lords Deputies, Lords Justices, Lords Bishops and Lords ALDERMEN, and all the Lords who have lorded over us, that it is sufficient to make us ... abjure the Name of Irishmen.[34]

Published in dated, more or less regular editions, with a masthead, it had the appearance of a newspaper; but in content, it was a continuation (under the pseudonym of 'Frank Somebody') of Lucas's increasingly incendiary pamphleteering. During the fiercely fought election campaign of the summer of 1749, the *Censor* was not alone in changing the Irish newspaper world; indeed, it was a response to an anti-Lucas periodical, *The Tickler*, and was in turn countered by *The Alarm Bell*. At sixteen pages *The Alarm Bell* was four times longer than most newspapers of the period, and was effectively a series of pamphlets; yet, like the *Censor*, it appeared in newspaper format, with a masthead and date.[35]

[33] Charles Lucas, *The Great Charter of the Liberties of the City of Dublin* (Dublin, 1749), ix.
[34] *Censor Extraordinary* (August 19–21, 1749).
[35] Anthony Litten, *The Cork Surgeon's Antidote against the Dublin Apothecary's Poyson for the Citizens of Dublin* 1 (Dublin, 1749), 5.

Irish newspapers, which had hitherto largely contented themselves with reprinting facts, would never be quite the same again. When Lucas returned to Dublin to found the *Freeman's Journal* in 1763 (which was to continue, in a variety of political liveries, until 1924), it was not dissimilar in some ways from the crusading newspapers of the next century, from the *Northern Star* in the 1790s to *The Nation* in the 1840s. Indeed, of the more than 100 Dublin newspapers founded before 1770, the *Freeman's Journal* would be only one of four (the others were *Impartial Occurences, Saunder's Newsletter* and *Hunter's Dublin Chronicle*) to survive later than 1780. Toning down the rhetoric of *The Censor*, the *Freeman's Journal* left readers in no doubt as to its editorial politics; but it also ran a variety of local and international news, upon which it commented with varying degrees of vigour, depending on the piece's relevance to the paper's own campaigns. If prior to 1750 the commentary and analysis in Irish newspapers took place in person, in the coffee house or scribbled in the blank half-sheets of early news-sheets, from 1749 onwards it increasingly appeared in the newspaper itself, moving the public sphere one step deeper into the medium of print.

'THE HARD LAWS OF DISTANCE'

As the role of print in Ireland changed, so too did its geography. Although there had been printing in Cork, Kilkenny and Waterford in the 1640s, there was no sustained development of printing in these cities until later in the eighteenth century. Instead, in the early decades of the eighteenth century, outside of Dublin the major centre for Irish printing was Belfast, where Patrick Neill began publishing religious works in 1694, and by mid-century there were a number of printers at work, publishing plays, pamphlets and almanacs. Elsewhere in Ireland, printing spread slowly: there was a newspaper being published in Limerick in 1716; the printer James Coulter was at work in Derry in 1724, and by the 1750s there were printers in Downpatrick, Drogheda and Carrickfergus, and Cork, which grew rapidly, eventually surpassing Belfast in the number of items printed outside of Dublin. Elsewhere, printworks did not appear until later in the century: for instance, Carlow (1773), Birr (1775), Ennis (1779), Wexford (1774), Youghal (1784) and Coleraine (1791).

In part, the spread of printing throughout Ireland was a case of an expanding industry moving into new markets. In the decade 1731–40, only 59 items were printed outside of Dublin; in the following decade, this figure almost triples to 144, and by the decade 1791–1800, there are

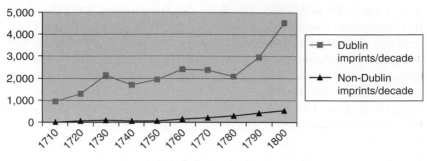

Fig 1. Irish imprints, 1700–1800.

more than 500 items printed in towns and cities outside of Dublin – roughly one per week. Moreover, printing generated printing. The Belfast printer Francis Joy, for example, began as a tailor, started selling the Dublin newspapers (about three days late), bought a press, and in 1737 founded the *Belfast Newsletter*. A decade later, he began making his own printing presses, and by 1748 he not only had presses operating in Newry and Armagh, he was also operating three paper-making factories, located in Randalstown and Ballymena,[36] creating a vertically integrated industry, albeit on a modest scale.

A small printer such as Joy would take any available work: lottery tickets, notices, playbills, pamphlets or sermons. However, such work was intermittent, and a newspaper at least provided steady employment, even if it was self-employment. So, as printing spread, so too did newspapers. Prior to 1750, there are only three Irish newspapers printed outside of Dublin: the first, the short-lived *Limrick News-Letter* (1716), and its equally short-lived successor, Andrew Welsh's *Limerick Journal* (1739); and Joy's *Belfast Newsletter* (1737). Then, at the endpoints of major post-roads, four new titles appeared in the 1750s: the *Sligo Journal* (1752), the *Connaught Journal* in Galway (1754), and two Cork papers, the *Cork Journal* and *Cork Evening Post*, both founded in 1755. Five new titles appear in the 1760s: two more in Cork (in 1765 and 1768), a first newspaper in Waterford (1765), *Finn's Leinster Journal* in Kilkenny (1766), and the *Limerick Chronicle* (1766). Of these early newspapers, three of the Cork newspapers, and the titles from Galway, Sligo and Waterford would all last until into the middle of the nineteenth century, while the *Newsletter* in Belfast, and the *Chronicle* in Limerick are both

---

[36] Munter, *Dictionary of the Print Trade in Ireland*, 151.

still being published today, making the *Belfast Newsletter* the oldest Irish newspaper in existence.

From the beginning, successful papers such as the *Limerick Chronicle* or *Finn's Leinster Journal* mixed Irish and international pieces with local news: local politics, reports from the local markets and fairs, land and stallions for sale, notices of absconded servants and occasional pieces on local history or culture. The formula was a tempting enough proposition that in the 1770s sixteen new titles were launched outside of Dublin; this was more than in the preceding three decades combined, and, for the first time, outpaced the twelve new titles that appeared in the capital in the same period.

Newspapers began appearing around Ireland at about the same time that improvements in the postal service made it possible, under ideal circumstances, for news from Dublin (and beyond) to trot towards a local newspaper on the Private Express post, introduced in 1765, at a dizzying five miles per hour. Even before then, however, the mid-century introduction of a daily Dublin–Limerick postal service meant, for instance, that Andrew Welsh's *Munster Journal* (Limerick) for January 23, 1755, contains news from Dublin dated January 21, London (January 14), Paris (January 3), Amsterdam (January 2), St Petersburg (December 13), and what it refers to as 'Plantation News' from Fredericksburg, Virginia, dated three months earlier, on October 28. In each case, the gap between an event and its reporting is more or less the same as we would expect from a Dublin newspaper of the period (adding only the three days travel from Dublin to Limerick), although it is equally possible that some (or indeed all) of the overseas news was arriving directly from a southern port, rather than through Dublin.

Between finding the fastest way between two towns, and publishing locally, the growth of newspapers in Ireland in the eighteenth century shows a new need to pare away the gap between an event and knowledge of that event. As the speed of information increased, Irish people began to glimpse the tantalising possibility of eliminating space. 'Hail Mystick Art!', proclaimed the printer Constantia Grierson, in 'The Art of Printing: A Poem', in 1764:

> With the hard Laws of Distance we dispence,
> And, without Sound, apart, commune in Sence...[37]

For news, where the time between the event and reading was crucial, the 'hard Laws of Distance' were still very real. On one hand, local

---

[37] [Constantia Grierson], *The Art of Printing: A Poem* (Dublin, 1764).

newspapers did begin to weave a shared informational zone, and for the first time in Irish history readers in Cork, Derry and Galway all learned of the Lisbon earthquake, or the accession of George III at approximately the same time. And yet, while this would eventually help weave the basis for at least conceptualising a shared island-wide consciousness, the local press reinforced existing local and regional loyalties, by giving them tangible form in print. This sense of local identity is neatly encapsulated by the woodcut that appeared in the masthead of the *Clonmel Gazette*: it is a wheel, at first glance like a globe or planetary sphere, but inscribed with 'Principal Counties in which This Paper Circulates Are: Clare, Tipperary, Kilkenny; Corke; Limerick; K[ings]. County; Q[ueens]. County; Count Waterford.' In short, the spread of print in the final quarter of the eighteenth century in Ireland created (or at least consolidated) worlds which were often intensely local; however, this happened just as a new kind of print culture was emerging, one that saw itself as embodying the idea of the nation.

THE PALLADIUM OF RIGHTS

On November 11, 1783, a new kind of newspaper appeared in the coffee houses and taverns of Dublin: the *Volunteer Evening Post*. On its front page, it laid out its creed: 'The Volunteers of Ireland consider the Liberty of the Press as sacred, and that it forms an essential part of that freedom for which they have so long and effectively contended.' In that same issue, its editors published an open letter 'To the Irish Nation':

It may be truly asserted, that since the Art of Printing was first introduced into this kingdom, the people were never so deeply interested in the conduct of the Press as at present. Every consideration that can possibly be dear to us, depends at this awful moment, on a faithful representation of public men and public measures; and which can only be communicated to the people at large through the medium that has been called the Palladium of all civil, political and religious rights.[38]

The *Volunteer Evening Post*, like the *Volunteer Journal*, which had begun publication in Cork a year earlier, were both part of a larger movement in Irish political life in the final quarter of the eighteenth century. Initially, the Volunteers had been founded as an unpaid militia during the winter of 1778–9, at a time when many of the regular troops were off trying to

---

[38] *Volunteer Evening Post* 1:1 (November 11, 1783).

put down the American Revolution. Raised locally, with officers generally drawn from the local gentry, they soon tapped into the sense of Patriot identity that had been slowly percolating since the 1720s, and by May of 1782 they were 60,000 strong, and capable of giving a physical presence to the campaign for legislative independence that led to the creation of an independent Irish Parliament in 1782.

In retrospect, the most visible indication of the Volunteer movement might appear to have been their public gatherings, where units dressed in their full military regalia would gather in fields and public squares to cheer speeches by their commanders and Irish political leaders. However, it is only possible to fit a limited number of people into a field. So, for many Irish people, the experience of these public meetings was mediated by print, as the various Volunteer newspapers devoted increasing amounts of space to printing speeches from the meetings. 'Resolved Unanimously at a General Meeting of the Boyne Volunteers Corps', reads a typical announcement in the *Volunteer Journal* on November 14, 1782: 'That those our Resolutions be published in the Cork Papers, and *Dublin Evening Post*.'[39] Not only resolutions appeared in its pages: full texts of speeches, complete with replies and responses, filled columns in the *Volunteer Journal*, alongside reports from London, Paris or New York, local news, verses and, paying for it all, advertisements. In short, Volunteers were a local movement by virtue of their public meetings; but they were a national movement by virtue of print.

There is a new sense not only of national culture in these newspapers; there is a new ability to imagine Ireland's place in an international informational order. When the *Volunteer Evening Post* began publication, it announced in its first issue that its primary objects 'shall be to protect the national character from the shafts of envy and malevolence, to faithfully convey to distant countries, and to the most remote parts of this kingdom, the sentiments and proceedings of our Military Associations', and to this end the *Volunteer Evening Post* claimed it would set up a network of newsgathering and distribution, with:

correspondents and agents at London, Paris, and Madrid, also in every principal city on the German continent, six in the American provinces, two at Philadelphia, two at New York, and two at Boston. Instructions were also given to employ competent people to vend the Paper throughout England and Scotland, and to effect a general distribution over this kingdom.[40]

---

[39] *Volunteer Journal* 1:3 (November 14, 1782).
[40] *Volunteer Evening Post* 1:1 (November 11, 1783).

There is, in fact, little evidence of this network of foreign correspondents in the paper's subsequent reporting. However, the realisation here is less important than the aspiration: in particular, where earlier Irish newspapers had carried news from North America under the heading of 'Plantation News' as reports from distant outposts, in the Volunteer press we see a remapping of the world that now included America as a republic that was if not contiguous to, at least was consonant with Ireland.

It is difficult to over-estimate the influence of the American Revolution on the Volunteers. 'If the example of the Americans successfully contending in the cause of freedom, can be of any use to other nations,' wrote George Washington to a delegation of Volunteers in 1783 (and duly published in the *Volunteer Evening Post*), 'we shall have an additional motive for rejoicing at so prosperous an event.'[41] Nor was it simply the case that Irish nationalists were discussing America; the opposite was also true. For instance, in 1795 the Philadelphia bookseller Thomas Stephens printed *Proceedings of the Society of United Irishmen of Dublin*, occasioning a reply from 'Peter Porcupine', entitled *A Bone to Gnaw*, taking issue with what he saw as a '*sans culotte* manual'.[42] In both directions, the growing influence of America on Irish public life in the 1780s was due in part to the change in the Irish media world. Whereas in the 1750s, news from North America appeared in Irish newspapers three or four months late, by the early 1780s, the increase in shipping across the North Atlantic was closing the informational gap between Ireland and the new cities of the American eastern seaboard. In the *Volunteer Evening Post* from November 20, 1783, for instance, there are news reports from London dated November 13, from Vienna dated October 21, and from New York dated October 11. The time lapse between Dublin and both London and Vienna is more or less as it had been sixty years earlier; New York, on the other hand, has crept closer on the informational map, until it is almost as close as Vienna. Moreover, it was not only news that was crossing the North Atlantic more quickly. When trade restrictions were lifted in 1783, many Irish printers and booksellers turned to the new American market, and there was a boom in Irish printing. It was the growth in trans-Atlantic commerce, for instance, which helps to explain why *Wilson's Dublin*

---

[41] *Volunteer Evening Post* 1:31 (January 20, 1784).
[42] Peter Porcupine, *A Bone to Gnaw, for the Democrat Containing 1st Observations on a Patriotic Pamphlet entitled 'Proceedings of the United Irishmen'* (Philadelphia, 1795).

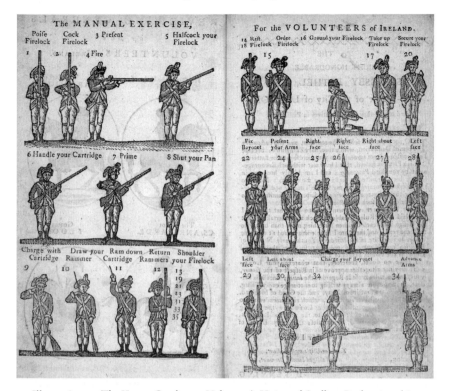

Illustration 3. *The Young Gentleman Volunteer's Universal Spelling Book*, printed in
Dublin by Patrick Wogan in the 1780s, contained instructions for the
two essential skills needed by a 'Young Gentleman Volunteer': literacy,
and the ability to handle a gun.

Directories shows an increase in Dublin-based book-trade businesses from
70 in 1781 to 118 in 1793.[43]

The book trade in Ireland – including trade with the United States –
had both an economic and a political dimension in the final decades of
the eighteenth century. In the wake of the American Revolution of 1776,
the Westminster Parliament imposed a series of restrictions on Irish
overseas trade, leading to a series of protests that culminated with a mass
protest of more than 3,000 Volunteers in College Green, demanding 'Free
Trade or Else' in November of 1779. Books were at the heart of the Free

[43] Vincent Kinane, *A Brief History of Printing and Publishing in Ireland* (Dublin, 2002), 20.

Trade debate, for the trade in books were both like other forms of trade (in that they had monetary value), and unlike them, in that they contained ideas. 'In this city, particularly,' wrote a correspondent to the *Volunteer Evening Post* in 1784, 'printers of newspapers have all at once commenced patriots.'[44] Consequently, any number of pamphlets and newspaper articles in those years argue – not without self-interest – for the importance of a free and economically viable press. 'The Liberty of the Press has been always considered the principal source of the superior degree of freedom and civilization of the British Dominions', writes 'A Private Gentleman' in his 'Observations' on 'the Liberty of the Press, the Volunteers, and Roman Catholics of Ireland' in 1784.[45]

The direction in which these arguments were heading is made implicitly clear by a little book published by Catholic printer, Patrick Wogan: *The Young Gentleman's Volunteer Universal Spelling Book; or, a New and Easy Guide to the English Language* (illustration 3), which by 1785 was in its seventeenth edition. Spelling books and guides to reading had been among the very first items printed in Ireland two centuries earlier; but this one was different. Its opening pages contain a series of woodcuts, showing the (possibly illiterate) Volunteer how to recognise his officers: the Duke of Leinster, the Earl of Charlemont and the Earl of Clanricarde. Woodcuts then demonstrate 'Manual Exercises for the Volunteers of Ireland' in the use of firearms: 'Poise Firelock', 'Cock Firelock' and so on.[46] However, the rest of the book is a reader, containing lists of words ('of two, three, four, five and six syllables'), and short moral tales and biblical texts for reading practice. The equation here is clear: a Volunteer must not only know how to handle his gun; he must also be able to read. By the mid-1780s, then, literacy was seen as a precondition both of liberty, and of nationality.

---

[44] *Volunteer Evening Post* 1:76 (May 1–4, 1784).

[45] *Observations on the Parliamentary Conduct of the Right Hon. John Foster; as also on the Liberty of the Press, the Volunteers, and Roman Catholics of Ireland* (Dublin, 1784).

[46] Daniel Fenning, *The Young Gentleman's Volunteer Universal Spelling Book: or, A New and Easy Guide to the English Language*, 17th edn (Dublin, 1785).

Media Event 2:
Postroads to liberty: January 22, 1793

Paris, Tuesday, January 22

Louis arrived at the foot of the Scaffold, at twenty minutes past ten. He mounted the Scaffold with firmness and dignity, he appeared desirous to address the people, but even this last wish was denied him, drums and trumpets gave the signal, and at twenty-two minutes past ten, his head was severed from his body.[1]

On January 22, 1793, Louis XVI was publicly executed in the centre of Paris. Eight days later the people of Belfast were reading accounts of the execution in the January 26–30 edition (which appeared on January 30) of the *Northern Star*. Interest in Belfast in events in Paris was intense that week, for when the French National Convention had voted to execute Louis XVI, the twice-weekly *Northern Star* reverted to the practice of printers earlier in the century, and rushed out a special news-sheet on Saturday, January 26, 1793, reporting on events in Paris a few days earlier. The effect was to create not only a sense of urgency and immediacy among Belfast readers for an event that had taken place in Paris, but also a sense of bearing witness to events as they happened. So, for instance, Louis's trial was published verbatim, as if it were a playscript:

President: Have you any more to say in your defence?
Louis [XVI]: No.
President: Sir, you are at liberty to retire.[2]

---

[1] *Northern Star* ɪɪ:9 (January 26–30, 1793).
[2] *Northern Star* ɪɪ:2 (January 2–5, 1793).

The time for news to travel from Paris to Belfast – eight days – may have remained the same for much of the century, but by presenting news in a style rich with dialogue, detail and minute-by-minute accounts, the *Northern Star* emphasised the immediacy of distant events, thereby creating a geography of the mind in which Belfast was a Paris *arrondissement*, to which the flames of revolution could easily spread.

Like the Volunteer movement before them, the United Irishmen were extraordinarily self-conscious and articulate about the centrality of the press to their political project. 'No maxim is more true than this: "That no Liberty can survive the Liberty of the Press"', declared the United Irishman Arthur O'Connor in his first editorial for *The Press* on September 28, 1797.

It breathes a soul into the body of the people; it forms their manners, and by teaching them their duties and their rights, and inspiring them with the sentiments of virtue, and courage by which they are to be enforced, introduces the empire of reason to the universe; it is the vestal fire upon the preservation of which, the fate of Nations depends.[3]

Indeed, calling a newspaper 'The Press' in 1797 was to make a statement that 'The Press' was more than a piece of machinery; it was an abstract principle. 'The invention of printing in the 14th century of the Christian era … altered not only the moral but the physical state of Europe', declared a correspondent signing himself 'William Caxton' in the October 5, 1797, edition of *The Press*. 'In the former crude state of the art of writing, it was easy for the tyrant to stop the progress of truth … Not so printing – by the press the writer could bay the tyrant in his den … The Press is the Palladium of Liberty.'[4]

The United Irishmen put an enormous amount of energy into realising this ideal of print as the foundation of a national culture. As Mary Helen Thuente has argued, 'newspapers, songbooks, and prose satires were central to the United Irish movement'.[5] *The Press* and the *Northern Star* in Belfast (as well as other shorter-lived titles that appeared throughout the 1790s) carried the staples of local news, international news, letters to the editor and advertising, as well as reports of meetings. However, they were much more than newspapers. The August 24–8, 1793, edition of the *Northern Star*, for instance, carried details of the Constitution of the

[3] *The Press* (September 28, 1797).
[4] *The Press* (October 5, 1797).
[5] Mary Helen Thuente, *The Harp Re-strung: The United Irishmen and the Rise of Irish Literary Nationalism* (Syracuse, NY, 1994), 89.

Republic laid down by the French National Convention in Paris. The paper also serialised the writings (and later, the trial) of Tom Paine. It printed original poetry and satires, and these were republished in song-books, such as the phenomenally popular *Paddy's Resource*. And, of course, the *Northern Star* was also responsible for publishing *Bolg an tSolair: or, Gaelic Magazine*, the first periodical to appear in the Irish language.

In other words, the form in which the *Northern Star* reported events such as the execution of Louis XVI, or the trial of Tom Paine, helped the newspaper cope with a gulf between idea and reality in the emerging equation between literacy and citizenship in the struggle for full citizen-ship in a culture with less than full literacy. Songbooks such as *Paddy's Resource* were one way of coping with this, in that printed songs and recitations could be memorised and sung, even by those who could not read. In other ways, as well, there is a new awareness of audience in a work such as Wolfe Tone's *Argument on Behalf of the Catholics of Ireland* of 1791, which largely dispensed with the classical allusion and presumption of an educated audience that had characterised the work of Addison, for instance. The writings of the United Irishmen, as Kevin Whelan points out, 'were a stylistic as much as a political triumph and set the tone for a flood of populist political writing',[6] and this was particularly true of the *Northern Star*. Although it sold an average of 4,200 copies per issue (and thus was at the higher end of circulation figures for the period), this still only represented a fraction of the Irish population for a paper whose project was the creation of a national audience. However, it has been claimed that many copies were read by more than one reader, and some were read aloud to those who could not read.[7] While it is difficult to prove this, it is certainly the case that the vivid narrative style of reporting Louis's execution, for instance, or the playscript-style transcription of his trial were written in a form that could easily be transformed back into an oral performance, taking place more or less simultaneously throughout the imagined nation.

However, these carefully formulated ideals constantly ran up against simple physical obstacles. Later, of course, both the *Northern Star* and *The Press* eventually encountered the most obvious form of physical obstacle, in the brute force of military censorship. However, even before

---

[6] Kevin Whelan, *The Tree of Liberty: Radicalism, Catholicism and the Construction of Irish Identity, 1760–1830* (Cork, 1996), 71.
[7] Thuente, *The Harp Re-strung*, 89.

soldiers knocked down the doors of the Belfast offices of the paper, and smashed its type, the *Northern Star* was struggling against the material realities of creating a national culture through print. We know this because, when it was closed down by the government in 1797, the military seized every piece of paper they could get their hands on, thinking (not incorrectly) that the newspaper's business records would provide a useful guide not only to the organisers of the United Irish movement (who were largely known in any case), but also to the wider circle of sympathisers who read the paper. As a result of this forcible archiving, we can trace not only democratic decision-making structures adopted by the paper's founders – all of whose decisions 'shall be by ballot in all cases without exception'[8] – but also the day-to-day struggles involved in distributing the paper.

Although it made some use of the existing postal system, the *Northern Star* also had its own distributors, who used specially adapted carrier bags to bring the paper from Belfast around the country. Even so, papers were often late, and sometimes went missing. When some newspapers went missing in 1792, the notebooks record that 'the Dromore post did not come in till 7 o'clock last night when he was quite drunk'. Later, when more problems cropped up in Dromore, the paper's agent reported that he was told 'that the delay is in the carrier from Dromore to Armagh & that William Caldwell the Armagh carrier, though he has a horse, only travels two miles an hour'. One subscriber in Meath told the agent that 'that paper was to be sent no more to him', because it was 'published more than a month before he got it'.[9]

All of this must have been enormously frustrating, for there is an entry in the notebooks, dated March 17, 1794, that shows the lengths to which the proprietors of the *Northern Star* were prepared to go to control the flow of news:

On Mondays, the Boys shall not go out with the Papers for Town Delivery before 5 strikes. No shop sale, nor delivery to Belfast subscribers till after the Boys are out. Except in the case of Country subscriber, also in the case of a Town Subscriber going abroad before the hour of sale (5 o'clock) – or of Carrier of Papers to the Country – any of whom may at discretion get a Paper as soon as it is at Press.[10]

[8] National Archives of Ireland, Rebellion Papers, 620/15/8/2.
[9] National Archives of Ireland, Rebellion Papers, 620/15/8/5, 10, 6.
[10] National Archives of Ireland, Rebellion Papers, 620/15/8/4.

Given the accidents that awaited them, it made sense to send the papers out into 'the Country' as soon as possible; at the same time, the decision to hold back the Belfast copies 'till after the Boys are out' suggests that the publishers did not simply want to speed up the delivery of news. They appear to have been equally concerned with orchestrating and regulating the flow of news, so that it appeared simultaneously in country and city. When news trickles out, it seeps into the public consciousness; when it bursts out all at once, from a single source, it becomes an event. When news burst on to the streets of Belfast fresh (or, at least, comparatively fresh) from revolutionary Paris, it would have created an effect greater than the mere arguments of political pamphlets. When the people of Belfast, together, at more or less the same instant, read of an execution or a resolution passed by the French National Convention, they were not simply digesting distant ephemera, an earthquake or a hanging, whose sequencing or currency were only matters of curiosity. They were taking part, vicariously at least, in a revolution, and as such had a sense of themselves as participants in a new sense of history as a sequence of events extending into the present, and projecting into the future. What is more, they could imagine themselves as part of a community of participants, spread all over Ireland – depending, of course, on the sobriety of the Dromore postboy.

And there the problem lay. Samuel Neilson, the proprietor of the *Northern Star*, and Arthur O'Connor, editor of *The Press*, were attempting to create a public sphere whose boundaries were not limited by the island of Ireland, but which extended to Paris, London, Washington and beyond. Such a sphere could only achieve this geographical extension when the time it took for information to reach Dublin, Belfast or Cork was no longer a factor, so that an event taking place in one part of this newly expanded world was also an event in another. When reporting of news first began in Ireland a century earlier, the concept of 'freshness' was already present, but as a relative notion, in which two- or three-week-old news was still news. By the 1790s, however, a new, insistent and distinctively modern demand to live in the present enters Irish print culture, and it is closely aligned to the formulation of modern republicanism. This is most obvious in newspapers such as the *Northern Star*, which imagine the existence of a sentient collective entity, existing in a simultaneous informational field, and progressing through sequenced time: the people. However, the reality of a simultaneous national informational field was a long way off in the 1790s, when fresh news could grow stale at the whim of a drunken postboy, or a two-mile-an-hour horse.

CHAPTER 3

Acts of Union: 1800–1890

ACTS OF UNION

'Why did America triumph over tyranny?' asked the United Irishman Arthur O'Connor in 1797: 'A journeyman printer [Benjamin Franklin] fulminated the decree of nature against the giants of England.'[1] When *The Press* and the *Northern Star* also began to 'fulminate' against 'the giants of England', the response was swift. The *Northern Star* was shut down in 1797, and new legislation passed by the Irish Parliament made it much more difficult to set up a newspaper by insisting that all new presses needed licences, which could be refused or withdrawn for a variety of reasons. 'It is a melancholy proof of the efficacy of the terror and that influence which the administration of this country have exerted since the agitation of the Union question,' lamented an anti-Union newspaper, the *Constitution* in May, 1800, 'that scarcely one public print in Ireland has boldly ventured forth to interpose, between the minister and the constitution, the shield of a free press.'[2]

By the end of July, 1800, the *Constitution* informed its readers that, the battle against the Act of Union lost, it too would cease publication. When the Act of Union went into effect five months later, giving Parliament at Westminster the authority to make legislation for Ireland, among the first batch of Irish bills to come before Westminster in 1801 was a new Copyright Act (41 Geo. III cap. 107), extending the provisions of the 1709 Act to 'any other bookseller printer or other person whosoever in any part of the said United Kingdom or in part of the British dominions of Europe' – which included Ireland.[3] English booksellers and printers had long complained of the legal advantage enjoyed by their Irish competitors

---

[1] William Caxton, 'To the Editor', *The Press* (October 5, 1797).
[2] *Constitution* (May 3, 1800).
[3] *An Act for the further Encouragement of Learning, in the United Kingdom of Great Britain and Ireland* (1801) 41 Geo. III, c.107.

in being able to reprint books without paying copyright; before the Act of Union in 1800, it would have been necessary to cajole or to bribe an Irish parliament to vote away such a privilege (which would have been difficult, since anyone voting for such a measure would have incurred the wrath of the entire political spectrum of the Irish press); after 1800, it could be done with the stroke of a pen.

The effects of the new Copyright Act in Ireland were immediate. Even though Stamp Taxes had been increased in the period between 1780 and 1800 in an effort to limit what was seen as an increasingly restless popular readership, Dublin printers rapidly increased the number of items they published in the final decades of the century. Buoyed to some extent by a growing export trade to the newly independent United States of America, the total number of published items increased from just over 2,000 items in the 1770s, to approximately 3,000 the following decade, to almost 4,500 in the final decade of the century. In the ten years immediately following the Copyright Act of 1801, that figure dropped again to less than 3,000 per decade. And the effects were long-lasting. Even with a rising population in the 1830s, the number of items published by Irish printers in the nineteenth century would not reach the levels of the 1790s, dipping to below 2,500 at one point, and only stabilising in the range of 3,000–4,000 items per decade after the Stamp Taxes were relaxed in the 1850s. Of course, these figures are not precise; and they do not reflect the size of individual print-runs (which, particularly in the cases of schoolbooks and newspapers, were considerably larger than their eighteenth-century counterparts); however, they do give us a sense of an industry that was knocked back by the legislative changes that followed the Act of Union. By the same token, the value of books imported from England increased from £7,000 in 1800, to £27,000 in 1815.[4]

Not surprisingly, many of the leading figures in the industry, including family businesses in their second or third generation, faltered at the beginning of the new century. Writing to a friend in Philadelphia on October 16, 1798, the prominent Catholic bookseller Patrick Byrne announced: 'After spending the better part of my life in trade in the Capital of this Kingdom, I am now determined to spend the remainder of it as an American Farmer.'[5] Within a few years, the situation was so

---

[4] Vincent Kinane, *A Brief History of Printing and Publishing in Ireland* (Dublin, 2002), 23.
[5] Cited in Charles Benson, 'Printers and Booksellers in Dublin, 1800–1850', in *Spreading the Word: The Distribution of Networks of Print, 1550–1850*, ed. Robin Myers and Michael Harris (Winchester, 1990), 47–60, 48.

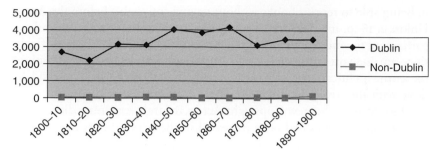

Fig 2. Irish imprints, 1800–1900.

precarious for many print-workers that the Dublin Typographical Provident Society was established, to 'afford relief to such of its Members as may, from time to time, be out of employment'.[6] In short, the legislative free-for-all of the eighteenth century was well and truly over. 'Has the printing of books in Ireland diminished or increased?' a Parliamentary Commission of inquiry asked a bookseller's agent, William Wakeman, in 1821: 'Since the Act of Union it is almost annihilated,' he replied. 'It was on the same footing as America previous to that time, and every new book was reprinted here; but since the Copyright Act has been extended, that cannot now be done openly.'[7]

EDUCATING THE LOWER ORDERS

Like so much that followed from the Act of Union, the 'annihilation' of the Irish print trade was the (predictable) side-effect of legislation whose primary purposes were to protect an English industry from Irish competition, and to prevent the recurrence of anything like the attempted revolution of 1798 by controlling public debate. The print industry did not simply churn out a product like linen or corn; ultimately, it produced and disseminated ideas – potentially revolutionary ideas. However, British policy towards Ireland after the Union was torn in two contradictory directions: while the Stamp Tax and Copyright Act made it more difficult for Irish people to afford books, the Commission set up to inquire into the state of Irish education in 1806 (46 Geo. III cap. 122) had the avowed goal of teaching more Irish people to read.

---

[6] *Constitution of the Dublin Typographical Provident Society* (Dublin, 1833), Art. 1.
[7] *Third Report of the Commissioners of Inquiry into the Collection and Management of the Revenue Arising in Ireland* (London, 1825) Appendix 2, 15.

The establishment of the Commission of the Board of Education in Ireland in 1806 was the beginning of a fundamental transformation of Irish education. By the time the Commission had issued its fourteenth report in 1812, the basis had been laid for the Irish Endowed Schools Act of 1813 (53 Geo. III cap. 107) to create 'new Establishments for the Education of the lower classes in Ireland'. Perhaps more than any other single factor, this would reconfigure the informational landscape of Ireland in the first half of the nineteenth century. While the print culture of the eighteenth century had been vibrant, it had been a confined vibrancy, limited for the most part to a closely knit little world of primarily urban readers, the efforts of the chapmen notwithstanding. Indeed, the passion of many of its controversies, and the speed with which they turned into personal attacks, was at least in part the product of this social intimacy.

This was not to say, however, it was going to be easy to create an educational system in the polarised, fiercely sectarian public world in the years leading up to Catholic Emancipation in 1829, in which many feared a blurring of the fine line between education and proselytising. The Commissioners, for their part, were acutely aware of these fears, insisting in 1812 that the 'leading principle' of the new educational system must be that 'no attempt shall be made to influence or disturb peculiar Religious Tenets of any Sect or description of Christians'.[8] Although these assurances did not quell debate, they did help an Irish educational system to take hold.

It is perhaps a measure of the effectiveness of the new educational system that, throughout the nineteenth century, print runs became larger, the periodical press diversified, and a market opened up for cheaply priced, popular editions of histories, poetry and fiction that went well beyond the limited stock of chapbooks that had been staples of the popular press of the eighteenth century. More directly, the educational system itself gave some Irish publishers the opportunity to operate on an unprecedented scale, by publishing schoolbooks. The pioneers in this regard were the Society for Promoting the Education of the Poor in Ireland (known as the Kildare Place Society), established in 1811, which managed to create a model for a school system that was sufficiently non-denominational to gain support from both Protestants and Catholics. It quickly established a publishing operation, and produced the first sequential series of schoolbooks in the British Isles, which sold

---

[8] *Report from the Commissioners of the Board of Education in Ireland: Fourteenth Report, view of the chief foundations, with some general remarks and result of deliberations* (London, 1812), 2.

in huge numbers. For instance, the first printing of 50,000 copies of their *Dublin Spelling Book* was exhausted by 1822; a further 50,000 were ordered later that year.

However, the political consensus that allowed the Kildare Place Society to operate collapsed in 1831, at which point the Commissioners for Education began to write their own schoolbooks. In a pattern that would repeat itself in an era of social planning with the Ordnance Survey (authorised in 1824), the organisation of the Royal Irish Constabulary (1836) and the Post Office (1831), the Commissioners for Education used Ireland as a kind of experimental testing ground for centralised state policy on a grand scale. The Commissioners followed the model of the Kildare Place textbooks in scrupulously avoiding offence to any set of political or religious sensibilities; so, for instance, in *Fifth Book of Lessons* the history of the period 1500 to 1800 was covered in six pages, without any mention of the Reformation. Still, for their time these books were, as one historian of Irish education has argued, 'probably the best set of school books produced in the British Isles'.[9] Printed primarily by the Dublin firm of Alexander Thom, these little volumes sold in even larger quantities than their predecessors, and by the mid-1830s were being exported to twelve countries. By 1851, Irish schoolbooks had a twenty-five per cent market share in England, a figure that would double by 1859 – at which point it has been estimated that a million Irish-produced textbooks were circulating in English schools.

Apart from carrying out a kind of reverse colonisation, and buoying the Irish print industry, all of this activity was teaching Irish people to read. Among those aged between 16 and 25 years old in 1841, 74 per cent of men and 67 per cent of women in Leinster could read, and the figures for Ulster are more or less the same, with women everywhere at a slight disadvantage. Further west, the rate of literacy dropped: in Munster it was 59 per cent for men and 44 per cent for women, while in Connaught it was as low as 46 per cent for men and 30 per cent for women. An indication of the effectiveness of education for the younger generation can be found in the recognition that literacy rates across the country dropped with age, so the lowest rate of literacy in Ireland was among women older than 66 years of age, and living in Connaught, of whom only 12 per cent could read in 1841.[10] By the end of the century, the effect of this increase in

---

[9] Donald Akenson, *The Irish Education Experiment: The National System of Education in the Nineteenth Century* (London, 1970), 238.
[10] Niall Ó Ciosáin, *Print and Popular Culture in Ireland 1750–1850* (London, 1997), 38.

literacy on Irish society as a whole was dramatic. Writing in 1884, J. Pope Hennessy observed in the *Nineteenth Century* that 'Irishmen who return to their country after a few years' absence cannot fail to see, as one of the most noticeable changes, an extension of popular literature; a great increase in the number of readers, not, however, in the upper or middle classes, but in the lower classes.'[11]

Of course, part of the reason that so many elderly people living in the west of Ireland were classified as illiterate throughout the century was because they were Irish-speakers. In 1806, the philologist Whitley Stokes estimated that only about 20,000 people could read Irish (out of a total of about 1.5 million whose first language was Irish).[12] In the decades that followed, printing in Irish continued to be a mere trickle, never rising above about two or three books per year until the Gaelic League began its work in the 1890s, if we exclude the major works of philological scholarship that began appearing in mid-century. In terms of volume, however, a substantial proportion of Irish-language publishing was made up of tracts by evangelical groups, such as the Irish Society for Promoting the Education of the Native Irish through the Medium of their Own Language, who flourished in the 1820s. Given that the first Irish-printed book in the language – *Abidil Gaoidheilge agus Caiticiosma* back in 1571 – was an aid to proselytisation, in some respects the situation for Irish-speakers in the early nineteenth century with regard to print had not changed very much since the dawn of printing in Ireland.

CONTROLLING THE PRESS

'Education has taken a most extensive range', announced the *Dublin Evening Mail* at its launch in 1823; 'a Newspaper has become a necessity, not to be dispensed with by even the most homely appetite, instead of being, as in other countries, a luxury intended and reserved for the fastidious palate of the epicure.'[13] Even though the increases in Stamp Tax meant that the *Dublin Evening Mail* cost fivepence a copy (where the *Northern Star* thirty years earlier had cost twopence), the 'lower classes' were still getting their hands on newspapers; and so, as grievances over the Act of Union and rights for Catholics created an ever more divided

---

[11]   J. Pope Hennessy, 'What Do the Irish Read?' *Nineteenth Century* 15:88 (June 1884), 920–32, 920.
[12]   Ó Ciosáin, *Print and Popular Culture*, 157.
[13]   *Dublin Evening Mail* (February 3, 1823).

society, the government felt the need to exercise some control over the content of newspapers.

The system for controlling the press in nineteenth-century Ireland was complex, costly and not always very effective. When the Duke of Bedford became Lord Lieutenant in 1806, for instance, one of his first projects (within months of the first Education Commission) was to set up a government newspaper, the *Correspondent*, at a total cost of £1,200 per year. More importantly, at a time when the Irish newspapers still relied on the English and Dutch papers arriving three times a week on the packet boat from Holyhead, the *Correspondent* was given privileged access to the express post provided by government couriers. In spite of this, early in 1810 the *Correspondent* began biting the hand that fed it by criticising the administration, and promptly lost its subsidy and privileged access to the express packet. Sensing a slippage, the government began to increase the amount of money it paid to other Dublin newspapers, and resorted once again to the old expedient of increasing taxation, raising Stamp Duty by two pence per paper and one shilling per advertisement. The once-supportive *Correspondent* protested loudly against the 'tyranny of the tax-gatherer',[14] while in the House of Commons, Richard Brinsley Sheridan spoke against 'the mean, cowardly and circuitous attempt' to control the press 'by raising the price of cheap publications'.[15]

When bribery and taxation failed, there were always the libel laws. It is both paradoxical and entirely consistent with the contradictory policies of the period that two weeks after the Endowed Schools Act became law on July 10, 1813, the editor and proprietor of the *Dublin Evening Post*, John Magee, found himself on trial for libel. Opening the case for the prosecution, the Attorney General conjured up the spectre of 1798. 'We remember the state of the Press in the year which preceded the Rebellion', he warned the court.[16] Privately, Sir Robert Peel wrote: 'Most of the dissatisfaction in the country arises from the immense circulation of that nefarious paper the *Dublin Evening Post*. It is … read by those who can read, to those who cannot.'[17] Standing up to speak for John Magee, Daniel O'Connell picked up a refrain that had echoed through the previous century: 'When the art of Printing was invented, its value to every sufferer – its terror to every oppressor, were soon obvious; and soon were

---

[14] *Correspondent* (July 3, 1810).
[15] Brian Inglis, *The Freedom of the Press in Ireland: 1784–1841* (London, 1954), 129.
[16] *The Trial of John Magee, Proprietor of the Dublin Evening Post, For Publishing an Historical Review of the Duke of Richmond's Administration in Ireland* (Dublin, 1813), 68–9.
[17] Inglis, *Freedom of the Press*, 139.

means adopted to prevent its salutary effects.' No hymn to the liberty of the press was going to save John Magee, however, given that jury selection had been carefully managed by the prosecution, and he was duly convicted, and committed to Newgate Prison. Nonetheless, the situation did not rest there, for before he was bundled off to his cell, Magee made arrangements to print the transcript of the trial. 'We, therefore, lay this Trial before the Country, and means to propagate it in every part, not only of the British Empire, but of America. Nay, it shall go to the Continent, in the languages of France and Spain.'[18]

The interest generated by Magee's trial was not uncharacteristic in the years prior to Catholic Emancipation in 1829, when the courts constituted a kind of alternative parliament, where public speeches could be delivered (immune from prosecution for libel) and legislation debated. What is more, print preserved political debates of all kinds, including trials, so that cumulatively they grew into an evolving archive of political theory, which would ultimately begin to appear in anthologies later in the century. Equally, in a time before public-address systems, a person who may only have heard O'Connell's words dimly from the back of a crowded market square could speak with authority on his rhetorical style and on the nuances of his arguments. A few years later, standing up before Trinity's College Historical Society on June 24, 1833, Isaac Butt – then a student – told his listeners that 'states are now magnified into empires, and in the gigantic dimensions of modern communities it is necessary, to give any value to eloquence, that there should be a contrivance that will bring it home to every man's fire side.'[19] That contrivance, Butt told his listeners, was the press.

MAKING NEWS

The ascent of the courtroom lawyer as a cultural figure in early nineteenth-century Ireland was to reshape the ways in which news was reported. Prior to this, news came to the newspaper – not the other way around. A typical eighteenth-century Irish newspaper editor (often one person would own and more or less write the whole newspaper) sat like a not-very-nimble spider at the centre of an informational web; when the packet boat from Holyhead brought the English or Dutch papers, the editor

---

[18] *Trial of John Magee*, 91, 121, xxxvi.
[19] Isaac Butt, *Address Delivered before the College Historical Society on the Evening of Monday, June 24 at the Close of the Session* (Dublin, 1833), 15.

extracted nuggets for Irish readers. Shipping news, notices of servants lost, hangings, or horses stolen would be dropped into the office; in some cases, so too would opinion pieces, *belles-lettres*, perhaps the odd verse, and, depending on the paper's closeness to the administration, dispatches and proclamations from the Castle. Newspapers such as the *Northern Star*, aligned to a particular cause, would publish reports of resolutions from Volunteer meetings, usually recorded by a branch secretary; it was also common in such papers, going back to Lucas's *Censor*, for the editor/proprietor to pen his own opinion pieces. However, investigative journalism was rare and usually confined to pamphlets, where an author could take shelter from the threat of libel under the cover of anonymity. Only rarely would an Irish newspaper editor of the eighteenth century venture outside his premises in search of a story.

This situation began to change, at least in part, because when Daniel O'Connell stood up to speak in the Four Courts, there was no point in an editor sitting waiting in his office, hoping that an exclusive verbatim report might find its way to his desk before his print deadline: someone had to be sent out to write down the news. Indeed, according to the *Oxford English Dictionary*, the earliest use of the word 'reporter' (to mean a journalist), is from 1813, when the word is borrowed from the legal sphere (as in a 'court reporter' who transcribed trials), where it had been in use since the seventeenth century. Once Irish newspapers began sending reporters to the courts, and elsewhere, in pursuit of local news stories, a different kind of competitive field began to open up. The most important indication of this new environment was the launch of Michael Staunton's *Morning Register* in 1824. Supportive of the Catholic cause, critical of the government, but mindful of the libel laws, the *Morning Register* changed the face of Irish journalism by being, as it described itself, 'much more rare than the black swan – a Journal wholly original, and wholly dedicated to Ireland'. 'It has happened', wrote Staunton in an early editorial, 'that while we have had three reporters taking notes of law proceedings, we have had four in attendance upon the Catholic Association; the entire seven going through the business heretofore assigned by the economical prints to one individual.'[20] Years later, when Staunton was elected Lord Mayor of Dublin, he was presented with an illuminated scroll, pronouncing him 'Creator of the Irish Press'.

This may have been something of a hyperbolic honour; it is nonetheless true that, after 1824, Irish newspapers began to devote more time to

---

[20] *Morning Register* (November 12, 1824).

gathering news. In this regard, the papers outside of Dublin were often ahead of their rivals in the capital. After all, the main justification for the existence of a local newspaper was the reporting of local news. So, for instance, when John Scanlon was executed in Limerick's Gallows Green for the murder of Ellen Hanley in March of 1820 (a case that Gerald Griffin later used as the basis for his novel *The Collegians*), the *Limerick Gazette*, the *Ennis Chronicle and Clare Advertiser*, and *Chute's Western Herald* all had reporters present – including Griffin, who was working as a reporter at the time. Covering the execution of Scanlon's co-accused, Stephen Sullivan, later that year, the *Ennis Chronicle* presented the story in a style that emphasised the vivid, eye-witness nature of the report. 'On Thursday, at four o'clock in the afternoon, Stephen Sullivan, whose trial and conviction for the murder of Ellen Hanley in the Shannon, we gave in our last, was taken from the City-jail to Gallows-green, for execution.'[21]

With this kind of lively local coverage, provincial newspapers flourished. More than 200 titles were launched outside of Dublin in the first half of the nineteenth century, and by no means all of these were in the major cities of Cork, Limerick or Belfast. For instance, five newspapers were founded in Castlebar in this period: the *Mayo Constitution* (1801), *Telegraph; or Connaught Ranger* (1830), *Mayo Mercury* (1840), *Aegis* (1841) and *The Connaught Telegraph* (1834). The *Telegraph* would survive from this period, as would the *Drogheda Argus* (1834), the *Sligo Champion* (1836) and the *Cork Examiner* (1841), which has since become a national paper. Of course, many more sank from sight, or merged with rivals within a year or two of their first appearance. Nonetheless, when the new titles were combined with survivors from the previous century, such as the *Waterford Chronicle* (1765–1849) or *Kerry Evening Post* (1774–1917), the overall picture was extremely healthy. In total, according to the *Report of the Select Committee on Newspaper Stamps*, in the years 1837–50, there were no fewer than 102 titles in circulation outside of the capital (of which 16 were in Belfast and 7 in Cork). The larger of these newspapers achieved circulation figures comparable to their Dublin counterparts. The *Limerick Chronicle*, for instance, was selling in excess of 1,200 copies per issue in 1841, while in the same year the *Newry Telegraph* was selling more than 700 copies.[22]

In part, of course, the health of the newspaper industry outside of Dublin was a simple recognition that a local newspaper could target local

---

[21] *Ennis Chronicle and Clare Advertiser* (August 20, 1820).
[22] *Report of the Select Committee on Newspaper Stamps* (London, 1851), 558–64.

advertisers more effectively than a national newspaper, particularly in the first half of the century when distribution of national newspapers was still a slow and uncertain prospect. However, the unprecedented expansion in the number of titles in the early nineteenth century was also a product of the fissured political landscape. The Tory *Drogheda Conservative Journal* (1837–48) and the nationalist *Dundalk Patriot* (1847–8) may have served the same geographical area; politically, however, their respective readers were continents apart. Indeed, it is not simply the emergence of a distinctive Catholic press that is the defining characteristic of Irish media culture in the first half of the nineteenth century; nor is it purely the bitter acrimony between Catholic and Protestant, Repealer and pro-Unionist publications, and the sense that no faction felt itself complete without its own newspaper. Instead, the defining feature of the period is the sheer proliferation of periodical titles in nineteenth-century Ireland – almost 4,000 titles were in print at one point or another over the century as a whole – as a symptom of an increasingly mediated society that was becoming more complex on many different fronts.

In terms of simple demographics, pro-Catholic papers like the *Connaught Journal* or the *Morning Register* should have had a much larger readership than the government papers. However, relative differences in income meant that even with his team of seven reporters, Michael Staunton's *Morning Register* was never able to keep pace with the pro-Protestant government dailies, and the Castle-supported *Dublin Evening Mail* would remain as the Irish newspaper with the largest circulation in the period before 1840. Sunday newspapers aimed at a Catholic readership had a better chance because, it was argued, less prosperous Catholics could better afford to pay fivepence per week for a Sunday paper, than fivepence per day for a daily. The pro-O'Connellite weekly *Pilot*, for instance, steadily increased its circulation throughout the period, although it never sold more than 1,000 copies per week. However, another paper of a similar political hue, the *Comet*, was to claim in 1831 that it was selling 4,250 copies per week. Although it only survived for 136 issues (1831–3), the *Comet*, with its mixture of humour, satire (it was here that James Clarence Mangan began publishing), woodcuts and political commentary would point the way ahead for a popular press that was targeting the increasingly literate 'lower orders'. Nor were the publishers of these papers unaware of the potential impact of reaching this new readership, with the *Comet*'s elaborate masthead framing the words: 'Knowledge is Power'.

At the same time, the media world was not simply fracturing into politically antagonistic groupings: it was also diversifying. When the new

Theatre Royal opened in Dublin's Hawkins' Street in 1821, for instance, the city's revived theatrical life gave rise to no fewer than nine theatrical journals, including *The Theatrical Observer, The Drama, Dramatic Argus, Dramatic Review, The Stage* and *The Theatre* – implicit recognition that the standard four-page daily newspaper could not satisfy all interests. More substantial, and usually more enduring, were other specialised journals: the *Temperance Gazette, Racing Calendar, Farmer's Gazette, Sporting Calendar* and *Medical Press* – the latter only part of what was to become a well-established medical and scientific publishing industry in Ireland, including the *Dublin Journal of Medical and Chemical Science*, first published in 1832, followed a year later by the prestigious *Journal of the Geological Society of Ireland*. By the same token, in a period in which there was vigorous religious controversy (not least within the Established Church), Ireland supported a plethora of religious magazines. These covered the gamut from the populist *Protestant Penny Magazine* (which featured woodcuts with captions such as 'Transubstantiation disproved by a mouse') to its counterpart, the equally luridly illustrated *Catholic Magazine*, to monthly tomes in which the most arcane points of theology were debated by earnest (and possibly under-employed) clergymen.[23] Of these magazines, perhaps the most notable was Caesar Otway's *Christian Examiner* (1825–69), which also published travel writing and literature, including some of the earliest writings of William Carleton.

For many, the real sign of the health of the Irish print world would be the appearance of a magazine to rival *Blackwood's* (founded 1802) or the *Edinburgh Review* (founded 1817). There were a number of attempts to create such a magazine in the early 1830s, including the short-lived *Dublin Literary Gazette* (founded 1830), and the *Irish Monthly Magazine of Politics and Literature* of 1832–4 (which was unusual in this field, in that it was oriented towards a Catholic readership). However, real success came with the *Dublin University Magazine*, founded in 1833 by a group of former Trinity students including Isaac Butt, Samuel Ferguson and Caesar Otway. Writing from a Tory, pro-Union stance, it published historical, topographical and antiquarian writing by leading Irish scholars, as well as serial fiction by Charles Lever and Joseph Sheridan Le Fanu (both of whom served as editors), and poetry by James Clarence Mangan. In some respects, the *Dublin University Magazine* looks back to the *Dublin Weekly Journal* in

---

[23] See Barbara Hayley, 'A Reading and Thinking Nation: Periodicals as the Voice of Nineteenth-Century Ireland', in *300 Years of Irish Periodicals*, ed. Barbara Hayley and Enda McKay (Mullingar, 1987), 29–33.

the eighteenth century, in that its intense engagement with Irish culture was always placed within a wider international frame. A typical issue (such as that of February, 1847), for instance, contained not only part of a series on Irish rivers and a biographical sketch of Thomas Davis by Samuel Ferguson, but also articles on Portuguese history, Russian politics, and a review of recent books from America.

In other ways, as well, the world of the Irish media was becoming more diversified, more organised and more international. By the early 1830s, an advertiser could drop in to the Johnston and Co. offices at 1 Eden Quay, Dublin, and there, for a flat rate, place an advertisement in 'every newspaper in the British Empire'. Moreover, it was possible to order a subscription for 'every Newspaper in the United Kingdom, supplied by the earliest dispatch'. This meant that for the (admittedly substantial) sum of £10 per year, an Irish reader could have *The Times* delivered to the door every morning (as compared to £6 per year for the *Dublin Morning Post*); or, for a more reasonable 17s. per year, an Irish reader could take delivery of the radical weekly *Cobbett's Register*, or for 11s., the popular Sunday paper, *Bell's Messenger*. For these subscribers, the sense of feeling part of a larger polity – whether Great Britain or the Empire – was as tangible as paper and ink.

THE SPEED OF NEWS

In some ways, then, the Irish media landscape in the 1830s was beginning to assume some of the features that would be recognisable in the twentieth century, and beyond. However, by the end of that decade, a much more far-reaching change was in the offing. Although local news reporting was undergoing a transformation, in terms of international news, an Irish newspaper from the 1820s or early 1830s looked very much like an Irish newspaper from the 1720s. The reader picking up the leading *Dublin Evening Mail* on February 9, 1823, for instance, would have been told that 'The London Journals of Monday had not reached our Office at the hour of our putting to press (4 o'clock)', so there would be no London news. Indeed, the only foreign news that day came from Madrid, and was dated January 15 – a delay of twenty-two days, which was more or less what it had been a century before. Readers of the venerable *Freeman's Journal* on November 18, 1824, would have had news from New York dated October 24 – which was a considerable improvement over the previous century – but a report from 'the Isthmus of Panama' dated back to September 1.

The basic problem was that news could only travel as fast as the person carrying it, and, while roads had improved somewhat, news in 1824 did not travel significantly faster around Ireland than it had fifty years earlier. One of the main problems here was the Irish Post Office. At almost every level, contemporaries claimed that the Post Office was riddled with corruption, patronage and inefficiency. In one exposé of the abuses of the Irish Post Office, the author noted that it was common for rural postmasters who wanted to curry favour with head office in Dublin to throw a few pheasants or a brace of hares into the postbag, with the result that 'the letters oftentimes came besmeared with blood, and otherwise much defaced'.[24]

By the early 1840s, this was to change. Ireland was brought under the control of the Postmaster General for the United Kingdom in 1831 (1 Will. IV cap. 8), and in 1840 crusading Postmaster General Rowland Hill introduced penny postage, the iconic Penny Black stamp. The results were dramatic: the volume of Irish post almost tripled from 1839 to 1842, from 9 million to 24 million items annually; by 1870, more than 65 million items were posted every year in Ireland.[25] Indeed, the new service was seen as being so supernaturally quick that when Rev. Alexander R.C. Dallas, founder of the Irish Church Missions, wanted to demonstrate the suddenness of the Second Coming (which Dallas believed was due sometime around 1872) to prominent Irish Catholics, he used the most modern communications technology available to him: the Post Office. On January 14, 15 and 16, 1846, he posted copies of a pamphlet, entitled *A Voice from Heaven*, to prominent Catholics all over Ireland, timed so that the envelopes would drop through letter-boxes more or less simultaneously all over the island,[26] enacting with wondrous banality the suddenness and universality of the Messiah's return.

The drive to modernise the postal system was part of a wider transportation revolution. On March 28, 1814, the paddle steamer *Thames* left Dublin, making the first steam crossing of the Irish Sea with passengers and cargo. A few months later, on July 6, the first Bianconi cars – horsedrawn carriages running regular routes – began to operate between Clonmel and Cahir. In 1818, the *Rob Roy* made the first steam crossing between Belfast and Glasgow. When the world's first railway, the Stockton

[24] P.C. O'Neill, *A Brief Review of the Irish Post Office from 1784 to 1831 when Sir Edward Lees was Removed from that Establishment* (n.p., 1831), 56.
[25] Mairead Reynolds, *A History of the Irish Post Office* (Dublin, 1983), 72.
[26] Alexander R.C. Dallas, *Six Lectures on Protestantism* (London, 1852), 184.

and Darlington, began carrying passengers in 1825, there were already two bills before Parliament for the building of Irish railways (one from Kingstown to Dublin, the other from Limerick to Waterford). Within a decade, the first Irish railway opened on December 17, 1834, running six miles along the coast from Kingstown (now Dun Laoghaire) to Dublin. In real terms, it could not honestly be said to have revolutionised travel in Ireland (although London papers from the mail packet did reach city editors slightly faster). What it did do, however, was to create a new appetite: the appetite for speed. When it was under construction, crowds gathered along the route to watch the navvies at work on the track; after it opened, Dubliners marvelled as its two trains, the *Hibernia* and *Vauxhall*, hurtled its 300 passengers down the rails at a dizzying 20mph.

After seeing trains smoking along the Dublin–Kingstown railway's six miles of track, for some Irish people anything seemed possible. A Royal Commission on the Construction of Railways in Ireland was established in 1836, and at a meeting in London to mark the occasion, a speaker stood up and told the meeting that it was now technically possible to link London and Dublin within sixteen or fourteen hours. Not one to be bettered, Daniel O'Connell, who was also present, said it should be possible to link the two cities within twelve hours. There was even stronger support for this kind of development in Unionist circles. 'By opening to every part of that country the most direct and easy lines of communication with England,' wrote one pamphleteer in 1836, 'the IDENTITY of feeling and interest will be soonest attained, on which depend the prosperity and permanence of the UNION of the two countries.'[27] Across the political spectrum in the 1830s and 1840s, a new language emerges: distances are no longer measured in miles, but in days and hours.

The most immediate impact of the railway on Irish public life was what contemporaries called 'Railway Mania'. In part, this was a simple investment frenzy; there were huge fortunes to be made (and lost) in railways, and over the course of the nineteenth century at least 180 different railway companies existed in Ireland:[28] some took money from investors and built railways; others simply took money from investors, while others did not even get that far. And even though it would be almost a decade after the Dublin–Kingstown railway before any major projects got underway in Ireland, once started, railway construction was rapid. Indeed, by

[27] *Direct Communication between London and Dublin.* (n.p., 1836).
[28] H.C. Casserley, *Outline of Irish Railway History* (Newton Abbot, 1974), 20.

1844, the new industry even had its own periodical, the *Irish Railway Gazette*. By 1853 there were 840 miles of rail in Ireland (as compared to 990 in Scotland, for instance), carrying a total of seven million passengers annually. By the time the Boyne viaduct opened in 1855, finally linking Dublin and Belfast, the Irish rail infrastructure had effectively taken the shape it would hold into the twenty-first century.

The stampede to build railways was not purely about cashing in on a bonanza, however. The railways were emblematic of modernity, both a metaphor for the speed of change and its most striking physical manifestation. Conversely, the possibility that Ireland – or a part of Ireland – might be shunted on to a siding often could induce a sense of panic. When, for instance, plans to build a rail line from Dublin to Navan were going poorly, a Navan merchant, William Ford, wrote an open letter urging that the people of Navan must not 'lag behind their brethren in the race of improvement'.[29] That breathless phrase, 'the race of improvement', captures succinctly the sense of forward motion – and the danger of being left behind – that evolved so quickly in the 1830s and 1840s. The absence of a railway would not just be an inconvenience for the people of Meath: it would effectively cut them adrift from the advance of humanity, causing them to stumble in the great race. 'Hail, Mighty Steam!', enthused Robert Young on the opening of the Enniskillen railway in 1847:

> That every place
> Can time outstrip, and shorten space,
> As men pursue life's onward race,
> By ocean or by railway.[30]

The same technology – steam – that made it possible to move information more quickly than ever before also made it possible to print far more quickly and efficiently. In a period of just under three decades at the beginning of the nineteenth century, the technology of print changed more than it had in the previous three centuries. While there had been some earlier improvements in the design of presses, the process of setting lines of type, and manually operating the press in 1790 was still more or less as it had been in 1590. However, from the early years of the century, mechanisation moved into almost every aspect of printing. First, Lord Stanhope began experimenting with ways of producing paper by machine.

---

[29] William Ford, *A Letter Addressed to the Resident Landed Proprietors, Merchants, Farmers, Mill Owners, Shopkeepers, Mechanics, and Labourers of the County of Meath on the Important Subject of Railway Communication between the County Meath and the City of Dublin* (Dublin, 1845), 2.
[30] Robert Young, *The Poetical Remembrancer* (Londonderry, 1854), 90.

Over the ensuing decades, although the cost of paper would be kept artificially high through taxation, there would be a move from handmade paper to cheaper machine-made paper. In 1800, all 11,000 tons of paper made in the United Kingdom was handmade; by 1860, the total figure had increased to 100,000 tons, of which 96,000 was machine-made.

At the same time, presses themselves changed. At the beginning of the nineteenth century, presses were still made of wood, until George Clymer of Philadelphia designed and built an iron press, the Columbian, which was introduced into Europe in 1817. It was soon joined by the Albion, introduced a few years later. The greater strength of the iron press in turn permitted the process known as stereotyping, in which an entire page (or part of a page) of type could be imprinted on a plaster (and later metal) sheet, which could be used over and over again, thus making possible almost cost-free reprints. Finally, it became possible to exploit fully the new potential to produce more copies when Friedrich König replaced manual power with steam power in 1814 – 'the greatest improvement connected with printing since the discovery of the art itself',[31] according to *The Times*, which was the first major newspaper to adopt the new technology. 'The *Times* alone', exulted one writer looking back over the nineteenth century in 1894, 'at the present day, in a single year consumes more type and paper than the printing presses of the whole world produced from the day of Gutenberg to the French Revolution.'[32]

'There is no department of the printing business which has undergone a more thorough alteration than the Press Room, within the last twenty years', wrote the Dublin publisher and editor Philip Dixon Hardy in the May 10, 1834 edition of his *Irish Penny Journal*. Founded in 1832 as the *Dublin Penny Journal*, the *Irish Penny Journal* published articles on antiquarianism, science, Irish history and Irish topography by writers such as George Petrie, Caesar Otway and Samuel Ferguson, all packaged in 'a Weekly Publication suited to the pockets of the poorer classes of society'.[33] When Hardy bought it in 1833, he was determined to bring the magazine to an even wider readership: and so, in the spring of 1834, he began using Ireland's first steam press. 'The number of impressions produced per hour on the Columbian, Stanhope press … is two hundred and fifty per hour, by the joint exertions of two men', he enthused to his readers. By contrast, the new steam printing machine, operated by two

[31] S.H. Steinberg, *Five Hundred Years of Printing*, 2nd edn (1955; rpt London, 1996), 138.
[32] John Dickie, *A Sketch of Human Progress during the 19th Century* (Glasgow, 1894), 13.
[33] *Dublin Penny Journal*, Vol. 1, 1832 (Dublin, 1833), i.

boys, 'would produce seven hundred and fifty sheets printed on both sides – that is fifteen hundred impressions; and when two are worked together, as in the case of the *Penny Journal,* three thousand impressions in the hour.'

Hardy recognised that the challenge with this sort of dizzying twelve-fold increase in productivity is not producing a large enough print run to satisfy the market; it is finding a market big enough to absorb the burgeoning print run. A similar magazine in London, the *Penny Magazine,* Hardy claims, needs to maintain sales of 'sixty or seventy thousand copies' per issue in order to make the new machinery viable. In Ireland, the domestic market was simply not big enough. So, for Hardy – as for so many entrepreneurs in those years trying to find a market for goods that could be produced much more rapidly than ever before – the solution was to look overseas. 'Already *The Irish Penny Journal* has been sent to some of the most distant portions of the globe,' he claims: 'to Van Diemen's Land, the United States, North America, and the East Indies. It is not a month since we received an order from an English bookseller for Calcutta; and we feel certain, that before another year shall have rolled away, it will have found its way into the most remote regions of the earth.'[34]

In those same years, there were other technological developments taking place that would transform the ways in which Irish men and women experienced the world. On August 6, 1839, for instance, Francis W. Beatty published a letter in the *Belfast Newsletter* claiming to have made a 'photogenic drawing' of a bridge in Belfast; the following month, a London publisher issued the first English translation of Louis Jacques Mandé Daguerre's *History and Practice of Photogenic Drawing.*[35] While Daguerre was only one of a number of people in those years trying to find a way to capture (and to fix) images, the daguerrotype was the first photographic process to achieve widespread acceptance, and a few days after it was made public in Paris in August of 1839, one eye-witness remembers seeing 'opticians' shops crowded with amateurs panting for daguerreotype apparatus, and everywhere cameras were trained on buildings'.[36]

---

[34] Philip Dixon Hardy, 'A Familiar Description of Printing in All its Branches', *Irish Penny Journal* 2:97 (May 10, 1834), 357, 359.
[35] Louis Jacques Mandé Daguerre, *History and Practice of Photogenic Drawing on the True Principles of the Daguerrotype,* trans. J.S. Meme (London and Edinburgh, 1839).
[36] Marc Gaudin, *Traité pratique de la photographie* (Paris, 1844), 7.

By 1841, there was a photographic studio in Dublin, and not long afterwards Beatty opened his own studio in Castle Street, Belfast. By the middle of the decade, not only were ordinary men and women getting their portraits taken in the studios that were springing up around the country, but shops were also offering for sale photographic views, as well as portraits of the famous, including leading political figures, contributing to a new kind of political celebrity. In Dublin in 1848, for instance, Leon Gluckman was offering portraits of the Young Ireland leaders from his 'Daguerrotype Portrait Institution'. The following year, 1849, in a non-partisan spirit of entrepreneurship, he was selling photographs of Queen Victoria's visit, which he also marked by shining a massive beam of light down Sackville Street from the roof of the Rotunda Hospital, powered by the battery developed by Nicholas Callan of St Patrick's College, Maynooth. By 1851, the daguerrotype had been replaced by a wet-plate process, and spurred by the prominence of photography at the Great Exhibition in Dublin of 1853, sixty photographic studios would be in operation in Dublin by the end of the decade, with a further twelve in Belfast. Meanwhile, amateur photographers began taking pictures, and by 1855 there were enough Irish photographers to support a magazine, *The Dublin Photographic Journal.*

The daguerrotype and its successors produced a startling disruption in the field of vision, making it possible to see faces of people distant in space and time (although the latter effect would only become apparent in later years: there were no old photographs in 1841). And yet, photography was only one of the tangible changes in the field of vision in the 1840s. In 1845, William Parsons, the Third Earl of Rosse, built what for the next sixty years would be the largest telescope in the world, the seventy-two-inch 'Leviathan of Parsonstown', on the grounds of Birr Castle. Over the ensuing decades, he saw in ways that no person before him had ever seen, from the craters of the moon to the spiral of the Crab Nebulae and other deep-space objects.

LIFE IN TWO HEMISPHERES

By the middle of the 1840s, an accelerated media sphere was making tangible the sense of living in a world rushing forwards and upwards. A reader of the *Dublin University Magazine,* for instance, sitting in his train carriage, would have probably found it difficult to disagree with a writer in the magazine in 1851 who observed:

Of all the agencies of social change, none, perhaps of recent times, has been so influential as steam: The intercommunication of ideas and of tastes, of mental and material wants, is now becoming so rapid and so well established, that, notwithstanding some serious impediments to present progress, every nation must advance, and all are tending towards the common goal of a higher civilization.[37]

At the same time, if our reader had looked out the carriage windows on a trip, say, from Dublin to Cork, he might have seen a completely different world. 'I have met mothers carrying about dead infants in their arms until they were putrid,' wrote Mathew Higgins in *The Times* of April, 1847, 'refusing to bury them, in the hope that the offensive sight might wring charity from the callous townspeople'.[38] In all, more than a million people died of starvation, typhus, cholera and related conditions between the summer of 1845, when the potato crop failed for the first time, and 1852, when the rural economy began to stagger back to life. By then, more than 2 million Irish people would have emigrated, mostly to the United States, establishing a pattern of emigration that would not reverse until the late twentieth century. 'Famines and plagues will suggest themselves; ... tragedies acted in remote times, or in distant regions; the actors, the inhabitants of beleaguered cities ...', wrote Shafto Adair in his account of the winter of 1846–7. 'But here the tragedy is enacted with no narrower limits than the boundaries of a Kingdom, the victims an entire people within our own days, at our own thresholds.'[39] There had, of course, been earlier famines in Ireland: in the terrible winter of 1741, and again in 1817. Indeed, what is usually considered the major Famine novel – William Carleton's *The Black Prophet*, serialised in the *Dublin University Magazine* in 1847 – is in fact set during the 1817 famine. However, what made the famine of the late 1840s the 'Great Famine' (or even simply '*The* Famine') was not simply its scale and duration (as bad as that was): it was the extent to which a panoply of new technologies made it possible for it to become a media event.

Without in any way minimising the enormity of what took place, the events of the 1840s were able to etch themselves on a public consciousness – both at the time, and subsequently – because they took place under an unprecedented glare of media attention. A writer like Adair may speak

---

[37] 'Progress and Retrogression: The Works of Laing and Kay', *Dublin University Magazine* 37:217 (January, 1851), 67–85, 68.
[38] Mathew James Higgins, 'A Scene in the Irish Famine', in *The Cabinet of Irish Literature*, Vol. III, ed. Charles A. Read and Katherine Tynan (London, 1904), 44.
[39] Shafto Adair, *The Winter of 1846–7 in Antrim* (London, 1847), 10.

of discovering what is hidden – peering into darkened cottages, travelling to remote villages – but in fact little of what took place was hidden from view. The Midland Great Western Railway was built during the worst of the Famine, and was open as far as Mullingar by 1848; by 1851, it was possible to travel from Dublin to Galway by rail. While conditions in Donegal, for instance, may have still been off the map, the correspondent who wished to report on deprivation in Connemara was still only a day away from Dublin. In short, in Mayo and West Cork, people were dying in conditions that would have seemed primitive to a medieval peasant; and reports of those deaths could be whisked to Dublin and London by correspondents such as Higgins in a matter of days, if not hours, by a rail and postal network and printed on a steam press, all of whose speed were gleaming icons of modernity.

'This is horrible!' exclaimed *The Nation* in a piece probably written by John Mitchel in July of 1847. 'Are we living in the nineteenth century – amidst all the enlightenment, steam, philanthropy and power-looms of the illustrious British Empire?'[40] For many Irish readers, *The Nation*, first published by Charles Gavan Duffy, Thomas Davis and John Dillon on October 15, 1842, was the most important link in the informational chain during the Famine years. 'In Ireland', wrote Gavan Duffy in his autobiography, *My Life in Two Hemispheres*, 'there was no journal resembling the London *Examiner* or *Spectator* which were original, critical, and vital from cover to cover; and such a journal might, I believed, be created.'[41] Not only did *The Nation*, at sixteen pages, make a credible claim to be 'the largest newspaper ever published in Ireland'; Duffy would also later claim that 12,000 copies of the first issue were published. However, the first recorded Stamp Tax paid on the paper dates from 1844, when it was paying tax on 1,800 copies per week, and this figure rose to just over 5,700 in 1846. Even so, these figures put it well ahead of any other Irish newspaper of its time.

Apart from the usual channels of distribution, *The Nation* was disseminated through the Repeal Reading Rooms that dotted the country, where a single copy had many readers. Moreover, there is at least anecdotal evidence to suggest that the paper was read aloud to those who could not read – an image that passed into collective memory with Henry McManus's painting, *Reading 'The Nation'* (illustration 4). Of course, given the regional difference in levels of literacy, it was essential to *The*

---

[40] 'The Civilizer!', *Nation* v:248 (July 3, 1847), 617.
[41] Charles Gavan Duffy, *My Life in Two Hemispheres*, Vol. II (London, 1898), 59.

Illustration 4. 'To create and foster public opinion in Ireland and to make it racy of the soil.' The slogan adopted by *The Nation* found an iconic image in Henry McManus's painting, *Reading 'The Nation'*.

Nation's claim to be a truly national paper to foster the idea that it was read to those who could not read themselves (particularly native Irish-speakers in Connaught and Munster). It would later be said that at its peak *The Nation* had 'a quarter of a million readers'.[42] While there is no real way to count the actual numbers who read (or were read) the paper, there can be little doubt that in the years between its launch in 1842 and its suppression in 1848 it was the most influential Irish newspaper of its time.

'Nationality is our great object', declared the prospectus for *The Nation*. The obvious model for *The Nation* was the *Northern Star* of the 1790s; just as the earlier paper drew inspiration from the Volunteer press, but spoke for the more radical United Irishmen, *The Nation* began as the voice of O'Connell's Repeal Association, but led the split

[42] T.F. O'Sullivan, *The Young Irelanders* (Tralee, 1944), 44.

over the use of physical force in which the faction known as Young Ireland broke away in January of 1847 to form the Confederate Clubs, who ultimately staged an abortive rising the following year. Like the *Northern Star*, *The Nation* was published not simply to inform, but to forge a national identity. Its 'slow and silent operation', according to Gavan Duffy in the paper's first editorial, 'acts on the masses as the wind, which we do not see, moves dust, which we do see'. That first edition also carried news reports from India, Afghanistan and China, as well as an article by Thomas Davis criticising the attitude of the London press to the British Army's actions in Afghanistan, 'invading the territory of an independent and unoffending people, with no pretext save a lie'.[43]

Like the *Northern Star*, *The Nation* aspired to be a national newspaper, filtering news reports from Afghanistan to Athlone through the lens of nationality; however, unlike its predecessor, it existed in a time when communications networks made that aspiration just about possible. Where the *Northern Star* struggled against drunken delivery men and subscribers who refused to pay for papers arriving a month late, *The Nation* travelled around the country on a cheap and comparatively efficient postal system. Moreover, the improved flow of information worked both ways; *The Nation* also received fresh reports of Repeal meetings from around Ireland, and drew on eye-witness reports from a plethora of local papers, each with its own local reporters, which did not exist to the same extent in 1795. So, when the Famine was at its peak, *The Nation* regularly carried reports from local papers such as the *Tuam Herald* or the *Mayo Constitution*. The same was true of the more radical weeklies that followed *The Nation* after its suppression in 1848: John Mitchel's *United Irishman*, the short-lived *Irish Felon* and *Irish Tribune*, and Joseph Brennan's *Irishman* – all channelled a digest of local news through a nationalist editorial filter. Where the *Northern Star* had been national in ideology, but had struggled to reach a national readership, *The Nation* and its successors were national in both ideology and form because they were able to give the idea of nationality the tangible form of a unified informational territory by making conscious use of the new communications networks that were, ironically, the product of the same imperial state to which they were opposed.

If the idea of the nation exists in space as a geographical territory, it also exists in time, as a shared history transmitted, and in a modern culture that transmission takes place mainly through print. The editors of *The Nation*,

---

[43] *The Nation* 1:1 (October 15, 1842).

like the editors of the *Northern Star* before them, recognised this. Just as the poetry in the *Northern Star* was collected in volumes such as *Paddy's Resource*, so too did *The Nation* branch out into less ephemeral forms of print. In particular, James Duffy printed an anthology of *Nation* poetry, *The Spirit of the Nation* in 1843. It sold for 6d. (at a time when a daily newspaper cost 5d.), and was later claimed (quite credibly) to have been the best-selling Irish-printed book of the nineteenth century. It was followed in 1844 by an anthology of articles that had originally appeared in *The Nation*, collected as *The Voice of the Nation*, at 1s. 6d. a copy. Buoyed by this success, the editors of *The Nation* launched the Library of Ireland (again in partnership with Duffy) in 1845, and for the next two years published a series that included Gavan Duffy's *The Ballad Poetry of Ireland* (which went through thirty-eight editions, selling 76,000 copies in twenty years), John Mitchel's *The Life and Times of Aodh O'Neill*, Michael Doheny's *History of the American Revolution*, fiction by William Carleton (*Art Maguire*) and literary history (Thomas D'Arcy McGee's *Irish Writers of the 17th Century*). Duffy continued publishing popular Irish fiction even after the Library of Ireland project wrapped up in 1847, and by the end of the century his Prize Library, mostly of Irish books, ran to eighty-six volumes.

In the year that the Library of Ireland wound up, 1847, more than 200,000 Irish people emigrated, mostly to the United States; and this massive migration, by creating large Irish communities around the world, fostered a media culture that was increasingly international. 'England has been left in possession not only of the soil of Ireland, with all that grows and lives thereon,' announces John Mitchel at the beginning of his *Jail Journal* (1854), 'but in possession of the world's ear also. She may pour into it what tale she will: and all mankind will believe her.'[44] When an eighteenth-century writer used the phrase 'the world' in relation to public opinion, it referred to the exclusive little cliques who made up the fashionable 'world'; when Mitchel uses it in the 1850s, he means the globe, and this new sense would have a profound effect on the way in which Irish men and women saw themselves.

AMERICA'S EASTERN SHORE

In June of 1852, some of the emigrants leaning over the rails of Dublin mail packet may have noticed a slow-moving vessel in the waters, as the first telegraph cable between England and Ireland was laid between

[44] John Mitchel, *Jail Journal* (1854; rpt Shannon, 1982), xxxvii.

Holyhead and Howth. Among the passengers may well have been some who had seen an earlier form of telegraph, when Mr Haddock's Exhibition of Androides performing at the Mechanic Theatre on Dublin's Exchequer Street in 1833 had displayed a working model of the Paris–Lille visual telegraph. Opened in 1794, the French telegraph used a string of hilltop towers, from the tops of which moveable arms transmitted signals by visual code. While effective for sending military messages, it had drawbacks, in that it could not be used at night, or in fog or in heavy rain, and the messages were easy to intercept. So, almost from the time Alessandro Volta developed the battery in 1800, there were attempts to develop a working electric telegraph. In London, the first commercial telegraph line opened between Euston and Camden Town in London in 1837. In the United States, Samuel Morse sent his first message in 1844, and later that year, on the eve of the Famine, the first Irish telegraph line was run alongside the rails of the Dalkey Atmospheric Railway, just outside Dublin. By 1852, the Howth–Holyhead link was in place, and the Irish Magnetic Telegraph Company began operating Ireland's first commercial telegraph along the Midland Great Western Railway, from Dublin to Galway.

In 1851, an anonymous Irish commentator, writing as 'An Old and Almost Obsolete Loyalist', published a pamphlet entitled *England's Western, or America's Eastern Shore? Old Ireland or a New State?* 'I had rather be a Briton than an American', he announces; 'but I cannot conceal from myself that if England delays much longer to recognise our claims to the advantages which our geographical position entitles us to … there is a danger that she may perceive her mistake when she finds that Ireland has become the eastern shore of America.'[45] The first steamer to cross the Atlantic without the aid of sail, the *Sirius*, had barely touched the dock in New York on its journey from Cork Harbour in 1838 when rival ports on the west coast of Ireland began making their claims to become the steam gateway to America. In thinking of Galway or Kerry not as the site of atavistic poverty and starvation in the 1840s, but as the hub of a global transportation network – and to do so at the height of the Famine – we can see the germ of a radical reconceptualisation of Ireland's place in the world.

Indeed, when the first trans-Atlantic telegraph cable was laid from Valentia by the *Great Eastern* in July of 1866[46] it seemed for a few years

---

[45] *England's Western, or America's Eastern Shore? Old Ireland or a New State?* (Dublin, 1851), 2.
[46] An earlier cable, also connected to Valentia, had been laid to great fanfare in 1858; however, it only functioned for a few months.

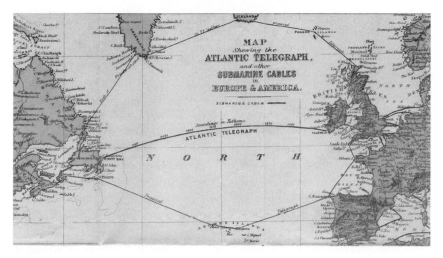

Illustration 5. The first successful trans-Atlantic telegraph lines, laid in 1866, ran from the west coast of Ireland to Newfoundland, in the process drawing a new informational map, with Ireland at its centre.

as if Kerry might well become the centre of the new informational map (illustration 5). One of the very first messages to have been carried across the Atlantic was a greeting sent from Mallow, County Cork, via Valentia, to the Mayor of New York. 'I have here', he told the crowd assembled in Manhattan, 'a message from a little village, now a suburb of New York.' In a sense, he was right. The telegraph created a new geography, and in terms of the time it took to send a message, Mallow was now a suburb of New York. For the first time, it was possible for a complex message to travel faster than a person could carry it; the effect was arguably the most profound since the development of moveable type. Celebrating the new dispensation, the poet Thomas Caulfield Irwin (who as a young man had written 'The Memory of the Dead' for *The Nation*), eulogised the telegraph with more enthusiasm than poetic ability in his 'Hymn of Progress':

Thought swift flashes through the wire as the nerve, over mountain, through main,
And the Telegraph narrows the round of our World to the size of the Brain![47]

[47] Thomas Caulfield Irwin, *Irish Poems and Legends: Historical and Traditionary* (Glasgow, n.d.), 145.

In 1700, the average time-lag for news from most European capitals to reach Ireland had been a week to ten days; in the early decades of the nineteenth century, this was still more or less the case. By comparison, the Dublin *Daily Express* of January 9, 1866, for instance, contains news from Paris, Madrid, Vienna and Florence dated the previous day (including a traffic report from Florence). In that same paper, commodity prices from New York, Bombay and Calcutta all appeared with a two- or three-day delay, and even these within a few years these would be replaced by same-day market reports. For the Irish reader in 1866, however, Australia and New Zealand were still beyond the reach of the telegraph, with the Dublin newspapers still carrying Antipodean news that was a month and a half old. However, when Australia was linked to the telegraph system by a submarine cable in 1871, along with Japan and China, it too entered the informational present of Irish readers, followed by South America in 1874, at which point the world would be wrapped in 650,000 miles of wire, 30,000 miles of it submarine cable.[48] Africa – geographically closer, but informationally remote – was finally connected in stages between 1879 and 1884. The fascination that this wiring of the world exerted on the press is to be seen in the titles of many of the newspapers launched in the period, even predating the electric telegraph: *Stewart's Telegraphic Despatch* (Dublin, 1832), *The Telegraph; or Connaught Ranger* (Castlebar, 1830), *The Telegraph* (Dublin, 1851) and the *Belfast Evening Telegraph* (1870), which would carry its name into the twenty-first century.

The telegraph effectively created a global informational field, eventually making it necessary to reconfigure the nature of time itself. Up until this point, time had been a local matter, because even with the railway it took so long to travel between two points that it made little difference if the clock in the train station in Dublin said 11 o'clock at the same moment that a clock in Glasgow read 11:15. With the telegraph, however, it was possible to communicate with people all over the world more or less simultaneously, so it suddenly became important to have some agreement as to what time it was. Beginning in the 1840s, the railways in England and Ireland began to adopt conventions on standardised time, which eventually led (after some local resistance) to the Statutes (Definition of Time) Act 1880 (43 & 44 Vict. cap. 9), 'to remove certain doubts as to whether expressions of time occurring in Acts of Parliament, deeds and other legal instruments relate in England and Scotland to Greenwich

---

[48] Tom Standage, *The Victorian Internet* (London, 2000), 97.

time, and in Ireland to Dublin time, or to the mean astronomical time in each locality'. The adoption of Dublin Mean Time meant that clocks all over Ireland were (legally, at least) set to the same time, but this was approximately twenty-five minutes earlier than Greenwich Mean Time (again, putting Ireland slightly off-centre in the Union of which it was ostensibly a full part); it would not be until 1916 that Ireland adopted Greenwich Mean Time.

The reconfiguration of time can be seen as part of a new, and particularly vigorous phase of globalisation, of which massive Irish (and, indeed, European) emigration was a part. In the second half of the nineteenth century, the Irish diaspora not only grew; it became increasingly well organised, not least because of the exile to the United States of a number of key nationalist leaders after the Fenian actions of 1867. In July of 1870, the Fenian John Boyle O'Reilly became editor of the Boston *Pilot* (whose name echoed the O'Connellite paper of the 1830s); in September of that same year, the tellingly named *Irish World and American Industrial Liberator* was launched in New York by Patrick Ford (who would edit it, remarkably, until 1913), while in 1875 an Irish newspaper, the *Southern Cross* began publication in Buenos Aires – and these newspapers were joined by others, in Canada, Australia and elsewhere. This in turn created a new geography of imaginary continuities, summed up by the masthead of the *Irish World*: in its centre was a globe being lifted by a radiant rising sun; to the left was a traditional Irish village, complete with round tower; to the right, a modern American metropolis. Each week, the *Irish World* carried a full page of snippets of local stories from around Ireland (with headings such as a 'Fatal Carriage Accident' in Antrim, or a 'Shifting Bog' in Clare), followed by a page of similar notices from around the United States. Its readers were, in a very real sense, living a mediated life in two continents.

The flow of information worked both ways, and Irish news was not only reported outside of Ireland; it now originated outside of Ireland. For instance, in 1868, the proprietors of the Dublin-based Fenian newspaper, *The Irish People*, were charged with 'seditious libel' for their reporting of Fenian meetings in the United States. Defending the case, Denis Caulfield Heron went straight to the heart of the substantive issue. 'The electric telegraph has united Europe and America', he told the court. 'The news of the day is a necessity of life. Free and fair commentary upon that news is an equal necessity. The press ought to be uncontrolled. Or, is all the liberty to be on one side?'[49] It was becoming increasingly clear that as

[49] Denis Caulfield Heron, *Irish State Trials, 1868* (Dublin, 1868), 1, 23.

there was more information in circulation, the old methods of controlling news within Ireland would no longer work. Commenting on the prosecutions, Karl Marx thought that the treatment of the accused was 'worse than anything happening on the Continent, except in Russia'.[50] And this was the new internationalism: a German, comparing conditions in Russia to the prosecution of an Irish newspaperman for reporting American news. In a paradox recognised by Heron, the claims of Irish nationalism were not threatened by the global flow of information; in fact, the opposite was true, and the more fully Ireland became enmeshed in a new informational order, the more difficult it was to suppress the spread of an idea of nationality.

Meanwhile, as the educational reforms of the early part of the century began to take effect, the proportion of the Irish population who were part of the new print culture was growing. Stamp Taxes, which for the first half of the century had kept the price of books and newspapers artificially high, were relaxed, beginning with the abolition of the tax on advertisements in 1853. Newspapers, which had typically been four pages long since the seventeenth century, began to get bigger, and cheaper, with the first major penny paper appearing on March 29, 1859, when the *Irish Times* was founded by Major Lawrence E. Knox. Reviving a title first used in the 1820s, Knox's paper originally appeared thrice-weekly, and could be priced at 1d. (or £2 per year), partly because it was printed on a four-feeder flatbed press that could turn out 5,000 sheets an hour. Fourteen weeks after the paper was founded, it was so successful that it went daily. By 1870, it had doubled to eight pages, and by 1873 was up to twelve pages, beginning to resemble, in its range of coverage, something like the newspapers of the next century.

There was also more to fill up the pages. With the telegraph, the days were gone when Irish papers had to apologise to their readers that there was no foreign news because the mailboat was late. From the very beginning, it was clear that the usefulness of the telegraph for sending personal messages would be limited by cost; however, for high value information – market reports, military dispatches and, crucially, news – it would radically increase the volume and speed of information, and hence its function. Indeed, it was an Irish journalist, W.H. Russell, who was arguably the first person to demonstrate that when an event was reported more or less as it happened, it changed the impact of that event.

---

[50] Marx to Engels, March 16, 1868, in Karl Marx and Friedrich Engels, *Ireland and the Irish Question* (Moscow, 1986), 150.

Although Russell had started his career in Ireland reporting Repeal meetings in the 1840s, by 1854 he was correspondent for *The Times* in the Crimean War, where his reports of the suffering of British soldiers, fresh from the battlefield, had an effect on public opinion that altered the conduct of the war. 'Your correspondent has shown the mistakes committed,' commented a reader on November 3, 1854, 'and due honour will be awarded to the press.'[51] Whereas in earlier conflicts, it would not have been until the wounded began to arrive on the quayside that questions would start, in 1854 the reading public were aware of what was happening as it happened.

Moreover, with the telegraph, the instantaneous sharing of news meant that stories (apart from investigative pieces) were less and less likely to be the exclusive property of one newspaper. This was particularly true after 1851, when Julius Reuter established a news agency that used a network of foreign correspondents to wire the news to subscribing newspapers. He was later joined by others, including the Press Association, which was founded in 1868, originally to help the English provincial papers to compete with the London dailies by sharing stories. When the British and Irish telegraph services were nationalised in 1870, the new body was brought under the wing of the Post Office, who applied the same public service ethos to the new medium that it had applied to postal service in the 1840s. Prices dropped, volumes increased, the number of newspapers subscribing to the wire services doubled,[52] and the newspapers found themselves inundated with information. For the Irish newspapers, the effect of this increased volume of news was proportionally greater than for the London papers, in that the flow of information from England to Ireland was usually greater than the other way around. The telegraph also carried more ephemera than had ever been available before. Andrew Dunlop, who was sub-editor of the Dublin *Daily Express* at the time, later recalled that, 'when the Telegraphs passed into the hands of the State, the quantity of "flimsy" to be dealt with increased to an enormous extent'.

Dunlop was freed from sorting through 'flimsy' in the 1870s, when he went from sub-editing to reporting, a job that involved racing around the country by rail, attending political meetings and trials, and then tele-graphing reports back to his office. In addition to writing for the *Daily Express*, Dunlop also sent a daily report on Irish affairs to the London

[51] Charles Shaw, 'The British Soldiers when Wounded in Action', *The Times* (November 3, 1854), 5.
[52] Paul Starr, *Creation of the Media: Political Origins of Modern Communications* (New York, 2004), 179.

Daily News from 1867 until 1889, and frequently filed reports for *The Times* as well. In other words, in a period stretching from the Fenian rising of 1867, through the founding of the Land League, to the defeat of Gladstone's second Home Rule bill, the telegraph allowed a single journalist – whose politics were firmly pro-Empire – to supply Irish news to not only one of the largest-circulating dailies in Dublin, but to two of the largest London papers as well. Dunlop later recalled: 'Mr. William O'Brien [editor of the Parnellite *United Ireland*] paid me the compliment, as I regarded it, of complaining … that I had, in my capacity of correspondent of *The Daily News*, done more to prevent Home Rule being granted than any other man in Ireland.'[53]

In short, Irish nationalism assumed its modern form in a period during which the media was undergoing a profound period of transformation that made a national media possible. However, the same technologies – steam and the telegraph – that created a national informational order also exceeded that order; a telegraph line that ran from Dublin to Kerry need not stop once it hit the Irish coast; it might just as easily carry on to New York, or Sydney, or Bombay. While this transformation took place at various points on the globe throughout the century, the Irish Famine of the 1840s and the consequent exodus of emigration that followed it meant that Ireland literally spilled over the edges of the island at precisely the moment that instantaneous electric telecommunications made it possible for the severed limbs, as it were, to maintain nerve links with the main body. From that moment on, Ireland ceased to be a nation bounded by geography; instead, it became an idea, to a large extent created, sustained and debated by a media culture that had absorbed one whole new dimension – speed – and was beginning to experience freedom from the constraints of another: distance.

[53] Andrew Dunlop, *Fifty Years of Irish Journalism.* (Dublin, 1911), 22, 205, 32, 277.

Media Event 3:
Parnellism and crime: April 18, 1887

Years later, in her account of their lives together, Katherine O'Shea remembered that on the morning of March 7, 1887 when Charles Stewart Parnell asked for his copy of *The Times*, she held it back from him. 'The *Times* is unusually stodgy', she told him. 'Do eat your breakfast first.' And so it was not until a few hours later that Parnell saw the first of the series of articles that *The Times* published as 'Parnellism and Crime'. 'Now, my King', Katherine told him, 'you must attend to the *Times*. You must take an action against them.' 'No,' he replied, struggling into his overcoat. 'I have never taken any notice of newspapers, nor of anyone. Why should I now?'[1]

Over the next few months, *The Times* would publish a series of articles (sixteen up to July 9, 1887) under the heading of 'Parnellism and Crime'. The timing of these articles was not coincidental: the Conservative Prime Minister, Lord Salisbury, and his Chief Secretary for Ireland, Alfred Balfour, were in the process of introducing the Criminal Law Amendment Bill – the so-called 'Coercion Act' – which, among other measures, would have allowed the introduction of martial law in any part of Ireland that was thought to be 'disturbed'. Meanwhile, Parnell was working more closely than before with the Liberal leader, William Gladstone, to find terms on which Home Rule could be achieved for Ireland. In that first article, and in those that followed, *The Times* set out to convince its readers of two things: that while Parnell might now be presenting himself

---

[1] Katherine O'Shea, *Charles Stewart Parnell: His Love Story and Political Life*, Vol. II (London, Toronto and Melbourne, 1914), 129.

as a statesman and a parliamentarian, he was in fact deeply implicated in political violence; and that that violence was being orchestrated and funded from America.

From the very outset, the 'Parnellism and Crime' campaign was not only conducted through the media; it was also, to a large extent, about the media. The first article, for instance, traces Parnell's contacts in the United States, focusing in particular on a group associated with the *Irish World and American Industrial Liberator*, whose columns provided *The Times* with much of its evidence. However, *The Times* also mined Irish newspapers for evidence of conspiracy. On April 12, for instance, the paper quoted from no fewer than nine Irish newspapers, including not only the nationalist *Freeman's Journal* and *United Ireland* (which was owned by Parnell's supporters), but also a range of local papers, including the *Leinster Leader, Midland Tribune, Sligo Champion, Tipperary Advocate, Enniscorthy Guardian, Munster Express* and *Kerry Evening Post*. 'The man who hangs fire is in secret alliance with the people's enemies,' it quoted the *Midland Tribune* as having declared on January 20, 1887, 'and the people will know how to deal with him when their ranks are closed in.'[2]

The Times was able take such a wide view of Parnell's organisation through the press because there were more nationalist papers in existence in 1887 than at any previous point in Irish history. Indeed, their numbers were increasing, going from forty-one in 1880 to fifty-five in 1886,[3] giving Parnell a more complete national information network than earlier nationalist leaders. From one point of view, it was the existence of this developed media world that made the national movement possible in the first place. On the other hand, the fact that newspapers could be archived made it possible for *The Times* to dig up articles from the past, juxtapose them with the present, and equate past allegiances with present actions. Equally importantly, quoting from such a range of Irish newspapers had an implicit rhetorical effect: it suggested to readers of *The Times* that the conspiracy to conduct 'a war of murder against the Empire' was well enough organised to have its own network of newspapers, stretching not only into every town and village in Ireland, but also across the Atlantic to the United States.

[2] 'The National League at Work', *The Times* (April 12, 1887), 6.
[3] James Loughlin, 'Constructing the National Spectacle: Parnell, the Press and National Leadership, 1870–1886', in *Parnell in Perspective*, ed. D. George Boyce and Alan O'Day (London, 1991), 221–42, 225.

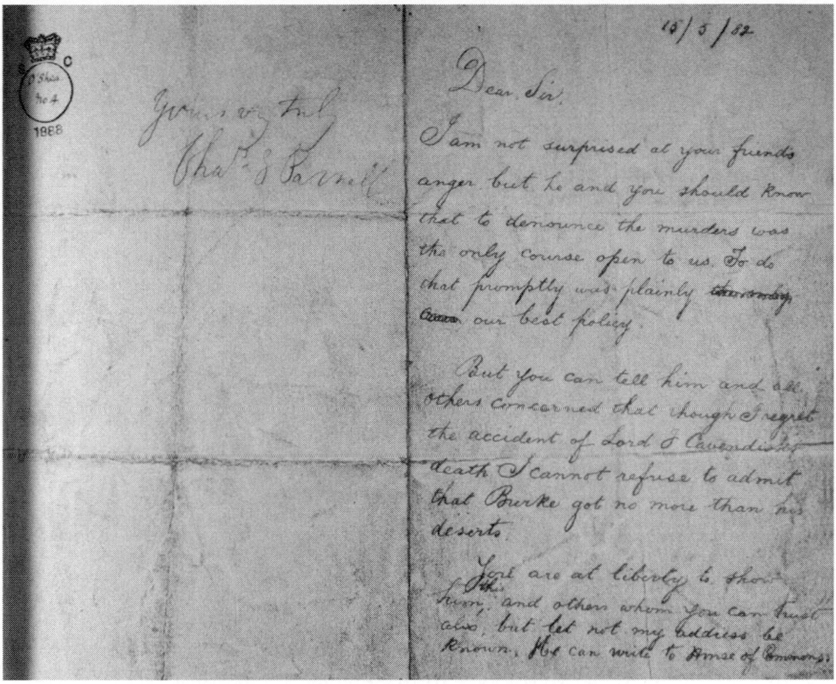

Illustration 6. On April 18, 1887, *The Times* published a facsimile of a letter in which Charles Stewart Parnell appeared to condone the Phoenix Park murders five years earlier. Apart from the political storm that it provoked, the visual nature of the facsimile caused consternation in media circles in an age when news circulated by telegraph.

On the morning of Monday, April 18, 1887 – the day on which the vote on the second reading of the Criminal Law Amendment Bill was to be held – *The Times* took the unprecedented step of moving beyond dredging up material from old newspapers, and under the heading 'Mr. Parnell and the Phœnix-Park Murders', published a facsimile of a manuscript letter that it claimed had Parnell's signature attached (see illustration 6):

15 May, 1882

Dear Sir,

I am surprised at your friend's anger but he and you should know that to denounce the murders was the only course open to us. To do that promptly was plainly ~~the only~~ our best policy.

But you can tell him and all others concerned that though I regret the accident of Lord F. Cavendish's death I cannot refuse to admit that Burke got no more than his deserts.

You are at liberty to show him this, and others whom you can trust also, but let not my address be known. He can write to House of Commons.

Yours very truly,

Chas. S.Parnell[4]

On 6 May, 1882, the newly appointed Irish Chief Secretary, Lord Frederick Cavendish, and the Under-Secretary, T.H. Burke, were stabbed to death with long surgical knives in Dublin's Phœnix Park by a militant nationalist group calling themselves 'The Invincibles'. These particularly grisly murders evoked horror in England, and had forced the Liberal Prime Minister of the time, Gladstone, to maintain a form of martial law not unlike that which was once again before Parliament in 1887. In 1882, Parnell had been shocked by the murders, and had publicly denounced them; however, *The Times* letter of April 1887, allegedly addressed to one of the *Irish World* group, Patrick Egan, suggested that his real sympathies lay with the murderers.

Where the earlier attacks on Parnell in *The Times* were not significantly more vitriolic than the ordinary cut and thrust of political journalism at the time, this was something different, and it provoked a media storm. Parnell denounced it late on the night of April 18 in the House of Commons, as well as giving an interview to a telegraph news service, the Central News Agency, in which he pointed out differences between the facsimile, and his own writing. In Dublin, the *Freeman's Journal* was well accustomed to keeping its readers up to date with the late-night sittings of the House, using both its own 'Special Wire' as well as the 'ordinary telegraph'. Accordingly, its Tuesday edition of April 19 published both the full text of the letter as it had appeared in *The Times* and Parnell's repudiation of it in the Central News interview. 'Yesterday morning,' it told Irish readers, '*The Times* created a bubble sensation by publishing a forgery.'[5] On the other side of the political fence, the Dublin *Daily Express*, a sister paper to *The Times* in London, asserted that 'notwithstanding Mr. Parnell's disclaimer, it is affirmed that the letter is a genuine document'.[6] The *Irish Times*, meanwhile, kept slightly aloof from the fray; while retaining *The Times*' original alarmist headline, 'Parnellism and Crime', it printed in full a Press Association telegram, in which Parnell pronounced the letter to be 'nothing more or less than

[4] 'Parnellism and Crime: Mr. Parnell and the Phœnix-Park Murders', *The Times* (April 18, 1887), 8.
[5] 'The Latest "Times" Canard', *Freeman's Journal* (April 19, 1887), 4.
[6] 'Editorial', *Daily Express* (April 19, 1887), 4.

a clumsy forgery'. 'The signature reproduced in the *Times* is much bolder and freer, and the long letters are marked by considerable irregularity. The initial letter Mr. Parnell declares to be written in a style never adopted by him.'[7]

By the late 1880s, newspapers had been using the telegraph for more than thirty years, and Irish readers were used to hearing about events in London or New York as quickly as they would hear about events in Dublin or Cork. Indeed, the telegraph was arguably the key piece of informational infrastructure that allowed Parnell to conduct a campaign for Irish Home Rule in the British House of Commons, funded (at least in part) from New York. In the age of the telegraph, Westminster was as close as College Green – or New York. And, indeed, in the days immediately after the publication of the letter, the trans-Atlantic telegraph wires were buzzing. For instance, Patrick Egan, to whom the letter was allegedly addressed, was contacted in Lincoln, Nebraska, from where he gave an interview to one of the wire services that made it into most of the English and Irish dailies on April 20. By the same token, the weekly *Irish World*, which *The Times* had claimed was pulling 'the wires that set the puppets dancing, each after his kind, from Westminster to Chicago', gleaned what it could from the telegraph for its April 23 edition, where it denounced the 'stupid forgery', as well as picking up a piece on the affair from the North American Cable News service, originally published in the *New York Tribune*.

However, by printing a facsimile of the controversial letter – in other words, by printing the handwritten letter as an illustration – *The Times* disrupted the trans-Atlantic informational geography that the telegraph had created. Simply put, it was impossible to telegraph a picture. Indeed, even the *Freeman's Journal* in Dublin had to wait until Wednesday, April 20, for the mailboat to dock before it could get its hands on a copy of *The Times* to reproduce the facsimile. For the Irish-American press, the wait was even longer. On April 20, Byron Stephenson of the *New York Herald* wrote to the Clan na Gael organiser John Devoy, telling him: 'I suppose we shall have the *Times* about Friday week'[8] – which would have been April 29. Hence, the *Irish World* had to wait until its May 7 edition before it could reproduce the actual facsimile letter, and it would not be until May 14 – almost a month after the original letter was published – that the

[7] 'Parnellism and Crime: Mr. Parnell and the Phœnix-Park Murders', *Irish Times* (April 19, 1887), 5.
[8] William O'Brien and Desmond Ryan, eds, *Devoy's Post Bag 1871–1928*, Vol. II (Dublin, 1948), 304.

paper published a facsimile of *The Times* letter alongside copies of Parnell's autograph.[9]

At that point, few people doubted that the letter was a forgery, and fingers began to point at Richard Pigott, a veteran journalist whose career had started with *The Nation* in the 1840s, but whose politics in the 1880s had turned against what he called 'a socialistic movement for the attainment of an impossibility'.[10] Meanwhile, allegations of collusion between *The Times* and the Conservative Party began to circulate, leading to the establishment of a Commission in the summer of 1888. Pigott was brought before the Commission on February 25, 1889, where his guilt became clear in a dramatic cross-examination; the following day he fled, and on March 1 shot himself in a Madrid hotel room. Although Pigott's disgrace would seem to have vindicated Parnell, much of the testimony brought forward at the Commission's hearings produced an impression of guilt by association, and some later historians would argue that perhaps the whole affair had been an elaborate libel trap, with the publication of a blatant forgery designed to propel Parnell into a public forum in which he could be linked with dynamiters and assassins.[11] Even if this was not the case, the controversy made one point abundantly clear: Irish politics in the age of a press connected by telegraph was no longer bounded by the island of Ireland. Instead of being a geographical entity, Ireland was now a network of telegraph wires, an informational field in which a letter published in a London newspaper alleging an Irish politician's involvement with an American newspaper would become an event that resonated throughout a new trans-Atlantic field.

---

[9] 'The Forged Signature: Six Genuine Autographs and the Forgery by the London "Times"' Jim the Penman', *Irish World* (14 May, 1887), 5.

[10] Richard Pigott, *Personal Recollections of an Irish Nationalist Journalist*, 2nd edn (Dublin and London, 1883), 437.

[11] Margaret O'Callaghan, 'Parnellism and Crime: Constructing a Conservative Strategy of Containment 1887–91', in *Parnell: The Politics of Power*, ed. Donal McCartney (Dublin, 1991), 102–24. The incident was, however, later an embarrassment to *The Times*. See *A History of the Times*, Vol. III: *The Twentieth-Century Test 1884–1912* (London, 1947), 38–49.

CHAPTER 4

Casual miracles: 1890–1920

SPEECH HAS BECOME IMMORTAL

When Thomas Edison completed the sketch on November 29, 1877, there was a general scepticism in the Menlo Park laboratory. The drawing showed a simple device, in which a cylinder, covered in foil and attached to a hand crank, captured the impressions of a needle connected to a vibrating diaphragm. It was meant to record sound. One of Edison's assistants bet him a cigar it would do nothing of the sort. So, when Edison bellowed 'Mary had a little lamb' into the diaphragm, rewound the cylinder, and heard a tinny – but recognisable – version of his own voice serenade him, everyone in the room was astonished. 'I was never so taken aback in all my life', Edison later recalled. 'I was always afraid of things that worked the first time.'[1]

Work it did. Edison was soon locked in a series of patent wars with Alexander Graham Bell, who developed an improved gramophone in 1886; a year later, in 1887, Emile Berliner introduced the flat disc that would become standard for the next century. 'By the supernatural genius of the wizard of Menlo,' wrote a contributor to *The Phonogram*, a magazine launched in 1893 as part of an emerging recording culture, 'transient speech has now been rendered not merely material and permanent, but capable of being transported through geographical space, like any other product of nature or art.'[2] Or, to put it another way, speech was now like print: a commodity to be produced, traded and saved. This in turn meant that it was possible for the first time in a market economy to

---

[1] Matthew Josephson, *Edison: A Biography* (New York, 1959), 163. It should be noted that Edison's invention of the phonograph is not uncontested; a Frenchman, Charles Cros, seems to have developed it almost simultaneously.
[2] Douglas Archibald, 'On the Phonograph', *The Phonogram: A Monthly Journal Devoted to the Science of Sound and Recording of Speech* 1:2 (June 1893), 22.

have a media culture that was, to some extent, based on the spoken rather than on the printed word.

Considered in this light, the phonograph might have seemed like precisely the technology for which Ireland had been waiting since the sixteenth century. Print had been introduced to Ireland in the sixteenth century as the medium of religious conversion and colonial administration; its antithesis, in this cultural configuration, was an indigenous oral culture, which in turn was intertwined with a manuscript culture. Although print was thoroughly indigenised by the eighteenth century, throughout much of the intervening period the trauma of its original introduction continued to reverberate, largely because the Irish language remained largely outside of print culture, with only a trickle of items (many of them continuing the proselytising mission of the seventeenth century) printed in the language. Indeed, it was only in precisely the same years that the phonograph appeared that Irish really started to appear in print, when the Gaelic League (founded in 1893) began publishing Irish-language material in any volume, so that in the period 1890 to 1910 the number of items published in Irish increased tenfold, from two or three volumes per year to twenty or thirty. Likewise, where there were only a few short-lived Irish-language periodicals prior to 1895, by 1920 there were nine different titles.[3]

In spite of all this activity, however, the perception persisted that Irish-language culture was primarily an oral culture, a richness glimpsed tantalisingly just beyond the edges of the printed page. 'Strange as it may seem,' the founder of the Gaelic League, Douglas Hyde, wrote in 'Some Words on Irish Folk-lore' in 1890, 'there existed until recently in our midst millions of men and women, who, when their day's work was over, sought and found mental recreation in a domain to which few indeed of us who read and write books, are permitted to enter.'[4] Recalling an old Sligo man who had claimed to be tormented by the fairies, W.B. Yeats tartly observed: 'The Spirit of the Age had in no manner made his voice heard down there. ... The "Spirit of the Age"' is never heard 'outside the newspaper offices ... of the city.'[5] In the work of Hyde, Yeats and others in those years, a curious inversion of the role of print suddenly becomes possible. Print, which had once been seen as a medium of preservation,

[3] Niall Ó Ciosáin, 'Creating an Audience: Innovation and Reception in Irish Language Publishing, 1880–1920', in *The Irish Book in the Twentieth Century*, ed. Clare Hutton (Dublin, 2004), 5–15.

[4] Douglas Hyde, 'Some Words on Irish Folk-lore', *Providence Sunday Journal* (August 24, 1890); rpt in Douglas Hyde, *Language, Lore and Lyrics*, ed. Breandán Ó Conaire (Dublin, 1986), 122.

[5] W.B. Yeats, *Selected Criticism and Prose* (London, 1980), 414–15.

that which would fix and keep secure a culture for all eternity, could now be identified with the newspaper, which was the epitome of the ephemeral. An old folk-tale was to be hoarded, remembered and passed on through the generations. An old newspaper, on the other hand, was fit only for wrapping fish. As a result, rather than being peripheral to the mainstream print culture, oral culture became the ungraspable core of a phantasmic Irishness, idealised because it could not be commodified.

This new configuration of the Irish media world put Irish music in a curious, but powerful, situation. Lacking a sustained tradition of composers in the classical tradition, Irish music in the 1890s had become virtually synonymous with traditional music in performance, and this in turn meant that Irish music *per se* was perhaps the most potent emblem of an essential Irishness beyond the mediated world, the purest form of oral culture. 'Music itself had become by the 1890s so closely identified with and symbolic of the culture of Gaelic civilisation,' argues Harry White, 'that it became useless to consider the concept of "Irish music" in any other meaningful way.'[6] Logically, this could have meant one of two things: the phonograph might have been embraced as the medium for which an essentially oral Irish culture had been waiting; or, alternatively, it might have been viewed with suspicion, as the medium that would commodify a culture whose value and distinctiveness was precisely due to its location outside the corrupt marketplace of modernity, the one cultural form that could not be bought and sold. As it happened, however, the place of recorded sound in Irish culture was ultimately the product of larger forces.

The phonograph was effectively the first mass medium in which the patent-owners dominated the industry. With the exception of Pathé, which was based in Paris (and Berliner, who based some of his operations in Germany), all of the major patent-holding companies were American, with a global network of regional offices that spanned the entire planet. What is more, these companies thought globally. 'You know,' boasted F.M. Prescott, President of the Universal Talking Machine Company, 'the world, in so far as the sale of their products is concerned, has been divided between the Gramophone & Typewriter Ltd, of London, England, and the Victor Talking Machine Co., of Camden N.J.'[7] Where Britain had been able to use its imperial reach to dominate the telegraph

---

[6] Harry White, *The Keeper's Recital: Music and Cultural History in Ireland 1770–1970* (Cork, 1998), 66.
[7] Oliver Read and Walter L. Welch, *From Tin Foil to Stereo: Evolution of the Phonograph* (Indianapolis, 1976), 147.

business (which had always been, to some extent, part of its military infrastructure), the gramophone industry was the first mass medium where that domination shifted significantly to American companies operating globally. To put the scale of the new industry in context, as early as 1903, the Victor Company alone sold 2 million discs in the United States; by 1910, the annual sale of recordings worldwide is estimated to have been about 50 million, with England, Germany and the United States accounting for about sixty per cent of this total.[8]

In this new globalised business, Ireland did not even merit a regional sub-office. So, the first Irish music was recorded in the United States, and it did little to upset the view of Irish culture that Edison himself might have formed from his frequent visits to vaudeville shows. The earliest catalogues of Edison pre-recorded cylinders date from 1889 – the same year that Douglas Hyde published his first collection of folk-stories, *Leabhar Sgeulaigheachta* – and in the June 1889 Edison catalogue, there is an 'Irish Medley'. It was followed in July of that same year by what is possibly the first of innumerable versions of John Michael Balfe's 'Killarney'. Similarly, the first Columbia catalogue in 1891 offered Marine Band marches, 'artistic whistling', as well as music marketed as 'Negro' and 'Irish' (making 'Irish' music among the first genres of recorded music). Up until 1896, phonographs were largely heard in phonograph parlours, or displayed by travelling showmen; however, when the first phonographs for home use appeared on the market in 1896, among the very first cylinders cut by the Edison Concert Band was a 'Medley of Irish Airs'. By the end of the nineteenth century, Edison and Columbia both offered a large selection of cylinders by Irish tenors and baritones, as well as Irish comic songs, monologues and sketches, with titles such as 'Arrah, go on!', 'Drill, ye Tarriers' and 'The Ballymoney Conversations'.[9] In short, Irish culture occupied a place in the early recording industry not unlike African-American culture; it existed in an instantly recognisable, but caricatured, form on the music-hall stage, which could be easily transferred to a two-minute cylinder. There was no need to go to Ireland to record Irish musicians; there were plenty of musicians and comedians labelled 'Irish' to be found just off Broadway.

---

[8] Pekka Gronow and Ilpo Saunio, *An International History of the Recording Industry*, trans. Christopher Moseley (London, 1998), 12.

[9] *Catalogue of the First Series (Brown Wax) Edison Bell Two Minute Cylinder Phonograph Records* (London, n.d.); Ed2169 'Arrah, go on!'; Ed2186 'Drill, ye Tarriers, drill!'; Ed2193 'The Ballymoney Conversations'.

The European recording companies, on the other hand, had a strong bias towards opera and classically trained voices. So, when Fred Gaisberg, Berliner's London representative (and the man who was to record Enrico Caruso, the biggest-selling artist in the early years of recorded music), took a couple of days to travel through Ireland on a talent-scouting expedition in September of 1899, he was disappointed. There were 'very few good singers at all' in Belfast, he later wrote, and the singers he heard in Dublin were 'a poor, conceited lot'.[10] Gaisberg only really got excited by an Irish voice in 1903, when people began mentioning a twenty-one-year-old singer named John McCormack – 'not as a celebrity,' Gaisberg later recalled, 'but as a provincial singer of Irish ballads'.[11] McCormack cut his first cylinders that year (three each for the rival Edison and Columbia labels),[12] and his selection of songs – including the ubiquitous 'Killarney' – fit very neatly into what had come to mean 'Irish music' in record catalogues for more than a decade.

Although McCormack cut his first cylinders in 1903 immediately after winning a medal for his singing at the 1902 Feis Ceol, their release preceded his Dublin professional debut by three years and his London debut by four years. As McCormack's career took flight on the stages of the world's opera houses, away from Ireland, discs and cylinders increasingly provided the primary way for many Irish people to hear the country's most famous voice. In short, McCormack was not only the first major Irish recording artist; he was more than that. He was the first singer to exist most fully for many Irish people through the new medium, reversing the priority of live and recorded, and establishing an often extraordinarily intimate relationship with many thousands of Irish people around the world who would never actually see him in the flesh.

As McCormack's star rose, and 'Come Back to Erin' echoed out of gramophones all over the world, it might seem that something like a repetition of the polarisation between a mass-produced and an oral culture that had taken place with print back in the sixteenth century opened up between the kind of popular Irish music that McCormack sang, and Irish music more purely rooted in a folk tradition of performance, such as *sean-nós* singing or music played on the uilleann pipes or

---

[10] Jerrold Northrup Moore, *A Matter of Records: Fred Gaisberg and the Golden Era of the Gramophone* (New York, 1977), 39.

[11] Fred Gaisberg, *Music on Record*, in Gordon T. Ledbetter, *The Great Irish Tenor* (London, 1977), 41.

[12] *Edison Two Minute Cylinder Records: The Complete Catalogue of the Edison Two Minute Wax Cylinder Records*, Vol. IV: *The Edison Standard Gold Moulded Records. British Series*, ed. Sydney Carter and H.H. Annand (n.p., 1964).

bhodhrán. However, such divisions are rarely so clear-cut in reality. In 1899, for instance, an uilleann piper named James C. McAuliffe cut four tracks for Edison in New York: 'Minstrel Boy', 'Miss McCloud's Reel', 'Donnybrook Fair' and 'Stack of Barley', the first of seventeen he would record.[13] Some of these early two-minute cylinders still exist, pre-dating McCormack by four years, and making McAuliffe possibly the earliest Irish-born musician to have become, as it were, immortal. A few years later, the Loughrea-born piper, Patsy Touhey (who had emigrated to New York as a child), began advertising a mail order service, offering 'Original Phonograph Records of the Irish Pipes Made to Order by the Best Irish Piper in America', delivered for $1 each.[14]

However, McAuliffe and Touhey remain isolated Irish figures in the early history of recorded sound, struggling to etch out a career in the United States. In Ireland in the same period, there are only hints of an Irish recording industry. In 1906, for instance, John O'Neill, a bicycle manufacturer on Dublin's South King Street was offering gramophones, phonographs and zonophones for sale, as well as ten-inch Zonophone disc recordings of patriotic songs such as 'The Memory of the Dead', 'The West's Asleep' and 'Bantry Bay'. The following year, when the Gaelic League held its annual Oireachtas, O'Neill had Zonophone dispatch a recording engineer from London to record the performers. 'Close on one hundred records were made', reported the *Evening Telegraph*, 'including speeches in Irish, traditional songs, Scotch-Gaelic songs, flute solos and pianoforte solos.'[15] Sound on many of the recordings was reportedly 'excellent', and the discs were given labels and Zonophone catalogue numbers. And yet, even though a selection of these recordings survived (discovered stacked in the back of a Dublin shop in the late 1970s), they were never released commercially.

Just why those 1907 recordings spent seventy years gathering dust is not easy to understand. When the key Edison patents lapsed in 1904, ethnic recording labels proliferated. In England, these included at least two minority-language labels (Hesse's Hebrew Recordings, and the Welsh-language Cambrian), as well as Noble, a label specialising in Scottish music. This in turn was only a faint echo of the increasingly multicultural hue that the industry was to assume in the United States, then in a period

---

[13] Richard K. Spottswood, *Ethnic Music on Records: A Discography of Ethnic Music Recordings Produced in the United States, 1893 to 1942*, Vol. v (Urbana, 1990); Ed7229–Ed7231.

[14] A selection of Touhey's recordings are available on CD: Patsy Touhey, *The Piping of Patsy Touhey* Na Píobarí Uilleann. NPUCD 001, 2005.

[15] Harry Bradshaw, *The Irish Phonograph: The Monaco Radio Contest* (Dublin, 1984), 3.

of boom immigration, where there were entire labels specialising in Greek, Turkish, Chinese and Arabic music. There is no uniquely compelling reason why this could not have happened with Irish music in New York, London – or in Dublin. But it did not. It may have been the case that the hugely successful mainstream genre marketed as 'Irish' music, such as that sung by John McCormack, filled (or at least was seen to fill) any demand for Irish recordings. It is also possible, given that this 'Irish' music was often marketed in the US in the recording companies' domestic catalogues, that Irishness was an invisible ethnicity, and as such was not seen as meriting a separate label (in contrast, for instance, to Hebrew or to Greek music). Whatever the full explanation, just as had been the case with print in the sixteenth century, recording came to Ireland late, and, with very few exceptions, the place of recording in Irish culture consolidated the sense, going back to the sixteenth century, that traditional Irish culture was defined by its distance from a mediated modernity, for better or for worse.

'ON THE LIMITS OF VISION'

The sense that Ireland was on the periphery of new media industries could sometimes disguise the fact that, for some Irish men and women in the final decade of the nineteenth century, the cutting edge of the new technologies was a visible horizon. For instance, there was correspondence between members of the Royal Dublin Society and Thomas Edison in 1878 to request 'any such objects' as might prove relevant for a planned 'exhibition of objects of interest in Science and Art'; they also wrote to Alexander Graham Bell, who sent along a telephone, which was demonstrated by a member of the Society, Professor W.F. Barrett. Barrett later dismantled Bell's telephone, and suggested some improvements (particularly in relation to reducing electrical interference on lines) noting in one of his publications that as early as 1865 an Irish inventor had produced a modified version of the telephone that in many ways prefigured Alexander Graham Bell's breakthrough in 1876.[16]

We get a sense of the speed with which such scientific wonders became domesticated in those years, by noting that four years later, in 1880, Dublin had its first telephone exchange. Run by the United Telephone Company (yet another merger of Edison and Bell interests) from a switchboard in Dame Street, it began with a total of five subscribers. Initially, a boy was hired to connect the callers; but there were so few calls

---

[16] W.F. Barrett, 'On the Electric Telephone', *Proceedings of the Royal Dublin Society* 1 (1877–8), 81.

that he quickly became bored, and was discovered one afternoon playing with marbles in the courtyard outside. After his dismissal, 'a lady operator' was hired, bringing the staff to six (a manager, an operator, three clerks and an electrician); within twelve months, they were serving twenty customers.[17] By 1888, however, there were 500 lines in Dublin and a trunk route between Dublin and Belfast; in 1893, the first submarine telephone cable out of Ireland was laid between Port Patrick, in Scotland, and Donaghadee, in County Down. This meant that with a little luck (and a complex set of negotiations involving half a dozen switchboards), a Dubliner could speak to a Londoner, and the imaginative geography of Ireland was once again realigned.

In those same years, the perceptual world of Ireland was changing in other ways as well. Sir Howard Grubb, for instance, spoke frequently to the Royal Dublin Society about his work as a telescope-maker, and by the early 1880s his Dublin-based family firm could boast that it had sold large telescopes on every continent of the world (with the exception of Antarctica).[18] The title of one of G. Johnstone Stoney's contributions to the Royal Dublin Society from the mid-1890s sums up the overall sensation of pushing at the boundaries: 'On the Limits of Vision'.[19] Earlier, Johnstone Stoney, along with Grubb, had explored the technical problems inherent in photographing extremely distant objects in space,[20] while Professor John Joly, an engineer, geologist and physicist who was to play an influential role in the teaching of science at Trinity College Dublin, published papers on using photography to detect stars not otherwise visible to the naked eye.[21] In 1892, Joly was able to lay claim to the invention of the world's first practical process for producing colour photographs.[22] And here, once again, in the *Transactions of the Royal*

---

[17] A.J. Litton, 'The Growth and Development of the Irish Telephone System', *Statistical and Social Inquiry Society of Ireland* (December 15, 1961), 3.

[18] J.E. Burnett and A.D. Morrison, *'Low, Vulgar and Mechanick': The Scientific Instrument Trade in Ireland, 1650–1921* (Dublin and Edinburgh, 1989), 105.

[19] G. Johnstone Stoney, 'On the Limits of Vision: With Special Reference to Insects', *Proceedings of the Royal Dublin Society*, Vol. VIII (1893–8), 228–43.

[20] Howard Grubb, 'The Construction of Telescopic Object-Glasses for the International Photographic Survey of the Heavens', *Transactions of the Royal Dublin Society*, Vol. IV (1888–92), 475–80; G. Johnstone Stoney, 'Mounting for the Specula of Reflecting Telescopes for Celestial Photography and Spectroscopy', *Proceedings of the Royal Dublin Society*, Vol. VIII (1893–8), 266–71.

[21] J. Joly, 'On a Photographic Method of Detecting the Existence of Variable Stars', *Proceedings of the Royal Dublin Society*, Vol. VIII (1893–8), 184–5; and J. Joly, 'On Shutters for Use in Stellar Photography', *Proceedings of the Royal Dublin Society*, Vol. VII (1891–2), 196–200.

[22] J. Joly, 'On a Method of Colour Photography', *Transactions of the Royal Dublin Society*, Vol. VI (1896–8), 127–38.

Illustration 7. One of the earliest practical processes for producing colour photographs was developed in Dublin in 1892 by Professor John Joly of Trinity College. Interestingly, he chose an image that was iconic of tradition – an Irish peasant girl – to demonstrate the process in the pages of the *Transactions of the Royal Irish Academy*.

Dublin Society, pushing the boundaries of technologies of perception, we find a new medium rendering phantasmic a rural Ireland that was imagined as existing just beyond its grasp: one of the illustrations that Joly published to illustrate his innovative technique was a colour photograph of a painting, entitled 'Irish Peasant Girl' (illustration 7).

The Irish interest in these emerging technologies of vision, and their potential to change the ways in which it was possible to see the world, was also evident in the work of Dublin-born Lucien Bull. Bull was a keen amateur photographer, who in 1895 moved to Paris to work with Etienne-Jules Marey. Marey also knew Eadweard Muybridge, another pioneer in high-speed photography, and was carrying out research along lines similar to Muybridge, using high-speed photography to create images that appeared to arrest motion. By the time Bull joined him in 1895, Marey had developed a technique known as chronophotography that allowed him to shoot at speeds of up to 120 images per second. In Bull's subsequent research, taking over the running of the Institute Marey after Marey's death in 1904, he developed faster and faster cameras (as well as the electro-cardiograph). In 1903, he recorded the flight of a housefly at 2,000 images per second; in 1914, he photographed a revolver being fired at 15,000 images per second; and, in the 1940s, he had developed an apparatus that could record 1 million images per second.

Although Bull's work would have been little known outside of the scientific community, the kind of research he was doing was reaching Irish men and women in more direct ways. For instance, on the evening of February 12, 1890, Muybridge exhibited his zoopraxiscope at the Ancient Concert Rooms in Dublin, at the invitation of the Photographic Society of Ireland. For those Irish men and women present, it would have been the first time that they saw the motion of a running horse, for instance, broken down into individual split-second images. In one sense, this must have been a revelation, a wonder.

At the same time, the 1890s were the age of the casual miracle, and for many in the audience, Muybridge was probably just one of a regular succession of showmen. Indeed, it had been more than fifty years at that point since Irish audiences had started watching magic lantern shows, which had been given a new lease of life in the 1870s when slides began to incorporate photographic images. 'Perhaps nothing could have enlivened the spirit of lantern exhibitions so much as photography,' advises *The Magic Lantern Manual* in 1878, 'for now we are able to procure at a cheap rate photographic slides of almost every country in the world.'[23] In the same decades that the telegraph brought the world to the local newspaper, and changes in print technology were making visual images more widely available and cheaper than at any previous point in history, photographic magic-lantern slides (often hand-tinted) brought the world into middle-class drawing rooms and lecture halls in glowing, vibrant colour.

The magic lantern not only brought visions of the world to Irish halls and homes; it also placed Ireland within this world of the glowing image. There were a number of producers of Irish slides, in particular the Dublin-based 'photographic publisher', William Lawrence, who offered for sale an extensive range of Irish slides in the closing decades of the nineteenth century: 'Selected Views of Irish Scenery' (1,200 slides), 'Comic Sketches of Irish Life and Character' (70 slides), 'Scenes of Eviction (Ireland)' (60 slides), 'Scenes of Irish Life and Character', 'Copies of Paintings (Religious and Secular)', 'Portraits of the Hierarchy and Leading Clergy of Ireland', 'Portraits of Noted Irishmen, Past and Present' and 'Portraits of the Irish Parliamentary Party'. Setting up in a meeting room or church hall, the typical lantern lecturer would read from a script accompanying the slide sets to create a narrative. For instance, one

---

[23] W.J. Chadwick, *The Magic Lantern Manual* (London, 1878), 10.

of Lawrence's scenic Irish slide sets begins with the viewer arriving in Belfast by ship, and travelling, scene by scene, through Ulster. 'It has been said that people know less of Ireland than any other part of Europe', begins the script. 'Ireland is looked upon as wild, ungovernable, and uncivilised.' A small parenthetical note then helpfully suggests that this section is 'only to be read by the lecturer when delivered out of Ireland'.[24] For a medium such as the magic lantern, this kind of local adaption was possible because it involved a form of live performance. However, by the mid-1890s, there was already a medium in existence much less adaptable to the sensibilities of a local Irish audience, but far more seductive.

'THE MOST MARVELLOUS INVENTION'

On the week of May 21–8, 1895, notices appeared in the newspapers inviting Dubliners to attend the Ierne Grand Bazaar in the Royal Dublin Society's showgrounds in Ballsbridge. Taking its theme from one of the mythological names for Ireland, the bazaar created a pastiche world of Irish antiquity, treating visitors to 'Representations of Old Irish Buildings', 'A Magnificent Historical Picture', as well as offering the usual stalls, water chute, 'Brilliant Illuminations' and 'Endless Amusements'. As they strolled past scale models of the Rock of Cashel and round towers, visitors to Ierne also had a chance to listen to a phonograph, or to be among the first Irish men and women to watch a moving picture on an Edison kinetoscope.

The kinetoscope may have been the latest technological marvel when it was exhibited at Ierne; however, it still did not top the bill, perhaps because it had been on display in Dublin for about six weeks at that point. The first advertisement for an Edison kinetoscope in Ireland appears in the Dublin newspapers on April 4, 1895, where visitors to the Kinetoscope Company's 'kinetoscope parlour' at 68 Dame Street were invited to watch 'a barber's shop, a cock-fight, a skirt dance, [strongman Eugene] Sandow exercising, and a scene from the Wild West Show'.[25] However, for most of these very first Irish moving-picture audiences, the real attraction was not only the films as such; it was the kinetoscope itself.

---

[24] *Ireland in the Magic Lantern: Lecture III Belfast & Antrim Coast including The Giant's Causeway* (Dublin, n.d.), 5–6.

[25] 'Edison's Kinetoscope', *Evening Telegraph* (April 4, 1896), 3. The films can be identified as follows: *The Barber Shop* (1893); *Cockfight No. 2* (1894); *Annabelle Butterfly Dance* (1894); *Sandow* (1894); *Annie Oakley* (1894); all produced by W.K.L. Dickson and William Heise, 50 feet. Available on *Edison: The Invention of the Movies*, 4 DVD set (New York, 2005).

In the same weeks that Ireland's first kinetoscope was being shown in April of 1895, in Paris two brothers, Auguste and Louis Lumière, first exhibited an invention that would eventually render the penny-in-the-slot kinetoscope obsolete, by combining moving images with projection of the sort that had been used by magic lantern showmen for decades. The Lumière cinematograph was first shown at the Société d'encouragement à l'industrie in Paris on March 22, 1895, followed by a second exhibition at the Sorbonne on April 17. By the end of the year, the first public exhibitions were taking place at the Grand Café, by which point the cinematograph had made the familiar – and painless – transition from scientific innovation to popular entertainment. Within a few years, and following a trajectory not unlike the development of the phonograph in those same years, a small number of key players, based in the major imperial powers – the Lumières and later Pathé in France; and the ubiquitous Edison, American Mutoscope and Biograph in the US – were attempting to create a vertically integrated industry (like the phonograph industry) in which a relatively small number of companies built patent-protected cameras, projectors and, in some cases, manufactured film stock, with which they shot and distributed their own films. However, as was the case with the phonograph, once cameras and projectors were available to purchase, it became impossible for any one company to control the new medium. So, in England, film production companies came into being, such as Warwick and Northern Photographic Works, quickly followed by smaller, in some cases local, film-makers and exhibitors, such as Mitchell and Kenyon.

Unlike the first cylinder recordings (which had be recorded individually), cinematograph films were a true mass medium, capable of being quickly and easily reproduced. This in turn meant that cinema, by its nature, was continually seeking new markets, since it would always be possible to produce more copies of a film than could be watched in any one place. The films themselves could be transported cheaply, the apparatus could be sold and set up easily, and the existing network of theatres, halls and exhibitions provided a readymade network of venues, and would continue to do so even after dedicated cinema buildings began to appear after 1908. Film companies thus became multi-nationals very quickly. The American Mutoscope and Biograph Company, for instance, was established in the United States in 1895; by 1897 it had established a British offshoot, was producing films in England, France and Germany, and was using the London office to distribute films not only throughout Europe, but also throughout the British Empire, in India, Australia and South Africa. So, as had happened with the phonograph, Ireland was once again a distant province of a regional office; as one early British film distributor commented, in contrast to the lucrative industrial cities of the north of England, 'Scotland and Ireland do not count for much.'[26]

Nonetheless, it was in the nature of the cinema to travel quickly, even to minor markets such as Ireland, and the first Lumière cinematograph arrived in Ireland four months after it opened to the public in Paris, and two months after its London debut. On April 20, 1896, Dan Lowrey's Theatre of Varieties (situated near both the first kinetoscope parlour and the Dublin telephone exchange) was offering to its patrons what the *Irish Times* would initially herald as an 'invention [that] is beyond all doubt one of the most marvellous of the century'.[27] In retrospect, we might be tempted to imagine that first cinema audience experiencing a moment of revelation, seeing the world as it had never been seen before; however, the audiences who regularly filled the stalls and boxes of Dan Lowrey's Theatre were used to marvels. It was for marvels that they paid their sixpences and shillings. So rather than revelation, the anonymous reporter who joined that first Irish cinema audience to watch a series of short films (including one that featured boxing cats) was impressed, but nonchalant about a device that seemed naturally to belong in a world of entertainments that it would soon come to dominate. 'All the figures were in motion,' noted the *Irish Times*, 'but it may be questioned whether the cinematograph is at all an improvement on the kinetoscope, except in the enlargement of the figures with the aid of a screen.'[28] It soon became clear to the Lumières that, even for the 'most marvellous invention of the century', it was going to take more than thirty seconds of boxing cats to hold the attention of an audience. So they discovered – as did their competitors in England and the United States – that what audiences really wanted to see on the big screen was themselves.

In September of 1897, the Lumières sent a cameraman – probably Jean Alexandre Louis Promio – to Ireland, where he filmed street scenes in Belfast and Dublin. The Dublin film survives. Shot from the left side of the O'Connell Bridge, facing north (to what was then Sackville Street), the O'Connell monument dominates the frame (illustration 8). Pedestrians swarm all over the street, not bothering to look or to pause when a horse and trap trots across the camera's range of vision; a woman

---

[26] Nicholas Hiley, s.v. 'Great Britain', in *Encyclopedia of Early Cinema*, ed. Richard Abel (London, 2005), 282.
[27] 'Star Theatre of Varieties', *Irish Times* (April 20, 1896), 6.
[28] 'Star Theatre of Varieties', *Irish Times* (April 22, 1896), 6.

Illustration 8. In September 1897 the Lumière cameraman Jean Alexandre Louis Promio, shot the first moving images of Ireland including this footage of a very empty Sackville Street taken from O'Connell Bridge in Dublin.

in a dazzling white blouse passes a man in black, his bicycle a gleaming icon of modernity, while in the background an uncertain exposure makes Nelson's Pillar fade in and out, its disappearance like some ghostly premonition of its later fate. The whole thing lasts less than thirty seconds; and, in very different ways, for us today as for those early cinema audiences in 1897, it is at the same time banal and irresistibly fascinating. In some respects, this first film of Ireland is unique; in other respects, it is just one of hundreds of such films from the period made all over the world into which cinema seeped so quickly: workers leaving factories, the bustle of a main boulevard, holiday-makers on promenades, fire brigades, sports teams. 'Have you seen yourself at Edison's', asked an advertisement in 1901, when the Edison Animated Pictures came to Dublin's Rotunda.[29]

[29] 'Edison Animated Pictures', *Irish Times* (December 6, 1901), 4.

The cinema, which initially took up residence in the same theatres that had been performing the plays of Dion Boucicault and presenting magic lantern lectures, thus fitted quite easily into an increasingly porous culture in which Irish audiences watched themselves as residents of an exotic tourist destination, aware, as they were watching, of an imagined community of others around the world also watching. At times, this experience must have been less than edifying, as when in 1899, the Biograph Syndicate sent William Dickson to Portrush, where he shot 27 feet of film of pigs feeding from a trough – a film released as *Irish Peasant Scene*. A few years later, the English film production company Warwick issued a series of 28 films, collectively entitled 'The Bioscope in Ireland' (also titled 'The Emerald Isle') ranging from 50 to 125 feet in length (or from about 30 seconds to just over a minute). The subject matter of this series says much about the way in which Ireland would appear on film, and about the place of early cinema in Irish culture. Many of the films market the pastoral image of Ireland as a land of happy, but primitive, peasants: *Scenes of Irish Cottage Life, Market Day in Kenmare* and *Working a Peat Bog*. Others are much more directly a form of virtual tourism: *Trip to the Giant's Causeway, Waterfalls of Glengariff* and even *Tourists Leaving the Lake Hotel*. And, reinforcing the idea of cinema as a form of virtual travel, six of the films deal with either rail, steamer or coach travel.

'Cinema,' argues Rebecca Solnit, 'can be imagined as a hybrid of railroad and photography. ... The sight out of the railroad window had prepared viewers for the kinds of vision that cinema would make ordinary.'[30] It was not only the succession of scenes, shuddering soundlessly (apart from the roar of steam) past the window that linked the railroad to the silent cinema (which, in a noisy auditorium with musical accompaniment, was far from 'silent'); it was the way in which both railroad and cinema were collapsing the time between places. Not only were audiences in London suddenly brought closer to Killarney; audiences in Ireland were being brought closer to the rest of the world – or at least closer to that part of the world that was of interest to the Edison or Biograph companies. So, when the first Edison films were shown in 1901, Irish audiences watched *Toils and Perils of Deep-Sea Fishing off the Newfoundland Coast* and a film about Switzerland, of which one journalist present noted that 'the railway journey through Switzerland was also a most enjoyable trip and was generously

---

[30] Rebecca Solnit, *River of Shadows: Eadweard Muybridge and the Technological Wild West* (New York, 2003), 219.

applauded'.[31] Just as the telegraph, by effectively reducing to zero the time it took for information to travel between Ireland and the rest of the world, had remapped Ireland's place in the world, so too did the cinema (and the kinetoscope before it) remap the imaginary world for Irish people. Switzerland was now somewhere at the top of Sackville Street.

The link between the cinema and the railway – and more generally between film and space – meant that speed came to be a factor in the reception of early actuality films, and hence the physical speed at which films could be transported became a factor in their reception. For instance, when the White Star Liner *Oceanic* was launched in the ship-yards in Belfast, on January 14, 1899, the event was duly recorded by at least two British film companies, including Warwick, who, as *The Optician* reported, filmed the launch at 11:30 a.m. on Saturday, and were showing copies of the film in six London theatres by Monday afternoon, fifty-two hours later. A year later, in April of 1900, an Irish film-maker and exhibitor, who gloried in the name of Professor Kineto, closed the gap further when Queen Victoria visited Dublin. 'He started from Belfast by the early train', reported the *Irish Playgoer*:

He got into position along the route of the Queen's procession in Dublin, took two separate films in perfect style, left Dublin by the quarter to three train, got to Belfast at six, carried out all necessary developments in a remarkably quick time, and at ten o'clock the same night the Queen's entry into Dublin was exhibited in the Empire Theatre in Belfast. This is undoubtedly a record.[32]

THE COMEDIAN'S ARCADIA

While Professor Kineto was rushing back to Belfast, there was already a cinematic Ireland taking shape, primarily in the United States. For its first few years it would owe much to the phonograph (and together both media would continue to draw on vaudeville). So, in September of 1900, for instance, the American Mutoscope and Biograph Company would release a short (ten-foot) film version of *Drill, Ye Tarriers, Drill* (a comic story in which Irish workmen, using dynamite, blow themselves up, but escape unharmed) – which was a visualisation of a sketch that had been released by comedian Russell Hunting on an Edison brown wax cylinder (Ed2186) a few years earlier. Indeed, Hunting's stage-Irish

---

[31] 'The Thomas Edison Animated Pictures at the Rotunda', *Irish Times* (December 3, 1901), 4.
[32] 'Our Record Cinematographer', *Irish Playgoer* (April 19, 1900), 7.

phonograph persona, Michael Casey, makes a couple of other early cinema appearances, including *The Finish of Michael Casey* (Edison, 1901) (which also involves an exploding Irishman), the self-explanatory *Michael Casey and the Steamroller* (Edison, 1902) and *Casey's Nightmare* (Edison, 1904), in which Casey's drunken hallucinations provide a framework for a series of trick shots, including a demonically possessed hatstand. Casey was joined in this early cinematic world of stage Irishry by Happy Hooligan, the hero of a series of films in 1903, and by their exploding female counterpart, Bridget, an Irish serving-girl, who blew herself up with kerosene in a popular film from 1900, *How Bridget Made the Fire* (Mutoscope and Biograph, 1900).

The transitional year, as far as Irish films were concerned, was 1906. While yet another Irishman who had been a star of phonograph sketches was comically exploding in *Brannigan Sets off the Blast*, Edison's innovative cinematographer, Edwin S. Porter, was filming *Kathleen Mavoureen*, based on an Irish play by William Taver. Taver's play had been on the stage more or less constantly since it first appeared in the 1860s, and Porter's film version, at just over 1200 feet, was the longest Irish film to that point. It is important not only as one of the earliest (arguably the earliest) extended Irish narrative film, but also for establishing 'the Irish play' (as melodramas such as *Kathleen Mavoureen* were known) as the structural model for more than one future generation of Irish films. At that point, the Irish play, of which Dion Boucicault would become the leading exponent, had evolved into a dramatic genre with clearly defined stock characters, situations and romantic scenery of ruined abbeys and thatched cottages. It also had an established narrative structure, usually involving a romance between a well-meaning Englishman (often an army officer) and a feisty Irish colleen, with a parallel subplot involving a trickster character – of which Boucicault's Shaughraun is perhaps the best known – and a villain (usually Irish, and usually a land agent or informer), who is banished at the end. Developed at a time when the theatre world was based on touring, the Irish play was a flexible form, equally capable of playing to Irish and non-Irish audiences alike. It was designed so that an audience in Paris with no particular Irish allegiances could appreciate its 'humours', without offending either a fiercely partisan audience of Irish expatriates in New York, or a London audience brought up on *Punch*. As such, it was the perfect raw material for a multi-national medium like the cinema. *Kathleen Mavoureen* was followed by Vitagraph's version of Boucicault's *The Shaughraun* in 1907, Selig Polyscope's *A Daughter of Erin* in 1908 (which Kevin Rockett suggests is based on Boucicault's

Colleen Bawn),[33] followed in 1911 and 1912 by versions of the same two plays filmed in Australia, and a version of Boucicault's *Robert Emmet* made by Thanhouser in New York in 1911.

The first feature films made in Ireland drew from this same well of material. *The Lad from Old Ireland*, directed by Sidney Olcott for the Kalem Film Company of Florida in 1910, was not based on any one play as such; although it partially resembles John Baldwin Buckstone's *Green Bushes* of 1845, it is perhaps best understood as a sort of generic distillation. Billed as the first feature film to have been shot on two continents, *The Lad from Old Ireland* follows an Irish peasant, Terry, who emigrates to America, rises through hard work to become wealthy, and is elected mayor; on the night of his election victory he receives a letter from Aileen, his all-but-forgotten sweetheart back in Ireland, who is about to be evicted from her farm. Terry returns home (and in one memorable trick-shot sequence on board the ship, conjures up a vision of Aileen), pays her rent, banishes the grasping black-hatted landlord and marries Aileen. In more than one respect, *The Lad from Old Ireland* is a paradigm for much that will happen in Irish cinema over the following decades: indeed, John Ford's *The Quiet Man* (1952) and Ron Howard's *Far and Away* (1992) both tell more or less the same story.

Filmed around Killarney – consecrated in more than a century of Irish visual culture from lithographs to photographs as the epitome of Irish landscape – *The Lad from Old Ireland* effectively absorbs the content of the early travel actualities as its backdrop, at the same time providing in Terry a protagonist who is both Irish and American, and would thus, presumably, appeal to audiences on both sides of the Atlantic. At the same time, *The Lad from Old Ireland* continues the cinematic reconfiguration of time and distance. Just as the early train films could render an entire train journey in a matter of minutes, in *The Lad from Old Ireland*, Terry in America and Aileen in Ireland are only a few minutes apart from one another. This is not to say that an audience who watched *The Lad from Old Ireland* were confused as to the actual duration of a trans-Atlantic crossing in any literal sense. At the same time, something happens to the imaginative place of Ireland in the world, not unlike what happened when the first trans-Atlantic telegraph message was sent half a century earlier: the Atlantic Ocean parts, and it is possible to glimpse New York in the next parish.

---

[33] Kevin Rockett, *The Irish Filmography* (Dublin, 1996), 243.

'Among the many worthless arguments set up for the continuance of the Irish Members in the British Parliament,' argued the New York-based *Gaelic American* in 1907, 'one of the most mischievous is that which claims that Ireland thereby commands "the ear of the world". … And yet there is no foundation whatever for the claim. It is a relic of conditions that existed thirty or more years ago, but which have now absolutely disappeared.'[34] With the proliferation of new media at the beginning of the twentieth century – cinema, the phonograph, telegraph and telephone – it was possible to speak directly into 'the ear of the world'; however, as the Irish experience of the phonograph and the cinema were to show, channelling what was heard by the world would prove more difficult in practice than in theory, as control of these new media either followed the contours of the old imperial territory, or set up new market-driven geographies of trade – in both of which Ireland was, once again, off the map.

A WEEKLY INSURRECTION IN THE INTELLECTUAL ORDER

The Ireland into which the phonograph and the cinema arrived may have had a carefully nurtured fantasy of itself as a fundamentally oral culture; in reality, however, by the 1890s Irish public culture existed in a frenzy of print. Indeed, the simple fact is that while the existence of an oral culture may have provided the ideal for much of the writing of the literary revival that included Yeats, Synge and Lady Gregory, Ireland's publishing and bookselling industry gave it a material basis. Even if it could be argued that major literary figures such as these would have found a publisher elsewhere, standing in their wake are the legions of lesser known figures, many of whom were published (at least initially) in Ireland. For those who had problems with Irish publishers (such as James Joyce), or who wanted wider distribution, proximity to London (or, in Joyce's case, Paris) provided ample opportunities.

In other words, the printing industry in Ireland at the time was not simply the vehicle for the literary revival; it was a constituent part of it. The Dublin-based Maunsel and Company, for instance, from its founding in 1905, advertised that its books were printed 'on Irish paper' (a feature that would influence Synge to publish with them[35]); they would

---

[34] 'The "Ear of the World" Fallacy', *Gaelic American* (August 24, 1907).

[35] Clare Hutton, '"Yogibogeybox in Dawson Chambers": The Beginnings of Maunsel and Company', in *The Irish Book in the Twentieth Century*, ed. Clare Hutton (Dublin, 2004), 36–46, 36.

later publish the works of both Synge and Pearse, as well as the literary periodical *The Shanachie*. The Dun Emer Press, founded by Elizabeth Yeats to produce fine printing, issued a prospectus in 1903 in which it announced: 'Though many books are printed in Ireland, book printing as an art has been little practised here since the eighteenth century.'[36] Its first imprint was a collection of poetry by her brother, W. B. Yeats, *In the Seven Woods: Being Poems Chiefly of the Irish Heroic Age*.

If it was true that literary culture was primarily a print culture, it was even more true that political culture was newspaper culture. In the period between 1885 and 1910 there were, at one point or another, just under 300 different newspaper titles in print in Ireland,[37] to which can be added even more monthly or bimonthly periodicals, ranging from the widely influential *Irish Homestead* to specialised journals, such as *The Arrow*, the organ of the Irish Literary Theatre, which ran for three occasional issues in 1899 and 1900. Among the newspapers of the daily or weekly press, some were venerable survivors from the eighteenth century, such as the *Freeman's Journal* and the *Belfast Newsletter*; others were the victors of the penny-press revolution brought by steam and the telegraph in the mid-nineteenth century, such as the *Irish Times, Daily Express* and *Belfast Telegraph*.

However, more than half of the newspaper titles published in Ireland between 1885 and 1910 – just under 150 titles – were founded in those years. As had been the case in the past, the attrition rate was high; some lasted only a few years, a few months or a few issues. And yet, a significant number survived, and many of the most important regional titles of the following century were first published in the closing decades of the nineteenth century. *The Wicklow People* began life in 1882, the *Carlow Nationalist and Leinster Times* first appeared in 1883; the *Limerick Leader* was published first in 1889; the *Southern Star*, serving County Cork, first went on sale on July 5, 1890; in Mayo the *Western People* and the *Mayo News* began publishing in 1883 and 1892, respectively; both the *Meath Chronicle* and *Longford Leader* first appeared in 1897; the *Clare Champion* evolved out of the *Clare Man* in 1903; *The Kerryman* was founded a year

---

[36] Elizabeth Yeats, 'Prospectus for Dun Emer Press', cited in Nicola Gordon Bowe, 'The Book in the Irish Arts and Crafts Movement', in *Irish Book in the Twentieth Century*, ed. Hutton, 16–35 25.

[37] A precise number is difficult to obtain; in some cases, what was effectively the same newspaper changed its title for a short period; in other cases, only single copies of short-lived periodicals survive. Counting all titles in *Newsplan*, there were 289 titles in print in the period 1885–1910, of which 147 were first published in the period. James O'Toole, *Newsplan: Report of the NEWSPLAN Project in Ireland*, rev. edn, Sara Smyth (Dublin, 1998).

later, while the *Connacht Tribune* began in 1909. All of these titles would be thriving parts of the Irish regional press a century later.

In part, these new regional papers were made possible by technological changes. Just as steam and the rotary press had opened up new possibilities in the nineteenth century, by the beginning of the twentieth century Irish newspapers were beginning to use Linotype machines, a process that allowed a typesetter at a keyboard to set an entire line of type at once – with obvious savings in labour that were immensely attractive to a small newspaper run by a handful of staff. The *Longford Leader*, for instance, had a Linotype machine from the start, the *Southern Star* had one by the end of the 1890s, and the *County Down Spectator* used one from its first edition in 1904. Indeed, with some provincial newspapers, Linotype machines bought in the first decade of the twentieth century were still doing service in the 1950s and 1960s. In the case of the *Anglo-Celt* in Cavan, the newspaper not only had the same machine in 1967; it also had the same compositor, James Donoghue, who worked for the paper for sixty-nine years.

At the same time, it was not technology alone that brought alive new papers, and gave new life to older ones; it was their growing centrality in Irish political culture. The *Longford Leader*, the *Meath Chronicle*, the *Southern Star*, or the *Carlow Nationalist* were not simply regional papers; they were nationalist-regional newspapers. On the face of it, the idea of a nationalist-regional newspaper may seem like something of an oxymoron. However, as the vitality of these newspapers suggests, this combination of the regional and the national, while it might seem contradictory, reflected the structure of Irish political life as it was taking shape in the final decade of the nineteenth century, where strong local loyalties, personalities and issues drove local political organisations whose affiliations were national. Hence, readers bought the *Carlow Nationalist* or the *Longford Leader* not just as a way of finding out what was happening locally; the local nationalist paper was a badge of identity, a flag of affiliation. Buying a nationalist newspaper was, in its own right, a political act, and in that sense Irish newspapers were not simply the medium through which politics were reported: to a certain extent, Irish newspapers *were* politics.

A career as a journalist with a nationalist newspaper, then, was a political career. Of the many Irish men and women of this period for whom the newsroom composing table was the political front line, William O'Brien of Cork can stand as something of an example (insofar as any one individual can be said to be emblematic in the complex and divisive political world of the period). O'Brien began his career writing for

the *Freeman's Journal* in 1876, working under its vigorous editor, Edmund
Dwyer Gray, for whom he published an influential investigative series on
conditions on an estate in the Galtee Mountains in 1880. However, as
O'Brien's political views on land ownership and Home Rule became
more clearly defined – he would later become one of Charles Stewart
Parnell's closest allies – he found that 'the views of the *Freeman* were
sometimes (and for reasons which the vastness of the property at stake
easily suggested) of too indecisive a hue in National crises to make it
possible for me to undertake any personal responsibility for them.'[38] This
is an astute analysis: a large-circulation Irish national newspaper (or,
indeed, a major nationalist-regional newspaper) had to keep on board
a delicately balanced and far from homogeneous constituency, whose
primary interests could be any combination of the various hues of Home
Rule, Catholicism, the land issue, the Irish language or simply their own
economic well-being. Collectively, this assemblage of readers and advertisers made up 'the vastness of the property at stake' – and they all had to
be kept more or less happy, which meant that taking a stand against any
particular interest could upset the whole precarious applecart.

Tired of trying to balance so many interests, O'Brien took the opportunity to become editor of the Parnellite *United Ireland*, whose politics
were far less conciliatory than the *Freeman*'s. The first edition appeared on
August 12, 1881, only a few months after the Peace Preservation Act had
been imposed; Gladstone's Second Land Act would be passed the
following week, and by October, the Land League would be outlawed
and Parnell arrested. 'The paper that made its appearance at this critical
hour was, from crest to spur, a fighting organ.' Later, after his own arrest,
O'Brien would edit *United Ireland* from Kilmainham Jail. 'To all intents
and purposes', O'Brien later wrote of *United Ireland*, 'the paper proposed
to create a weekly insurrection in the intellectual order.'[39] Later again in
his career, in January 1910, after yet another split in nationalist politics,
when former colleagues-turned-adversaries prevented him from speaking
at a party convention, declaring that 'no one with a Cork accent' would be
allowed on the platform, O'Brien promptly returned to Cork and
founded his own party and newspaper. He called it *The Cork Accent*.

The pattern of political parties fissuring and newspapers proliferating
also happened at local level, where politics were often even more subtly
complex. To take one example, two brothers, John and Florence Sullivan,

---

[38] William O'Brien, *Recollections* (London and New York, 1905), 185.
[39] O'Brien, *Recollections*, 315–16.

founded the *Southern Star* in 1889 in West Cork, which advertised itself as 'the recognised Nationalist Organ of South and West Cork', taking its place alongside the established unionist West Cork paper, the *Skibbereen Eagle*. 'It was started solely as a commercial speculation', John Sullivan later claimed; however, when he sold his share in the *Southern Star*, Father (later Monsignor) John O'Leary became the principal shareholder, and he had the newspaper's board pass a motion declaring that 'nothing shall appear in the *Southern Star* either editorially or by way of report in any way disparaging to the Bishop'.[40] With the *Southern Star* thus established in the clerical nationalist niche in the political spectrum, the way was opened for a series of less clerical Cork papers, including O'Brien's *Cork Accent*, and its successor, the *Cork Free Press*.

So, in the ferment of political ideas that was Ireland at the dawn of the twentieth century, Irish newspapers proliferated. The resulting web of influences and relationships was often extremely complex. For instance, in the final years of the century, a printer-turned-journalist (and later politician) Arthur Griffith founded the *United Irishman*, which articulated his particular brand of cultural nationalism, with his strong support for the Gaelic League, and his distain for what he called the 'Reptile press' (in the form of the *Daily Independent* and *Evening Herald*), constitutional nationalist papers whose politics were not radical enough for Griffith. However, for one of Griffith's contemporaries, D.P. Moran, Griffith was not sympathetic enough to Catholic business interests, and a tad too anticlerical; so he founded his own influential newspaper, *The Leader*. Later, they would be joined by *Sinn Fein*, which spoke for the Gaelic League, which in turn would be outflanked in terms of its militant stance by *The Republic*. Taking the long view of this tangle of vigorously shifting allegiances and antagonisms, there is a strong sense that Ireland in these years was, indeed, to use W.B. Yeats's words, 'soft wax',[41] waiting to be shaped by the right combination of printed words.

For the unionist press, the task was keeping the wax firm. Although not as extensive as the nationalist press, the unionist newspapers lined up along a spectrum that in many ways mirrored their nationalist counterparts. Like the *Freeman's Journal* on the other side of the national divide, the *Irish Times* upheld a liberal unionist line, while at the same time

---

[40] Liam O'Regan, 'A Century of Service', *The Southern Star: Centenary Supplement 1889–1989* (Cork, 1989), 2–3.
[41] Diarmaid Ferriter uses Yeats's phrase to characterise the politics of this period: *The Transformation of Ireland 1900–2000* (London, 2005), 28–31.

judiciously balancing its views so as to carry along a fairly wide range of readers and advertisers. However, other unionist papers were far less restrained, and for some the unholy allegiance of land reform, Home Rule, assertive Catholicism and resurgent Gaelicisation would produce a tone of editorial comment that verges on hysteria. *The Union*, for instance, which first appeared in January 1897, was jointly published in London and Dublin, and made its political point through its dual place of publication. 'In times of war every volunteer is of service', it proclaimed in an introductory editorial, 'and to-day in Ireland it is the bounden duty of every loyal man to bestir himself and take the field.'[42] On a weekly basis, it raised the alarm for its already-alarmed readers with headlines such as 'Boycotting a Regatta', 'The Agrarian Outrage near Killarney' and 'Firing on Bailiffs' (all July 16, 1897).

Unionist politics were almost as fissiparous as nationalist politics, however, and various shades of unionist opinion gave rise to no fewer than seven new newspapers in County Down alone in the period between 1880 and 1904. Here, too, the nuances of local politics were subtle. The *Ulster Gazette*, for instance, was particularly uncompromising on the land issue (at one point it suggested that the lynching of eight African-Americans in North Carolina could usefully be adopted as a technique for dealing with Land League protestors).[43] However, while its editorial view on trade unions appeared only slightly less hardline, it was clear that the newspaper relied, to some extent at least, on readers who were members of trade unions, for its reportage of strikes and labour disputes was often more balanced than the editorial stance would suggest.

When the *Ulster Gazette* stood firm with the lynch mobs of North Carolina, we see a symptom (admittedly, in this case not a very edifying one) of a new awareness of Ireland's place in the world. Although the wire services had been making available news from around the world for decades, if one were to read only the more deeply politicised Irish newspapers of this period, wrapped up in their intense political debates, it is easy to form an impression of a culture with little interest in world events, other than those which could be used to draw some lesson for the more engrossing debates of local, party or national politics. Griffith's *United Irishman*, for instance, ran a weekly column, headed 'Foreign News', but written as an editorial, in which he drew lessons for Ireland

---

[42] 'Introductory', *The Union: Journal Devoted to the Maintenance of the Union of the Three Kingdoms* 1:1 (January 29, 1897).

[43] 'Lynch Law in the States', *Ulster Gazette* (January 18, 1890).

from events overseas. 'What the Irish party cared about was not Egypt or the Sudan,' an Irish Party MP, T.D. Sullivan, told a meeting in Mullingar, 'but about Ireland and their own countrymen.'[44] And yet, for those newspapers whose concerns were more commercial than political (and hence whose views tended be more politically moderate), this was less true, and papers such as the *Freeman's Journal* and the *Irish Times* made extensive use of the telegraph and the wire services to report on international events. Moreover, on weekends, readers were offered an increasingly large array of heavily illustrated weekend editions, for whom the more exotic the story, the better (and the better the pictures). Not only among the English papers, but also for the unionist press and even for some moderate nationalist papers, the Empire provided not only a telegraph network to carry reports from the far-flung corners of the globe; it also provided a steady stream of exotic stories: Gordon at Khartoum, opium wars in China, Scott in the Antarctic and so on. For many Irish readers of all political hues, the rich fare provided by these illustrated papers must have been a glamorous (if illicit) pleasure compared to the speeches of local politicians, however impassioned.

So, in spite of the inclination to be more interested in Mullingar than Khartoum (or even to consider an interest in Khartoum as evidence of creeping imperial sympathies), the Irish news media in the early twentieth century became ever more globalised. Trans-Atlantic steam travel and the increasingly well organised Irish diaspora in the United States meant that not only raw news, but also the views of papers from around the world became regular features in a growing number of Irish newspapers of the early twentieth century. In some respects, this made the Irish press both more global, and more insular. Griffith, for instance, ran a series of articles in 1902 on the Irish-American press, praising the San Francisco *Leader*, the Boston *Hibernia*, O'Donovan Rossa's New York-based *United Irishman*, as well as the *Southern Cross* of Buenos Aires. 'With thousands of miles between them, half-a-dozen Irish journals are fighting to save the Irish from extinction'.[45] For a different set of Irish readers, *The Union* ran a regular column reprinting articles from these same newspapers, proffered up as evidence of the global conspiracy that Irish landlords were facing. 'It is suggestive to try to see ourselves as Irish-America sees us',

---

[44] *Freeman's Journal* (June 2, 1884), cited in Felix M. Larkin, 'The Dog in the Night-Time: The *Freeman's Journal*, the Irish Parliamentary Party, and the Empire, 1875–1919', in *Newspapers and Empire in Ireland and Britain: Reporting the British Empire, c. 1857–1921*, ed. Simon J. Potter (Dublin, 2004), 113.

[45] 'The Irish-American National Press', *United Irishman* (March 8, 1902).

commented *The Irish Peasant*, an agrarian nationalist paper founded in Navan in 1903, when commenting on an article in the *Gaelic-American*, published in New York. In short, the Irish mediascape often managed to be intensely local while deeply entangled in events half a planet away.

While William O'Brien, D.P. Moran and Arthur Griffith were turning out their 'weekly insurrection in the intellectual order', a revolution of a different kind was taking place across the Irish Sea in England. Newspapers such as the *Daily Mail* (founded in 1896), the *Daily Express* (founded 1900) and the *Daily Mirror* (founded 1903) were using new print technology to entertain readers with more illustrations, more features, punchier news and – perhaps most importantly – a more exacting relationship with advertisers, who for the first time began to be supplied with reasonably accurate circulation figures. Once circulation became an object of scrutiny, every effort was made to make it soar – and it did, on an unprecedented scale. The *Daily Mail*, for instance, was selling approximately 1 million copies per issue by 1899.[46] This more intense relationship with advertisers made newspapers into a big business, and, in what later became known as the 'Northcliffe Revolution' (after the leading press baron, Lord Northcliffe), ownership began to concentrate in the hands of a few increasingly powerful individuals who had the money to found new newspapers and magazines, and to buy out competing titles, sometimes simply to shut them down. In the United States, meanwhile, something similar was happening, as figures like Joseph Pulitzer (publisher of the *New York World*) and William Randolph Hearst built up vast media empires.

Ireland's smaller, more politically volatile and splintering market meant that its Northcliffe Revolution would have to wait. This is not to say that there were not attempts in Ireland to follow the example of Lord Northcliffe. Cork-born William Martin Murphy, for instance, used a fortune made in railway investments to take control of the *Irish Catholic* and the *Irish Daily Independent* in 1904, partly as mouthpieces for his own pro-business, conservative Catholic nationalist views, but also with a view to building up a profitable media empire. The extent to which Murphy was modelling his newspapers on English papers is most evident in his weekend edition, the *Irish Weekly Independent*. Published on Saturdays, it was heavily illustrated, featured large, elaborately illustrated advertisements, and regularly had two or three serialised novels running at one time. It targeted its readership with precision, featuring weekly special

---

[46] Lyn Gorman and David McLean, *Media and Society in the Twentieth Century. A Historical Introduction* (Oxford, 2003), 11.

interest columns for farmers, women, civil servants and children, as well as a weekly report on Irish industries. It covered organisations such as the United Irish League sympathetically, contained detailed coverage of the Gaelic Athletic Association, but also featured international news. As a businessman with extensive business interests outside of Ireland, Murphy had little time for Irish-Ireland insularity: 'We are to ignore the time spirit which is infusing into progressive peoples a sentiment of international solidarity,' he retorted to criticism from the *United Irishman,* 'and are bidden to take an antiquated and unamiable provincialism as our ideal.'[47]

Murphy was, of course, much more than a newspaper proprietor. As founder of the Dublin Employers' Federation, Murphy precipitated a vicious conflict with the Irish Transport and General Workers' Union (ITGWU), culminating in the Dublin Lockout of 1913, one of the most traumatic events in the public life of Ireland in the years immediately before the 1916 Rising. We get a sense of the centrality of the press in these events by noting that the founder of the ITGWU, James Larkin, was also the editor of a newspaper, *The Irish Worker. The Irish Worker* was only four pages long, written largely by one or two people, depended on classified ads from a small list of stalwart advertisers, and, apart from an elaborate masthead (a garland of hearty workers and tools radiating out of a rising sun), featured few illustrations, and had production values best described as functional: its role was purely political. The *Irish Weekly Independent* was twenty-four pages long, was the work of a large production team, and drew heavily on wire services. It was profusely illustrated using the most modern technology, laden with advertisements, and was run as a business. If we take *The Irish Worker* and *Irish Weekly Independent* as opposite poles of the newspaper world, they also define two opposing attitudes to the media *per se* in pre-Independence Ireland.

Larkin's paper is unselfconsciously old-fashioned in its form; in some respects, it could have been published at any point in the previous half century or more. Murphy's, on the other hand, with its illustrations (some in colour) and mixture of fonts, wants its readers to marvel at the form of the newspaper itself. 'As a mere feat in printing, the appearance of the *Irish Independent* speaks for itself ... produced by the most modern equipment of machinery to be found in any newspaper office in the

---

[47] *Irish Weekly Independent* (February 18, 1911), cited in Patrick Maume, 'The *Irish Independent* and Empire, 1891–1919', in *Newspapers and Empire*, ed. Potter, 136.

world',[48] enthused Murphy's paper when its daily stablemate, the *Daily Independent*, began publication on a new Goss press, the cutting-edge technology of its time. The *Irish Weekly Independent's* fascination with the mechanics of its own production extended to regular coverage of other innovations in new media – something that one would never find, for instance, in *The Irish Worker*, which was taken up with what it considered to be more urgent matters (particularly after Larkin was imprisoned). The *Independent* ran a weekly column on photography (an amateur enthusiasm that had blossomed in the 1890s), and reported breathlessly on new inventions, such as 'the wireless telephone', which it accompanied with an illustrated profile of 'Signor Marconi', 'the great scientist and inventor who brought wireless telegraphy into practice'.[49] Other articles regularly told readers of what one characteristic article calls: 'The Latest Wonder in Electricity'. Where Larkin's paper argued for a vision of what Ireland's future could be in social terms, Murphy's wrote as if that future had already arrived in technological terms.

From one perspective, the period from 1916 to 1922 is one of political ferment: from the executions that followed in the wake of the Rising, through to the establishment of the First Dáil in 1919, to the War of Independence and the Civil War. From the perspective of Ireland's media, however, the revolution took place earlier, in the 1890s and the first decade of the twentieth century. By 1916, the technologies that would dominate the next half century were already in place. The telephone had become an ordinary part of life, at least in urban areas. The phonograph and the cinema had both settled into the recognisable shape of multi-national industries, attracting listeners and viewers with songs and stories, rather than with their status as technological marvels. Where there had been literally hundreds of new newspapers founded in the final decade of the nineteenth century and the first decade of the twentieth century, in the period between 1916 and 1919, there was only one new Dublin newspaper: *The Irish World and Industrial Advocate* (1917–19). In the new world of the advertising-driven press, movies, movie stars and songs would become staples of the news, and flows of international news would increase even further. In short, on the eve of achieving its political and economic independence, Ireland was more intimately and complexly connected with the rest of the world than at any other point in its history.

---

[48] 'An Irish Welcome: New "Independent": A Gigantic Success: Several New Records', *Irish Weekly Independent* 14:1 (January 7, 1905).
[49] 'Signor Marconi', *Irish Weekly Independent* 14:1 (January 7, 1905).

Media Event 4:
Broadcasting the Rising: April 24, 1916

The first radio broadcast was an accident of war.

On the morning of Easter Monday, 1916, about 1,500 members of the Irish Republican Brotherhood fanned out over the streets of Dublin. Some took possession of St Stephen's Green; others took up positions near Mount Street Bridge to prevent British soldiers marching into the city from the Beggar's Bush Barracks. The main body of rebels, including Patrick Pearse and James Connolly, established themselves in the General Post Office. From its portico, they read out a Proclamation announcing the birth of an Irish republic to the few startled passers-by who happened to be on the streets on an Easter Monday. At almost the same time, printed copies of the Proclamation were being pasted up around the city, unconsciously echoing one of the first uses of print in Ireland in the early 1600s.

Among those who took over the Post Office on Easter Monday was Fergus O'Kelly, a member of the 2nd Battalion of the Irish Volunteers. O'Kelly was no sooner inside the Post Office, than he was given orders to lead a group of men, including Abbey actor Arthur Shields, to take over the Irish School of Wireless Telegraphy, which was located across O'Connell Street on the corner of Abbey Street. O'Kelly and his men scampered across O'Connell Street, and throughout the rest of that day they worked to erect an aerial and repair a transmitter that had not been used since 1914. By late afternoon, the area was swarming with British snipers, and the final work on the aerial had to be left until after dark, while another unit from the 2nd Battalion was dispatched to try to secure some of the surrounding buildings. As snipers' bullets pinged off the roof tiles, the men worked on the aerial, and by Tuesday the transmitter was

Illustration 9. O'Connell Street, immediately after the 1916 Rising. The Irish School of Wireless Telegraphy, from which the world's first radio broadcast was attempted, is the pile of rubble in the foreground on the right.

operational. At that point, James Connolly sent over from the Post Office the text of a message to be broadcast. 'As far as I can remember,' O'Kelly later recalled, 'the first message announced the proclaiming of the Irish Republic and the taking over of Dublin city by the Republican Army.'

However, in spite of their best efforts, the Volunteers found that they could transmit, but not receive messages, which meant that 'it was not possible to get in direct touch with any station or ship'. Not to be deterred, O'Kelly's men sent out their proclamation 'on the normal commercial wavelength in the hope that some ship would receive it and relay it was interesting news [*sic*]'.[1] The position continued under heavy fire until the following day, when it had to be abandoned, at which point the transmitter was manhandled down the stairs of the Telegraphy School, loaded onto a dray cart, hauled across O'Connell Street under heavy fire, and left in the Post Office, where it was destroyed in the conflagration that ended the Rising (see illustration 9).

[1] Fergus O'Kelly, WS 351, Witness Statements, National Archives of Ireland.

This unlikely combination of a faulty receiver and 'interesting news' resulted in what is possibly the first radio broadcast anywhere in the world.[2] Admittedly, no ships at sea heard the Irish Republic declared; but then, no one was expecting messages to be simply scattered into the ether. In 1916, all wireless messages were sent point to point, from one sender to one receiver.

In fact, it was point-to-point communication that spread the news of the Rising. While Fergus O'Kelly's unit were struggling with the aerial of the School of Wireless Telegraphy, another group of men led by J. J. Walsh were dispatched to the telephone exchange on Dame Street, where they used the telephones to spread word around the country. Meanwhile, the father of Volunteer Tom Ring, who worked for Western Cable in Valentia, County Kerry, had been given a coded message to send on Easter Sunday to John Devoy, the Clan na Gael leader in New York: 'Ted operated on successfully' (presumably a sly reference to King Edward VII). News of the operation turned out to be premature as the Rising was delayed until the following day, so that with the five-hour time difference between Kerry and New York, Devoy (who had convened a press conference for the occasion) had news of the Rising before the first shots were fired. It was later claimed that the British government in London first heard reports of the Rising from the British Consul in New York, who saw the headline in the *New York American* proclaiming: 'Revolution in Ireland, says Cipher Cable.'[3] 'The British were frightfully perturbed at the news of the Rising reaching New York so quickly', one of those involved later recalled, 'and had failed to get any evidence, despite many efforts on their part, as to how word had reached America. They treated the incident as a major mystery.'[4]

While it might seem obvious to us today that seizing the local radio station is the first thing any self-respecting rebel should do, it took a considerable act of imagination to make use of the new medium of wireless telegraphy in 1916. Indeed, it could be argued that apart from anything else, the Rising was a media event as much as it was a military operation,[5] particularly in terms of James Connolly's argument that 'once a stand was made, however brief, in Dublin, the country would turn in

---

[2] The most notable proponent of this claim was Marshall McLuhan. See *Understanding Media: The Extensions of Man* (New York, 1964), 266.
[3] Maurice Gorham, *Forty Years of Irish Broadcasting* (Dublin, 1967), 3. This account is also given by Mortimer O'Connell, WS 326, 5. NAI Witness Statements, 1916.
[4] WS 804: Mortimer O'Connell; Member IV, 1913–16; Clerk, Dáil Éireann, 1919.
[5] See James Moran, *Staging the Easter Rising: 1916 as Theatre* (Cork, 2005).

mass against the British government and overthrow it'.[6] In other words, success of the Rising depended upon its transmutation into a form of information that could be spread widely and quickly. Assigning key members of the 2nd Battalion to work on the transmitter, and to protect its position, suggests that leaders of the Rising understood that its success or failure depended as much upon it becoming a news event as upon any military action. Indeed, in its basic structure – the actions of a few reaching and influencing the masses – the 1916 Rising mapped perfectly to the shape of a new media world that had emerged with the telegraph, but in 1916 was getting ready to change yet again.

The Volunteers may well have been led to what was possibly the world's first radio broadcast because of Ireland's central place within an informational geography created by the telegraph, which in turn was a product of the country's location, at the geographical nexus between Europe and America. In other ways, as well, Ireland was at the heart of the new geography of electric communication. For instance, while a number of people were exploring wireless telegraphy (as it was initially known) in the final decade of the nineteenth century, the key figure – both in terms of public imagination, and patent holding – was Guglielmo Marconi. Marconi may have been Italian, but his mother, Annie Jameson (of the Jameson distilling family), was Irish, as was his first wife, Beatrice O'Brien. As a consequence, when Marconi first applied for a patent for wireless telegraphy in 1897, the company he subsequently formed was started with a healthy infusion of Irish money, and had a board made up largely of Dublin businessmen. Marconi's first demonstration of the possibility of transmitting messages without wires may have been on England's Salisbury Plain; however, the major test of what many considered to be the new medium's real use – transmissions from ships at sea – took place in Ireland, on Rathlin Island, on July 6, 1898. What is more, while Marconi was in Ireland conducting the experiments off the Antrim coast, his equipment was brought to Kingstown (now Dun Laoghaire) on July 20 for the annual yacht regatta, where it was set up to transmit shipboard reports to a telegraph office in the harbour, and hence to the *Evening Mail*, who commissioned the experiment. More than 700 messages were sent over the course of the two-day regatta, marking the first time that radio transmissions were used in news reporting anywhere in the world. 'The present is an epoch of astounding activity in physical science', enthused the *Mail*'s reporter. 'Progress is a thing of months and weeks,

---

[6] Eoin O'Neill, in Roy Foster, *Modern Ireland 1600–1972* (Harmondsworth, 1988), 478.

almost of days. The long lines of isolated ripples of past discovery seem to be blending into a mighty wave, on the crest of which one seems to discern some oncoming magnificent generalisation. The suspense is becoming feverish, at times almost painful.'[7] In 1898 and in the years immediately afterwards, there was a palpable sense that Ireland was at the crest of that wave.

Marconi's experiments on Rathlin Island showed that wireless signals could be sent from ships to shore stations. Ireland's geographical position, jutting out into one of the world's busiest sea lanes, meant that by 1901 there were wireless telegraphy stations in Crookhaven, County Cork, and Rosslare, County Wexford, transmitting out into the North Atlantic shipping lanes. Before long, Marconi was to show that it was possible to transmit radio signals for very long distances, and Ireland was once again in a strategic location on the edge of Europe. In 1907 Marconi built the European transmitter for the first commercial trans-Atlantic wireless service in Clifden, County Galway (its North American counterpart was in Glace Bay, Nova Scotia). By 1912 – the year in which the sinking *Titanic* used wireless to save many of its passengers – there were Marconi stations in Letterfrack, County Galway, and Ballybunion, County Kerry.

By the time the Rising erupted on the streets of Dublin in 1916, the Dublin Wireless Club had been in existence for three years, allowing early adopters to be trained in the new medium, while the Irish School of Wireless Telegraphy trained technicians for the new industry. In short, it was not a huge leap of the imagination to see wireless as a more or less direct informational pipeline to world – and more specifically American – public opinion. This perceptual shift subtly but significantly added to the redrawing of the map of the world that had been changing for half a century; its effects would be long-term, and would have a double-edged effect on Irish political life. On one hand, the telegraph had literally bound the British Empire together with copper wires, so that London, Bombay, Sydney and Dublin existed, for the first time, in the same informational field. With the telegraph, a far-flung empire had never been so intimately connected. At the same time, as the Irish diaspora – a large, vocal section of whom held strongly nationalist views – became increasingly woven into the fabric of American cultural life, Irish nationalists in Ireland felt less and less isolated in a world in which there was instant communication with 'the greater Ireland beyond the seas'. And, of

[7] The reporter was quoting a speech by Prof. Lodge; in Michael Sexton, *Marconi: The Irish Connection* (Dublin, 2005), 45.

course, all of this was happening in the same years in which developments in trans-Atlantic steam travel – of which the Belfast-built *Titanic* was to have been the apotheosis – was cutting the temporal distance between Ireland and America even further, making it possible to exchange more quickly than ever before books, newspapers, Edison cylinders, discs and movies.

Wireless telegraphy consolidated this new geography of shrinking time, giving imperial administrators, unionists and nationalists alike a tangible connectedness with a larger, trans-national network – whether Empire or diaspora, all circulating through the same communications infrastructure. Supporters of Home Rule could, with some limitations, use the new communications media as easily as supporters of Empire, each generating new, competing senses of Irishness that were no longer bounded by the coastline of the island. Indeed, when the trans-Atlantic wireless service commenced in October, 1907, among the first messages was one relayed from David Lloyd George, as President of the UK Board of Trade, to his opposite number in Canada, declaring that 'all well-wishers of the Empire will welcome every project for facilitating contact between Britain and the Great Dominion across the Atlantic'; this was quickly followed by an appeal from Henry Murphy, of Galway County Council, to Theodore Roosevelt, appealing for the American President's support for Home Rule.[8] In a sense, then, the rebels of 1916 were taking Henry Murphy's initiative to the next logical step. At the same time, their decision not to send a message to a specific ship, but to broadcast it generally shows an almost intuitive grasp of the new world that was coming into being. The rhetoric of some of the leaders of the Rising may have been self-consciously archaic; however, the medium through which that message was communicated (or at least through which communication was attempted), showed a consciousness of being part of a modern informational order.

---

[8] Sexton, *Marconi*, 83.

CHAPTER 5

Listening in: 1921–1960

On November 2, 1920, in what is generally considered to be the inaugural moment of the radio boom in the United States, radio station KDKA went on the air in Philadelphia to broadcast the results of the US Presidential Election; the previous night in Dublin, Kevin Barry was hung, becoming the first IRA man to be executed during the War of Independence. Over the next twelve months, as a guerrilla war was being fought in Ireland, the American Department of Commerce licensed five new radio stations. In the month that the Anglo-Irish Treaty was signed – December, 1921 – a new radio station began broadcasting in the US almost every day.[1] The following month, in January, 1922, the Marconi Company made the first English broadcast at Writtle, and by November of 1922, the BBC was on the air in England.

The Irish Free State was thus born simultaneously with radio, coming into being in a world in which the airwaves were wide-open spaces suddenly filled with voices and music, a great lost continent conjured into existence from thin air. It had taken print a century or more to weave networks of trade and production across Europe, and even cinema spent nearly a decade as a fairground attraction; in this context, only the telegraph comes close to matching the astounding speed with which radio went from being a technological possibility, of real interest only to the military and the curious, to becoming part of the fabric of cultural life across much of the world. With no local stations to mask them in those early years, signals flowed into Ireland from London, Manchester and later from high-powered transmitters in Hilversum and Toulouse, to be picked up by Irish men and women, even those with small, inexpensive

---

[1] Paul Starr, *The Creation of the Media: Political Origins of Modern Communications* (New York, 2004), 328, 331.

crystal radio-sets and a bit of ingenuity in rigging an aerial. For the first time in human history it was possible for Irish families, sitting at their kitchen tables, to hear voices from around the world. After sunset, radio waves travelled with even less interference, and owners of the more powerful valve radios spent evenings gently nudging dials, so that the voices flooded in. English, French, Spanish, Italian, Slavic: homes that had only ever heard English or Irish spoken were suddenly filled with accents, inflections and music from a babel of cultures.

In December of 1925, the *Irish Radio Trader* reported that, less than four years after Marconi's first broadcast in Writtle, there were 922 radio stations globally, located in every continent of the world; that same month, the *Irish Radio Review* was giving Irish readers hints on how to best tune in KDKA broadcasting from Pittsburgh.[2] It took no special instructions to tune in the BBC, however. It began broadcasting from Belfast under the call-sign of 2BE in September of 1924, where a young Tyrone Guthrie was one of the station's first announcers. A little over a year later, the BBC in England began transmitting as 5XX from the Daventry transmitter, which was the largest in the world, located only 350 kilometres from the east coast of Ireland, and which the *Irish Radio Trader* enthusiastically proclaimed could reach '23,000,000 persons within the crystal range alone'.[3]

'By a seeming paradox', declared an enthusiastic contributor to the *Irish Radio Journal* in 1925, 'this new weapon of nationalism (as an Italian paper calls it) is more apt to turn on its owner and become an invaluable weapon of attack for internationalism.'[4] The message here came through crisply and clearly: at the very moment that an independent Ireland had come into being in the name of a national culture, a new media technology had come along that challenged more profoundly than any before it the very idea of a self-contained national culture. In the years leading up to independence, organisations such as the Gaelic League had fought for an Ireland whose cultural cornerstone would be the Irish language. For many Irish people, then, there must have been a sharp jab of culture shock to find the *Irish Radio Journal* in 1925 promoting a world language, Esperanto, the adoption of which 'perhaps would mean that internationalism would take the place of nationalism'.[5] 'The radio abolishes time and

[2] 'How to Receive KDKA', *Irish Radio Review* 1:3 (December 1925), 86.
[3] 'Broadcast News', *Irish Radio Trader* 1:14 (December, 1925), 273.
[4] 'Radio Wipes out Boundaries in Central Europe', *Irish Radio Journal* 2:8 (March 16, 1925), 762.
[5] 'Editorial: International Radio Language', *Irish Radio Journal* 2:3 (January 1, 1925), 635.

space; it gives ubiquity and infinite variety with a very modest expend-iture', enthused R.J.P. Mortishead, Assistant Secretary of the Irish Labour Party and Trade Union Congress. 'It may internationalize knowledge in sufficient degree to induce us to carry internationalism further. That depends, of course, on an international language, and I am glad to see *The Irish Radio Review* emphasising the need for Esperanto.'[6]

It was clear that the government of the Free State had to do something; and it fell to the Minister for Posts and Telegraphs, J.J. Walsh to decide what should be done. There is a certain aptness to this key role falling to Walsh; a telegraphist by profession, in 1916 Walsh had led the unit who had gone to the central telephone exchange in Crown Alley, and relayed news of the Rebellion around the country by telephone. Walsh treated Ireland's belated entry to broadcasting as an advantage, in that it allowed him to assess the different models already in existence. 'In America and elsewhere, where broadcasting has been conducted as a private enterprise, a multiplicity of Companies has been found to lead to chaos and confu-sion and to an inefficient service', Walsh declared in the opening of the document that was to form the basis for broadcasting policy in Ireland, the *White Paper on Wireless Broadcasting* (1923). 'All experience has proved that there must be unified control in broadcasting if the public are to get an efficient service.' He thus came up with a proposal to create a company – the Irish Broadcasting Company – with 'unified control', 'the main capital of which should be provided by the chief firms interested in the industry'.[7]

In later years, the playwright Lennox Robinson would claim that the *White Paper on Wireless Broadcasting* formed one of the essential docu-ments in what he called 'the secret history' of the new state. From the beginning, it was clear that the Free State government looked with deep suspicion on the situation that had arisen in the United States, where a virtually unregulated market meant that by 1924 there were already nearly 500 radio stations. On the other hand, while there was clear admiration for the BBC model of funding radio through a licence fee, this was tempered by the pragmatic acknowledgement that Ireland's smaller (and relatively less prosperous) population would simply not be able to provide the kind of income through licencing that would allow an Irish radio station to compete with the BBC, who by the end of 1925 were gathering revenue from 1.5 million licence holders. 'The truth of the matter', Walsh

[6] R.J.P. Mortishead, 'My Opinion of Broadcasting', *Irish Radio Review* 1:2 (November 1925), 56.
[7] Richard Pine, *2RN and the Origins of Irish Radio* (Dublin, 2002), 180.

later conceded in his memoirs, 'is that we saw no hope of providing programmes from the limited cultural material of three million people, to stand the test of comparison with big populations in neighbouring countries, and we feared that this deficiency would lead to trouble.'[8]

The problem that faced Walsh and his colleagues was finding the money to fund the new service, and earlier approaches from both Lord Beaverbrook and Marconi had been rebuffed on the grounds that they would lead to a loss of state control. 'Capital is undoubtedly international,' concluded a member of the Committee set up to examine the matter, 'and the people who control it may have international views.'[9] Perhaps the most imaginative 'international' proposal came from Francis J. Lowe, of the Friends of the Irish Free State in New York, who wrote to the Wireless Commission, enthusiastically proposing the construction of a 1,500-foot-high transmitter on the Hill of Tara, 'in the form of a gigantic harp with five strings of different wire lengths so that it would be possible to broadcast … to the five continents'.[10] At that point, things were getting out of hand. In the end, it was decided that the broadcasting service was to be an arm of the Postmaster General's office, funded by the Department of Finance. In September of 1925 – less than a year after BBC had begun broadcasting from Belfast as 2BE – Seamus Clandillon was appointed as the first Director of the new station. The station was assigned the call-letters 2RN (reputedly because it sounded like the Thomas Moore song, 'Come Back to Erin'). After a series of tests in November and December of 1925, the new station first went on the air on January 1, 1926, with a speech from the man who had been a founder of the Gaelic League (and who would later be Ireland's first president), Douglas Hyde. 'It is the earnest wish of the Minister for Posts and Telegraphs', Clandillon wrote to Hyde, 'that you, above anyone else in Ireland, should do this for us.'[11]

The choice of Hyde to open the new station was far from random: apart from anything else, it was a signal to the internationalists and Esperantists. The Director General of the BBC, John Reith, had written an open letter to the new station when it had been announced in November of 1925, welcoming Ireland to the airwaves. 'We are now on the threshold of the international era, in the course of which the medium

[8] J.J. Walsh, *Recollections of a Rebel* (Tralee, n.d.), 66.
[9] Thomas Johnson, cited in Pine, *2RN*, 76.
[10] *First, Second and Third Interim Reports and the Final Report of the Special Committee to Consider the Wireless Broadcasting Report* (Dublin, 1924), doc. 127.
[11] Pine, *2RN*, 186.

of the wireless will permit a free exchange of thought and culture between all nations, continents and races.'[12] Delivered mainly in Irish, Hyde's speech managed to both endorse and refute this new internationalism. 'It is a sign to the world that times have changed when we can take our own place amongst other nations, and use the wireless in our own language,' he told that first radio audience. 'Éire is not completely saved yet, and will not be until the foreign influence is wiped out.'[13] Between Reith's 'international era', and Hyde's wiping out of 'foreign influences', battle lines were being drawn. One radio enthusiast, writing to the *Irish Times*, complained that the frequencies on which 2RN was transmitted had been chosen so as to block out signals from Manchester and Bournemouth, both of which were popular with Irish listeners. 'It is childish of Mr. Walsh, or anyone else in office, to dictate to Irish people what they are, or rather what they are not, to listen to. King Canute tried to sweep back the sea waves, and Mr. Walsh proposes to confuse the wireless waves.'[14]

However, when the giddy euphoria of those early years of radio began to settle, it became apparent that its effect on Irish culture would not be to give rise to a generation of Esperanto-speaking internationalists; nor, however, would Irish radio help to 'wipe out the foreign influence'. As the airwaves became more congested, the plethora of distant low-powered stations were increasingly blocked out, and radio listening for all but those enthusiasts willing to build elaborate aerials gradually resolved itself to a choice of the local station, or a few of the stronger overseas stations, such as 5XX, Hilversum and later Radio Luxembourg. What Irish people heard in that first broadcast of 2RN in 1926 would provide a good indication of what they could expect to hear for the next few decades. The evening began with the Army Band, followed by station director himself, Seamus Clandillon (an accomplished traditional singer in his own right), singing in Irish; and then the broadcast proceeded, by way of Chopin and Wagner, through a mixture of Irish and other European music. One of its later directors, Maurice Gorham, later wryly observed of 2RN:

It was expected not merely to reflect every aspect of national activity, but to create activities which did not exist. It was expected to revive the speaking of Irish; to foster a taste for classical music; to revive Irish traditional music; to keep people

---

[12] J.C.W. Reith, 'A Message from 2LO', *Irish Times* (November 11, 1925), 4.
[13] *Irish Independent* (January 2, 1926); in Pine, *2RN*, 147.
[14] Pine, *2RN*, 143.

on the farms; to sell goods and services of all kinds from sausages to sweep tickets; to provide a living and a career for writers and musicians; to reunite the Irish people at home with those overseas; to end partition.[15]

Although there was certainly a gap between the high hopes with which the station was launched and the content of much of what was broadcast, there was nonetheless a sense that the medium itself would change Irish life in fundamental ways. Writing on the eve of 2RN's first broadcast, George Russell, poet and editor of the *Irish Statesman*, had one of the more prescient views of the effect of radio on Irish culture.

Within a few years, I doubt if there will be any village in Ireland, any valley, however remote amid the hills, where it will not be possible for the country folk to be not only within hearing distance of Dublin, but also London, Paris, Berlin, and even the United States. Imagination fails in trying to realise the complexities, the myriad changes in the mentality of the country folk which may come within a generation.[16]

'A nation is made from the inside, it is made, first of all, by its language, if it has one,' Hyde told the first listeners to 2RN, 'by its music, songs, games and customs.' It was not so much that the content of radio was to challenge that traditional culture – at least, not initially in the case of Irish radio. The real transformation, powerful but almost imperceptible, was, as Russell saw, in the 'mentality of the country folk', seen by many as the repository of an authentic, unmediated Irish culture; what is more, in an opposition that went back to the sixteenth century, that culture was understood to be a fundamentally oral culture. Now, 'the country folk' suddenly found themselves immersed in a new kind of mediated community, which was also oral, although it would be what Walter Ong would later call a 'secondary orality', 'a more deliberate and self-conscious orality'.[17]

On both sides of the newly created border, radio thus began to weave the invisible fabric of a mediated oral culture. In the Irish Free State, a second studio began broadcasting from Cork as 6CK in 1927, and in 1933 Eamon de Valera officially opened a new transmitter in Athlone, giving more or less nationwide coverage to a service rechristened 'Radio Athlone' (changed again to 'Radio Éireann' in 1937, the year in which the Irish Constitution was adopted). As transmission spread geographically, it also

[15] Maurice Gorham, *Forty Years of Irish Broadcasting* (Dublin, 1967), 40.
[16] George Russell, 'My Opinion of Broadcasting', *Irish Radio Review* 1:2 (November 1925), 56.
[17] Walter J. Ong, *Orality and Literature: The Technologizing of the Word* (London and New York, 1982), 134.

began to fill up more time. As late as 1932, 2RN was only on the air for half an hour every afternoon, from 1:30 to 2:00 p.m., providing weather and some recorded music, returning from 6:00 to 11:00 p.m. with a mixture of live and recorded music, language lessons, a smattering of light comedy and – with increasing prominence – sports coverage, particularly Gaelic Games. In those early years, however, the station spent almost nothing on newsgathering, choosing instead to collect information from 'haphazard sources – government pronouncements, messages from the High Commissioners' Office in London, Morse broadcasts intended for ships at sea, and not infrequently the Dublin evening papers and news broadcasts of the BBC'.[18] In part this was simply due to a lack of money; but frugality was sustained by the belief (picked up in part from the BBC) that it was in poor taste for radio to broadcast anything 'controversial'. This attitude was only just beginning to wane in the late 1930s when the Free State's official neutrality during World War II brought with it strict limits on news reporting. Hence, it would not be until 1951 that the first unscripted political debate was heard on Irish radio.

In Northern Ireland, sectarian tensions meant that there was added reason to avoid anything controversial – a category that could unexpectedly blossom to embrace not only election broadcasts (tactfully avoided until the late 1940s), but also St Patrick's Day celebrations or the Irish language. In its early years, the BBC in Northern Ireland proceeded particularly gingerly, largely because it was never entirely clear whether its function was to establish a fully fledged regional broadcaster, or simply to extend the range of the main, London-based BBC service. Admittedly, for the first five years or so of its existence, 2BE was no more a fully regional service than 2RN was a fully national service, with the *Northern Whig* newspaper complaining as late as 1929 that the station could only be heard within a thirty-mile radius of Belfast: 'Not a single complete county of the six comes inside it. One-third of the area is taken up with the Irish Sea.'[19]

By the mid-1930s, however, the transmission range had increased, and in 1934, under the new directorship of George Marshall the BBC in Northern Ireland officially became a regional service, with a remit to provide 'a programme of local items, music, plays, talks, etc. reflecting the life of the province'.[20] Although the suspension of regional broadcasting

---

[18] Gorham, *Forty Years of Irish Broadcasting*, 46.
[19] *Northern Whig* (September 4, 1929); cited in Rex Cathcart, *The Most Contrary Region: The BBC in Northern Ireland 1924–1984* (Belfast 1984), 61.
[20] *Northern Whig* (October 2, 1934); cited Cathcart, *The Most Contrary Region*, 71.

during World War II would delay these plans, by the late 1940s Marshall had not only gathered a team that over the years included Denis Johnston, Sam Hanna Bell and John Boyd; the station had also acquired new technology in the form of mobile recording equipment. Travelling throughout the Ulster countryside, Sam Hanna Bell recorded the voices of ordinary people, so that by the end of 1949, the station could report that '260 programmes were broadcast from sources outside the studio in the cities, towns and rural districts of the Province'.[21] In that same year, the station launched a dramatic serial about a working-class Belfast family, *The McCooeys*, written by Joseph Tomelty, the series would gain a listenership of half a million (or approximately one in three of the population of Northern Ireland),[22] thereby becoming an intimate part of the fabric of many people's lives.

Meanwhile, in the Irish Free State the Minister for Posts and Telegraphs, P.J. Little, announced plans to expand the radio service to 'give a day-to-day picture of Irish events and activities, so that the constant listener may follow the everyday story of the new Ireland, spoken with its own voice'.[23] However, it was not a single new Ireland, nor even two distinct new Irelands that took shape in the airwaves of the two states on the island; it was a hybrid, as listeners on both sides of the border listened to one another's programmes, each the product of an increasingly distinct broadcasting identity, each both familiar and foreign to the other.

EVIL LITERATURE

'A natural urge to keep out the alien supported the Censorship', wrote Sean O'Faolain in 1941. 'World Radio replies night after night.'[24] It is no coincidence that Irish radio and Irish censorship in the Free State came into existence together. In the same months that radio was introduced to Ireland, George Russell was using his editorship of the *Irish Statesman* to fight a losing battle against a campaign that would reach legislative fruition in the Censorship of Publications Act in 1929. Indeed, it is possible to go further, and to say that the debate over the *White Paper on Broadcasting* that led to the first broadcast of 2RN in 1926, and the debate that led to the Censorship of Publications Act in 1929 were two

---

[21] Draft Report presented by Andrew Stewart, Northern Ireland Controller, to Board of Governors, 1949; cited in Cathcart, *The Most Contrary Region*, 156.
[22] Jonathan Bardon, *Beyond the Studio: A History of BBC Northern Ireland* (Belfast, 2000), 15, 83.
[23] 'Plan to Extend Radio Services Outlined', *Irish Times* (February 20, 1947), 1.
[24] Sean O'Faolain, '1916–1941: Tradition and Creation', *The Bell* 2:1 (April, 1941), 5.

sides of the same coin. In both, there is the same underlying sense of panic, a sense that the fledgling state that had justified its existence so powerfully in terms of an indigenous culture was suddenly being swamped by voices, music, words and images from all over the world. At the very moment when Irish culture should have been most self-contained, it suddenly seemed most porous.

Controlling the promiscuous airwaves by creating a state broadcasting service was a relatively simple solution to the problem of cultural integrity; the older medium, print, was so deeply interwoven into Irish society that controlling it was always going to be a trickier matter. And, to make a complex situation even more complex, at the very moment that the Irish Free State was taking shape, the world of print – particularly newsprint – was consolidating the effects of a revolution arguably greater than any since the invention of the steam press a century earlier. The transformation of newspapers from what had effectively been a cottage industry to a fully industrial form of production, begun in the late nineteenth century, had followed the logic of economies of scale, and by the early 1920s ownership of the British press would be concentrated in the hands of a few large companies. In the period between 1922 and 1937, four individuals (Lords Beaverbrook, Rothermere, Camrose and Kemsley) collectively gained such a stranglehold on the British media that at one point they controlled half of all daily local and national papers sold in England, and one in three Sunday papers, with a total combined weekly circulation of 13 million copies.

For these press barons, the changed political status of the Irish Free State was a mere detail; indeed, as the circulation war intensified throughout the 1920s between the two most vigorously competitive English dailies, the *Daily Express* and the *Daily Mail*, both made concerted efforts to increase Irish sales. Accordingly, their combined Irish circulation in 1926 was 49,119 copies; by 1931, it had increased to 60,707. To put this in context, the estimated circulation figure for the largest Irish daily of the period, the *Irish Independent*, was reputedly 90,000.[25] While the Catholic Truth Society would claim in 1926 that the Sunday *News of the World* was selling more than 130,000 copies in Ireland every week, the generally agreed figure for all English papers in Ireland by the end of the first decade of independence was somewhere between 180,000 and 200,000 copies every week – papers that were coming from an England that was to

[25] L.M. Cullen, *Eason & Son: A History* (Dublin, 1989), 347, 355.

draw even closer, after Aer Lingus began the first regularly scheduled flights between Dublin and London in September of 1936.

National independence was always going to be relative in a world of trans-national media. It was arguably Catholic activists who grasped this most clearly, defining the issue in moral terms. The *News of the World*, the Catholic Truth Society claimed, 'is devoted almost entirely to reports of murders, suicides, divorces, bigamy cases, indecent assault, incest, affiliation cases, and crime in general, and particularly sexual crime'.[26] 'In former times,' argued another Catholic polemicist, 'the poison of the bad Press was not spread everywhere, and, therefore, the antidote was not so necessary.'[27] As early as the spring of 1924 (in the same weeks that the Wireless Committee was finishing its report), the first official salvo fired at these 'offenders against our standard of public decency'[28] came in a series of Lenten Pastorals, released simultaneously by the Bishops of Dublin, Galway, Tuam and Clogher. The ground for the Pastoral had been prepared a few weeks earlier, in February of 1924, by an article in the *Ecclesiastical Bulletin* by a Fr. Richard Devane, S.J. Quoting the Bishop of Galway, Devane mapped out the campaign for a post-revolutionary Ireland. 'It was time that a great crusade was started', he urged, 'and instead of people devoting so much of their energies to politics and other matters of that sort, some effort should be made to save the soul of the Nation, which was being steadily destroyed by filthy publications coming from England, and he was sorry to say, from Ireland too.'[29]

The very name of the body established by the Minister for Justice to consider the issue loaded the dice from the outset: the Committee on Evil Literature. For Catholic activists such as Devane, the threat of evil literature was real. However, their campaign against newspapers like the *News of the World*, or advertisements for contraceptives, hit a much wider target, and the resulting piece of legislation was to cast its shadow over the cultural life of the next four decades. Initially, when the Bill was before the Dáil, there was some debate as to whether censorship should extend to books at all. However these nuances were swept aside in the ensuing crusade.[30] When passed, the Act provided for the banning of printed works on three grounds: that they are 'in ... general tendency indecent or obscene' (11:6), with 'indecent' glossed elsewhere as 'including suggestive

---

[26] *The Problem of Undesirable Printed Matter* (Dublin, 1926), 20.
[27] P. Ivers Rigney, 'The Modern Newspaper', *Irish Rosary* (June, 1926), 10.
[28] *Problem of Undesirable Printed Matter*, 20.
[29] R.S. Devane, *Indecent Literature: Some Legal Remedies* (Dublin, n.d.), 3.
[30] Michael Adams, *Censorship: The Irish Experience* (Dublin, 1968), 50–4.

of, or inciting to sexual immorality or unnatural vice or likely in any other similar way to corrupt or deprave' (1:2); that they devote 'an unduly large proportion of space to the publication of matter relating to crime' (11:7); or that they advocate 'the unnatural prevention of conception or the procurement of abortion or miscarriage' (11:6).[31] When Desmond Fitzgerald, the Minister for Defence, explained to the poet Ezra Pound that the Act was intended purely to 'make it a little less easy for people to read about every rape and incest performed in England', Pound replied that it might be a good idea to keep 'condoms and classics' separated in the statue books.[32] In practice, they were seldom far apart.

It was the task of the five-member Board who were to execute this legislation to consider any work brought to its attention by anyone, including offended members of an Irish public who were to show themselves adept at being offended. Reports of the Censorship Board show that over the first couple of decades of its operation, the number of what were categorised as 'informal complaints' received by the Board far outnumbered the number of books that Board members brought to their own attention. For instance, in 1946, the Board examined a total of 285 books, of which they prohibited 116. Of those 285 books, 233 had been brought to their attention on the basis of 'informal complaints'; only 35 were 'examined on the Board's own initiative'. However, of those 35, 28 (or 80 per cent) were banned, while only 76 (or a third) of the 233 informal complaints were upheld. The following year, 317 books were brought to their attention, of which 164 were banned; in 1948, the figure was 329, with 181 banned.[33] The cumulative effect of the annual banning of between 47 (1930) and 181 (1948) books every year (even taking into account that the same book was sometimes banned more than once, if it appeared in a new edition) was to form what was perhaps the defining feature of Irish print culture in the middle years of the twentieth century. In its first decade alone, the Board banned 1,200 books, and 140 periodicals.

Reading through the Board's reports, the first thing that becomes apparent is the extent to which the original aims – at least the originally stated aims – of censorship became a minimal concern. In the heady years

---

[31] Censorship of Publications Act, 1929 (Dublin).

[32] W.J. McCormack, 'Censorship: Some Uncomfortable Revisions', in *The Irish Book in the Twentieth Century*, ed. Clare Hutton (Dublin, 2004), 84–8, 85.

[33] *Annual Reports of the Censorship of Publications Board and of the Censorship of Publications Appeal Board for the Years Ended 31st December, 1946 and 31st December, 1947* (Dublin, 1947); *Annual Reports of the Censorship of Publications Board and of the Censorship of Publications Appeal Board for the Years Ended 31st December, 1948 and 31st December, 1949* (Dublin, 1971).

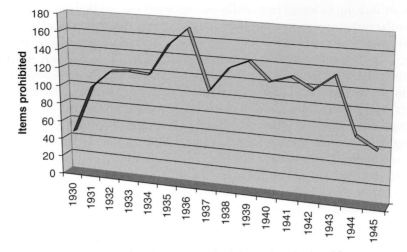

Fig 3. The number of books and periodicals banned in the first fifteen years
of censorship ranged from 47 to 171 per annum.

of the newspaper wars of the 1920s, there was a widespread (and by no means groundless) perception that in the battle for circulation figures, the reporting of crime (particularly sexual crime) in some English newspapers was designed to titillate rather than to inform. Indeed, there were Catholic activists who argued for the wholesale banning of all English newspapers, on the grounds that 'the British popular press is morally, nationally, and economically an evil'.[34] However, by 1947, while the legislation specifically allowed for a periodical to be banned for 'devoting an unduly large proportion of space to the publication of matter relating to crime', there were years in which no newspapers or magazines were banned under this heading. By the same token, there had been an argument that the aspects of Catholic moral teaching that were being put into legislation – particularly bans on artificial contraception and abortion – could only be effective if accompanied by censorship effectively precluding any debate whatsoever of these issues. However, while the latest edition of a family-planning manual by Marie Stopes was dutifully banned most years, the number of books or periodicals banned under this heading remained small, averaging about 12 per cent annually in the first decade of the Bill, and diminishing even further in later years. In the end, by far the greatest number of books were banned simply on the grounds that they were 'indecent or obscene'.

[34] Adams, *Censorship*, 71.

The list of books banned is impressive. Seven of William Faulkner's novels, including *As I Lay Dying* and *Sanctuary* (banned in 1931 and 1937, respectively); Volume II of Freud's *Collected Papers* (1944); Graham Greene's *Brighton Rock* (1939); Hemingway's *Farewell to Arms* (1936); Steinbeck's *Grapes of Wrath* (1940); just about everything by Aldous Huxley; four of H.G. Wells' later works; parts of Proust's *Remembrance of Things Past*; and, of course, Lawrence's *Lady Chatterley's Lover* (1932). In an irony not lost on observers at the time, a measure that was intended (at least in part) to protect Irish culture against 'foreign' influences was equally effective in protecting Irish people from Irish writers: Samuel Beckett's temptingly titled *More Pricks than Kicks* (1934); Austin Clarke's *The Bright Temptation* and *The Singing Men of Cashel* (1932 and 1936); Joyce's *Stephen Hero* (1944); O'Casey's autobiographical writings; Frank O'Connor's *Dutch Interior*, and his translation of Bryan Merriman's *The Midnight Court*; five of Liam O'Flaherty's titles; and Sean O'Faolain's *Bird Alone* (1936).

If writers can be relied on for anything, it is to be articulate; and so, the most memorable accounts of the effects of censorship are, not surprisingly, those of the authors. 'Under the feeble and apologetic tyranny of Dublin Castle we Irish were forced to endure a considerable degree of compulsory freedom', wrote George Bernard Shaw in 1928. 'The moment we got rid of that tyranny we rushed to enslave ourselves.'[35] 'The whole thing that I really resented when I was young', John McGahern later recalled, 'was that you had to go into exile if you were an Irish writer, like Joyce and Beckett.'[36] By the same token, Frank O'Connor had observed earlier that 'the most awful thing about the censorship is the way it perpetuates the negative attitude we oppose to every manifestation of intellect and scholarship'.[37]

Unravelling the debate on censorship as it evolved from the mid-1920s, through to World War II, it has sometimes appeared in retrospect as a purely ideological struggle between repression and resistance. In reality, however, the situation was considerably more complex. While the original arguments for censorship had concentrated primarily on newspapers and magazines, the Irish newspaper industry did more than hold its own in the decades after 1922. The real problem lay in the wider Irish publishing

---

[35] George Bernard Shaw, 'The Censorship', *Irish Statesman* II (1928); in Julia Carlson, ed. *Banned in Ireland: Censorship and the Irish Writer* (London, 1990), 133.

[36] John McGahern, 'Interview with Julia Carlson', in *Banned in Ireland*, ed. Carlson, 64.

[37] Frank O'Connor, 'Frank O'Connor on Censorship', *The Dubliner* (March, 1962); in *Banned in Ireland*, ed. Carlson, 155.

industry, particularly in relation to book publishing. *Thom's Directory* for 1926, for instance, lists thirty-one businesses under the heading of 'Booksellers and Publishers' in the city of Dublin, a conflation of trades that dated back to the eighteenth century, but which the increasingly international and industrialised publishing industry had rendered obsolete. So, at least half of those on the list were purely booksellers, and of those who did produce books, almost all were specialist publishers who made a living from a localised niche market, such as the Catholic Truth Society who published religious pamphlets, or Browne and Nolan, who published school textbooks. Outside of Dublin, there were smaller publishers: Dundalgan Press in Dundalk, the Forum Press in Cork, the Quota Press in Belfast, the Mourne Press in Newcastle, Cork University Press in Cork and O'Gorman in Galway, as well as regional newspapers that occasionally produced books, including *The Kerryman* and *The Waterford News*. Nonetheless, most of the stock in Irish bookshops originated from outside the island.

In the years between the two world wars, the global publishing industry consolidated, and increasingly worked from economies of scale, swamping Irish publishing. The groundwork for this had been laid by J.M. Dent, when it introduced its Everyman Library in 1906; however, the real revolution came when Penguin began publishing its paperback editions in 1935. With offices in the main publishing centres and distribution directed at chains such as W.H. Smith, the publishing industry – particularly in the area of fiction – was increasingly driven by volume of sales. 'Irish publishing houses are now, alas, very few', noted Seamus O'Sullivan in the *Dublin Magazine* in 1924, 'and ... now the work of the best Irish writers must be sought for in the announcements of English publishers.'[38] A contributor to Frank O'Connor's *Ireland To-day* asked if 'Irish culture is possible'. 'I have heard it costs three hundred pounds to publish a novel', he replied. 'Four thousand copies must be sold to pay costs, and of these four thousand, four hundred at most may be sold in Ireland. From this fact it is obvious that an Irish novel is not possible to-day.'[39] A later contributor to *The Bell* went further, arguing that it was not in the Irish writer's interest to publish with an Irish press. 'For an Irish publisher, without the comprehensive catalogue and without the widespread organisation and connection, to attempt to publish, say, Bernard

[38] Seamus O'Sullivan, 'Notes of the Month', *The Dublin Magazine* 2:3 (October, 1924), 1.
[39] James Devane, 'Is an Irish Culture Possible?', *Ireland To-Day* 1:5 (October 1936), 23.

Shaw ... Sean O'Casey, or Maurice Walsh, would be disastrous for those authors. Nine-tenths of the sales would be lost.'[40]

The irony of this situation, as Sean O'Faolain chided readers of *The Bell* in 1943, was that 'Ireland's dependence on Britain for her books does not even hurt our national pride.'[41] The exception was in relation to printing in the Irish language, where a government committee had been convened in 1926 to consider publishing in the Irish language, leading to the establishment of a subsidised Irish-language publishing house, An Gúm. In the following twenty years, it published some 800 items, ranging from original fiction and poetry, to medical textbooks, dictionaries, as well as an ambitious programme of translation from a wide range of languages. Admittedly, most of the translations were from English, and there were frequent criticisms 'that readers of Irish will not read translations of books which they can easily procure in English'.[42] Nonetheless, by 1937, An Gúm had published almost 100 titles translated from languages other than English.[43] In its own terms, it was a success, providing a publishing outlet for authors working in the Irish language, even if there were complaints that it sometimes took up to seven years to approve a manuscript. Later, in 1948, the Finance Minister of the time, Frank Aiken, approved grants to Irish-language magazines, including *Inniú* (£4,900), *Comhar* (£1,150) and *Feasta* (£1,800), launched that year by Conradh na Gaeilge.[44] For English-language writers, however, it was irksome that while the state had no problem putting forward a cultural justification for subsidising Irish-language publishing, the possibility of subsidising English-language book publishing, which faced the equally daunting task of competing in a global marketplace, could only be seen in economic terms, and was thus left to shift for itself.

In spite of this, there was a lively print culture in Ireland during the middle decades of the twentieth century, largely because of the vigour of a magazine culture headed by *The Bell*, but also including George Russell's *Irish Statesman* (1923–30); the *Dublin Magazine* (1923–58), a literary monthly edited by Seamus O'Sullivan; the short-lived *Ireland To-day* (1936–8), edited by Frank O'Connor; *Envoy* (1949–51); and, in Belfast, *Rann* (1948–53). If these magazines constituted a kind of liberal opposition, there was also an equally vigorous Catholic magazine culture.

---

[40] A Dublin Master Printer, 'Publishing in Ireland', *The Bell* 6:4 (July, 1943), 318.
[41] Sean O'Faolain, 'Books and a Live People', *The Bell* 6:2 (May, 1943), 91.
[42] Séamus O'Neill, 'The Gúm', *The Bell* 12:2 (May, 1946), 137.
[43] Michael Cronin, *Translating Ireland: Translation, Languages, Cultures* (Cork, 1996), 157.
[44] John Horgan, *Irish Media: A Critical History since 1922* (London, 2001), 56.

Writing in the Catholic *Irish Monthly Magazine* in 1937, Patrick Gannon, S.J. noted: 'It seems fairly clear that already a chasm, both wide and deep, has been dug between the Church and a section at least of our "Intelligentsia".'[45] And yet, in some of the same Catholic journals that were supporting censorship, we find a serious and sustained debate about the kind of Irish society that was being created. Indeed, given that the *Dublin Magazine*, or *Ireland To-day* were primarily literary magazines, their focus was principally on print culture, whereas the Catholic press took a wider interest in the media as a whole.

For instance, running throughout the *Irish Monthly Magazine* in the 1930s was a debate on the new concept of 'leisure', criticising a culture in which 'the factory at one end and Hollywood at the other mark out the limits of "the leisured State".'[46] Indeed, in articles such as these, there emerges a clear sense in the Catholic press of being engaged in a struggle of global proportions. In a particularly astute analysis of the Catholic press published in *The Bell*, Conor Cruise O'Brien, writing as Donat O'Donnell, argued that the Catholic press recognised that the ground had shifted from the old colonial struggle with Britain. Ireland's new importance for Catholic activists, he argued, was in terms of its position in a new 'theopolitics', 'as the point half-way between the American and Soviet Middle Wests, the ultimate reservoirs of war', and site of the 'principal deposits of faith from which the Great Powers can be influenced towards Catholicism, or at least way from Materialism'. 'We cannot judge the Catholic Press correctly unless we keep this "theopolitical" background in mind.'[47]

'Everything is now commercialised, whether it is a good thing or not', wrote T.J. Ryan, S.J., in the *Irish Monthly* in 1941. 'When mechanical progress made it possible to produce huge quantities of papers at great speed it was inevitable that the papers would fall into the hands of those who thought more about profits than about the responsibility of directing public opinion.' The consequence, he concluded, is clear:

Freedom of the Press is little better than a myth. It means freedom from direct Government control, but it does not mean freedom from control from other interests, and it would be very difficult to find any paper which gives straightforward news and has not in mind in its presentation of it some special interests ...

[45] Patrick J. Gannon, S.J., 'Literature and Censorship', *Irish Monthly Magazine* (July 1937), 434.
[46] Stanley B. James, 'The Fallacy of the Leisure State', *Irish Monthly Magazine* (Sept. 1933), 571, 576.
[47] Donat O'Donnell [Conor Cruise O'Brien], 'The Catholic Press: A Study in Theopolitics', *The Bell* x:1 (April, 1945), 30–1.

whether it be the support of a certain political party, or the backing of big business, or the particular affiliations of the chief proprietor.[48]

TRUTH IN THE NEWS

Although T.J. Ryan was making a general point about the relative concept of press freedom in a market economy, his comments would have had a special pointedness in the Ireland of the 1930s, particularly after the founding of the *Irish Press*. Established in 1931 by Eamon de Valera, largely with funds raised by subscribers in the United States, the paper was created to provide his Fianna Fáil party with a newspaper that was sympathetic to its interests. Born out of members of Sinn Fein who had opposed the Treaty during the Civil War, Fianna Fáil would manage to combine a rhetoric of republican social idealism with a hard-nosed *Realpolitik* pragmatism that would keep them in post from 1932 until 1948. In many respects, the *Irish Press* mirrored this mixture. With its first edition emerging from presses ceremonially started up by Patrick Pearse's mother, its editor, Frank Gallagher, announced in his first editorial that 'other nations will have a means of knowing that Irish opinion is not merely an indistinct echo of the opinions of a section of the British press'. While the *Press* was not – at least officially – controlled by Fianna Fáil, there was little doubt that de Valera maintained a tight control over the paper. One writer would recall his father, a journalist on the paper, 'telling me stories about Dev phoning the newsroom every night to know what was coming out in the paper the next day. He often had no hesitation in changing copy, in changing a whole front page.'[49] However, even de Valera had to balance a range of interests. As Vivian Mercier noted at the time, the directors of the *Press* included a selection of Irish businessman: a distiller, a retailer and the chairman of a grocery chain. 'In other words, the *Irish Press* is almost as closely linked with the new Big Business of Ireland as the other two daily papers. ... it is not likely to expand on the mystical semi-revolutionary lines of its opening years.'[50]

The Irish newspaper world into which the *Irish Press* was launched had begun to settle into a shape that would last into the final decade of the twentieth century, with three national dailies dominating the Irish news-print market, all aligned to business interests: the *Irish Times*, the *Irish*

[48] T.F. Ryan, S.J., 'The Press of the World', *Irish Monthly Magazine* (February 1940), 65–6.
[49] Frank Kilfeather, *Changing Times: A Life in Journalism* (Dublin, 1997), 22.
[50] Vivian Mercier, '"The Times"', *The Bell* 9:4 (January, 1945), 484.

Independent and the *Irish Press.* Of these three, the largest was the *Irish Independent.* Founded by railway tycoon William Martin Murphy in 1905 (the same year as Northcliffe's *Daily Mail*), the *Independent* operated along more or less the same lines as its English counterpart, with a premium on high circulation and large advertising revenues. Its circulation figures dipped just below 120,000 in 1932, after the *Irish Press* entered the market; however, buoyed by the import duty on English papers introduced in the Finance Act of 1933, its numbers went back up again, and by 1939 they had reached 140,000. The *Independent,* as one contemporary put it, 'is the non-party organ of business interests in the country'; like the *Daily Mail,* commented *The Bell,* 'both papers are in themselves great businesses, with the natural interest of any great going concern in the maintenance of law and order'.[51]

Of the big three papers, the history of the *Irish Times* in the years immediately after 1922 is one of the more unlikely stories of the period. A cartoon in the satirical *Dublin Opinion* from the 1920s shows the office of the *Irish Times*: 'everybody down to the office boy wears a top hat. ... The only portraits on the office-walls are those of Nelson and Wellington. All admonitory notices are in Latin. Among the technical equipment of the office one notes an Italics Insertor and a Semi-Colon Scatterer.'[52] Founded in 1859 as a penny daily with liberal unionist politics, it would not have been unreasonable to expect that after 1922, the *Irish Times* would quietly fade away. 'When the British left Ireland in 1922,' wrote the paper's hugely influential editor, Robert Smyllie, who took over the paper in 1934, 'the bottom fell out of the world in which the *Irish Times* had previously existed. Quite frankly, we had been the organ of the British government. ... We had now to write for a totally different public. ... We pictured them, largely, I think, as young men and women just left school, just down from the universities – the people who were going to be the voters and the leaders of the future.'[53]

Under Smyllie's editorship, the *Irish Times* managed to create a role for itself as a newspaper of record. Although its circulation figures were not much higher than a flourishing regional weekly (estimated to have been around 20,000 throughout most of the 1930s and 1940s), and its traditional readership of middle-class Protestants had a diminishing hold on

[51] Donat O'Donnell [Conor Cruise O'Brien], '"The Irish Independent"', *The Bell* 9:5 (February 1945), 389.
[52] Mercier '"The Times"', *The Bell* 9:4 (January, 1945), 290.
[53] Anon., 'Meet R. M. Smyllie', *The Bell* 3:3 (March, 1941), 185.

elected office, its influence nonetheless remained disproportionately strong. In part, this was because the Protestant middle class who made up its readership continued to be influential in the business and professional worlds, thus ensuring the paper an advertising base that depended more on targeting a particularly affluent readership than on mass circulation. Toning down its reports on the doings of the titled, and making little editorial changes such as dropping the word 'Roman' when referring to 'Catholics', the paper gradually became the paper of record for all of the professional classes, regardless of religious denomination. 'The Fianna Fáil organ, *The Irish Press*, was not called to make any difficult transition or define any hard reality: it arrived when the battle was already over,' commented Vivian Mercier in 1945. 'The *Irish Independent* needed to make but a comparatively slight transition, from one nationalist movement to another; ... The *Times* alone was compelled to do some realistic thinking.'[54] 'Smyllie integrated the *Irish Times* and what it stood for with the Irish nation,' politician Todd Andrews later recalled, 'and he was more than welcomed by the ruling group, and by the civil servants in particular.'[55] This was particularly true during World War II, when reports of the war were vigorously censored, but nonetheless eagerly sought after, in neutral Ireland. Smyllie spent his war finding ways to outwit the censors, achieving a victory of sorts on VE Day, when he printed a series of photographs of the Allied military commanders in the shape of a large 'V' on the paper's front page.[56]

Meanwhile, the *Cork Examiner*, founded in 1841, had established itself as the largest newspaper in the Irish Free State outside of Dublin. Indeed, when the *Irish Times* began making public its circulation figures in the early 1950s, it became clear that the Cork paper outsold its avowedly national rival, with figures for 1953 putting the *Times* at around 35,000, and the *Examiner* at 45,000. In Northern Ireland, the pattern that had been taking shape before 1922 continued, with a press divided along sectarian lines. The *Irish News* of Belfast, which dated back to the politics of the 1890s, had always been Catholic, if not nationalist, in its politics, and it increasingly identified with the interests of the new state to the south. Meanwhile, the *Belfast Evening Telegraph*, founded in 1870, continued to be the main organ of moderate unionism, sharing a readership with the venerable *Belfast Newsletter*, which went back to 1737.

---

[54] Mercier, "'The Times'", 296.
[55] C.S. Andrews, *Man of No Property* (Dublin, 1982), 136–7.
[56] Mark O'Brien, *The* Irish Times: *A History* (Dublin, 2008), 119.

Meanwhile the *Londonderry Sentinel,* founded in 1829, became the main unionist newspaper in the northwest. Around the country, as printing technology became more affordable and the price of newsprint fell in the early 1930s, many of the key regional newspapers expanded or consolidated. In Galway, the *Connacht Tribune* launched a sister publication, the *Connacht Sentinel* in 1925; the *Kerryman* began to branch out into occasional book publication, and in Roscommon, the *Roscommon Messenger* folded in 1935, supplanted by a rival, *The Roscommon Champion,* founded in 1933. In short, although a number of papers were closed for a period during the War of Independence and the Civil War, for a country that had undergone violent upheaval at a time when the world media was undergoing an unprecedented transformation, the Irish newspaper press – both in their content and in their form – spoke to their readers of continuity. The only real victim was the venerable *Freeman's Journal,* founded in 1763, it folded in 1924.

'THAT IRELAND OF WHICH WE DREAMED'

That Ireland which we dreamed of would be the home of a people who valued material wealth only as the basis of right living, of a people who were satisfied with frugal comfort and devoted their leisure to things of the spirit – a land whose… whose firesides would be forums for the wisdom of serene old age.[57]

Eamon de Valera's St Patrick's Day radio broadcast in 1943 has become iconic of an authorised traditionalism in the middle decades of the twentieth century: a vision that spoke of tradition, continuity and community, rooted in an oral culture passed on by the firesides of 'serene old age'. However, it is worth remembering that de Valera's speech was made (and hence made possible) by radio. Moreover, shortly after it was broadcast, a recording was released as a pair of 78 rpm records by Parlophone ('The Irish Language, a characteristic mark of our Nationhood' and 'The Ireland We Desire')[58] to be sold to the Irish diaspora around the world. In other words, one of the clearest articulations of the traditionalist view of Irish culture was made possible by a multi-national media culture. As Irish men and women listened to de Valera's evocation of a pre-modern community on the radio, or crackling from the speaker

---

[57] Eamon de Valera, 'The Undeserted Village', in *Speeches and Statements of Eamon de Valera 1917–1973,* ed. M. Moynihan (Dublin, 1980), 47.

[58] IP364: 'The Irish Language, a characteristic mark of our Nationhood'; IP365: 'The Ireland We Desire'.

of a gramophone, they became part of a mediated community of isolated individuals, each sitting alone, and yet connected to thousands of invisible others, separated by geography; in the case of the 78 rpm records, this community was also separated in time, for the discs were still on sale in Ireland more than a decade after the broadcast.

These effects of recording on tradition were felt most strongly when traditional Irish music became a category in the record company catalogues. Up until the early 1920s, Irish music had been assimilated into the 'domestic' American catalogues of the major record companies. However, by the mid-1920s there were a number of small labels in the New York area, notably Emerald, Gaelic and Celtic, recording more traditional Irish music, which went beyond the comic songs, tenor ballads and orchestrated Irish airs that filled the catalogues of the big labels. However, by the end of 1923 (in the same months that the Wireless Committee were meeting in Ireland) the big three international labels of the period – Columbia/Regal, HMV and Parlophone – realised the value of this niche market, and began using new electrical recording techniques not available to the smaller labels to record and release traditional Irish music. In 1929 alone, Columbia released over 100 Irish 78s in their 33000-F Irish series, and they would release almost 600 more over the next decade.[59] Having said this, most tracks were recorded in studios in New York and Boston, using musicians who had emigrated to the United States. Indeed, it was not until 1929 that Parlophone eventually sent a team to Ireland to record Irish music in Ireland, and it would be a further eight years until EMI opened the first Dublin recording studio in 1937. It would take until the early 1950s before an Irish label started recording in Ireland, when a Dublin music store, Walton's, started the Glenside label. Glenside was followed towards the end of the decade by the subsidised Gael Linn label, whose first recording was of the unaccompanied *sean-nós* singer Seán 'ac Dhonncha in 1957.

From the moment that traditional musicians began to record in the early 1920s, the effect was not simply to preserve past performances; recording would equally affect future performances. For instance, when 15-year-old Michael Coleman emigrated to the United States from County Sligo in 1914, he brought with him his fiddle, and a repertoire of tunes from his local area around Ballymote. The very existence of a 'Sligo style' was only possible because in the years that Sligo fiddlers such as Michael Coleman, Paddy Killoran or James Morrison were learning their

---

[59] Pekka Gronow, *The Columbia 33000-F Irish Series: A Numerical Listing* (Los Angeles, 1979), 1–3.

craft, almost all of the music they would have heard would have been made by men and women they knew personally from their local area. A melody, a style of phrasing, or a technique for holding the bow; all manner of idiosyncrasies and local preferences would have been passed on, until a fiddler from Sligo, perhaps sitting in on a session in Kerry, would have been as instantly recognisable as if he was speaking a different dialect (which, in a sense, he was).

Coleman continued to cut sides for labels such as HMV up until just before his death in 1946, and these remained for sale in Ireland throughout the 1950s, until 78s were replaced by LPs. Coleman's 78 recordings – and those of his contemporaries – transformed traditional Irish music in a number of different ways. In the first place, one side of a 10-inch 78 rpm record plays for approximately three minutes. Longer classical recordings based on a written score adapted to this restriction by releasing a symphony, for instance, as a set of discs broken into shorter segments. Traditional Irish music, however, resided in the performer, not in the written score. Hence, when Michael Coleman stepped into a New York studio in 1930 to record 'The Morning Dew' for HMV (released as B3401), he knew that he had to record a version of the tune that lasted for no more than three minutes – so that is what he played. Once recorded and cut, the master of the three-minute version of 'The Morning Dew' would have made its way to HMV's London office, and from there to Ireland.

For fiddlers, pipers and singers from Dingle to Donegal, this had two immediate consequences. From the 1920s onwards, for the first time in the history of a centuries-old musical form, it became possible for a fiddler in Dingle or Donegal to learn a style of playing completely different from that in his local area, played by a musician he might never meet, simply by dropping the stylus in the disc, over and over again. This in turn detached tradition from time and sequentiality, for even after Coleman's death in 1946 his recordings remained in Irish catalogues. Secondly, the pieces that traditional musicians learned from 78 records were all three minutes long. Prior to the advent of recording, there had been no such thing as a standard length for a piece of traditional music; there now was a standard, and it was determined by technology. Indeed, three minutes would remain the standard length for a song (as it would in pop music) even after the introduction of the long-playing record in the late 1950s made longer tracks possible.

In addition, as the recordings of Michael Coleman and his contemporaries circulated around the world, and were played on the radio, Irish traditional music was no longer something that existed outside the mediated world, a remnant of an oral culture heard only by those who had personal contact with the musicians; instead, it became one more musical choice among many. The government minister responsible for Irish broadcasting in 1953, Erskine Childers, told the Dáil that the results of the first survey of Irish radio listeners had shown 'a tremendous interest in light music of American origin coming from abroad. A great number of the young people in the country have adopted light variety, operatic and Anglo-American dance music as their folk music along with our own melodies in the same way as other European countries.'[60] Looking through the Gramophone Company's Irish catalogue as late as 1957, for instance ('All These Records Are Made in Ireland by Irish Labour'), one finds that Coleman is still there, as is John McCormack; but in the alphabetical listing, Coleman shares the page with Nat King Cole and Perry Como. This is not to say that Irish music suffered for being recorded, or became any less important to those who played and listened to it; however, its place in the culture had shifted.

CINEMA AND THE CARAMEL OF AMERICANISATION

Perhaps to an even greater extent than with the radio or the phonograph, the cinema was being woven into the fabric of Irish life in precisely the years that an Irish nation was being defined, fought for and established – say, between D. W. Griffith's *Birth of a Nation* in 1915 and the first sound film, *The Jazz Singer*, released in 1927, the year in which Fianna Fáil first contested a General Election. In those years, and in the decades that followed, amid debates about the creation of an Irish Ireland, cinemas continued to open around the country, and Irish men and women attended those cinemas in growing numbers. In 1934, there were 190 cinemas in Ireland, with 18.25 million admissions annually (out of a population of just under 3 million, according to the 1936 Census).[61] Just over a decade later, in 1948, there were over 320 cinemas in Ireland, spread throughout the island. For instance, the town of Callan, in County Kilkenny, with a population of 1,508 in 1943 had a cinema, the Gaiety, with a seating capacity of 500 (which meant that roughly one in three of the town's population could watch a film at any one time). Similarly, Omagh, in County Tyrone, with a population of 5,741 had three cinemas,

[60] Victor Curran, 'What the Listener Wants II', *Irish Monthly Magazine* (August, 1954), 314.
[61] Lance Pettitt, *Screening Ireland: Film and Television Representation* (Manchester, 2000), 33.

with a combined capacity of more than 1,800.[62] By 1954, when cinema-going peaked in Ireland, there were a total of 54,100,000 admissions annually – which meant that, on average, every man, woman and child old enough to watch a film went to the cinema every three or four weeks.

By far the majority of the films that these Irish people saw originated outside of Ireland, overwhelmingly from the United States and, to a lesser extent, from England. In the newly independent Ireland this raised issues more complex, in some respects, than those raised by the importation of English newspapers. There were powerful Irish business interests who had very practical reasons for wanting to see constraints put on the import-ation of English newspapers, and were thus happy to have the case for import duties framed in moral and patriotic terms (that English papers were full of crime, smut, advertisements for contraceptives and anti-Irish prejudice). America, however, was different. If nothing else, the sheer number of Irish people who had emigrated to the United States in the century since the 1840s meant that in the Irish imagination, America was, quite literally, the promised republic, the screen upon which many of those who remained in Ireland projected their dreams. So, when America's own dreams began to be projected upon cinema screens all over Ireland, it was difficult to denounce them as foreign.

At the same time, the inundation of American films could not simply be ignored in a culture finely attuned to the impact of the foreign, for good or for ill. This meant that criticism of the dominance of American films on Irish screens came from the fringes of the mainstream, and sometimes produced some very odd bedfellows. For instance, there were small cinema clubs, such as the Dublin Film Society (which opened by showing *Battleship Potemkin* in 1929), and the Irish Film Society (founded 1936), both of which were attempting to counteract what film-maker and writer Liam O'Laoghaire referred to in 1929 as 'the monopoly of the public screens by the American Sound Film'.[63] This brought cinephiles who wanted to see more Soviet montage or German Expressionism strangely close to the cultural protectionists lobbying for increased censorship. So, for instance, in September of 1925 the *Irish Times* (still effectively a liberal unionist paper at the time), published a long article entitled 'Movies and the Irish Mind'; it was reprinted later that year by one of the most vociferous journals of the Catholic right, *The Irish Rosary*. 'Every Irish

[62] *Irish Cinema Handbook* (Dublin, 1943), 169.
[63] Liam O'Laoghaire, 'The Film Society Movement', *The Bell* 15:2 (November 1947), 56.

village has a picture house,' the author observed. 'What do Irish children learn in picture-houses?'

That America is the grandest and most adventurous country in the world; that wealth, fine houses, and luxurious motor cars represent the *summum bonum*; that the means by which such wealth is acquired need not be investigated too closely; ... over and above all these things, sexual passion is the pervading interest of life. ... The queerest feature of the whole business is the complacency towards it of the people whose ideal is a Gaelicised and isolated Ireland. They strain violently at the gnat of 'Anglicisation' but swallow the caramel of Americanisation without a murmur.[64]

This article in the *Irish Rosary* was part of a sustained campaign that was given momentum and a theoretical focus by an encyclical dealing with cinema issued in 1936 by Pope Pius XI, *Vigilanti Cura*. 'The motion picture must be not merely not immoral', declared Pius XI. 'It has a positive function to perform as an auxiliary of instruction and education.'[65] 'How useless it is for Mr. de Valera to insist on the particular soul of Ireland,' chided a commentator in the *Irish Monthly Magazine* in 1936, 'when Hollywood is busy making it like the soul of Los Angeles.'[66] For such Catholic activists taking their cue from *Vigilanti Cura*, Ireland was simply one front in a world-wide battle where enemies lurked on all sides, allegiances were complex, and sometimes Soviet godlessness and American materialism merged into the same target. Beginning in the early 1920s, Fr. Richard Devane, S.J., one of the architects of the Censorship of Publications Act, was warning against the dangers of what he saw as Bolshevism in Hollywood film. When a number of prominent Hollywood stars aligned themselves with the Republican cause during the Spanish Civil War (in which the Catholic Church was a firm supporter of the opposing Nationalists of General Franco), it confirmed his suspicion that Moscow was somewhere in the Hollywood hills. Meanwhile, in the United States itself, the campaign that resulted in the Hayes Code (in which the industry regulated itself) was led largely by Catholic organisations, particularly the Legion of Decency, in which Irish-Americans were prominent. Ideas and literature flowed back and forth across the Atlantic, a case in point being a pamphlet published in Thurles in 1949 by Mícheál

[64] 'Hollywood and Ireland', *Irish Times* (September 5, 1925), 6.
[65] Gearoid Mac Eoin, 'Vigilanti Cura: A Commentary on the Famous Encyclical of His Holiness, Pope Pius XI, on the Cinema', *Irish Cinema Handbook*, 9.
[66] John Desmond Sheridan, 'The Flight from Leisure', *Irish Monthly Magazine* (May 1936), 287–92, 291.

Ó Tuathail for the Catholic Cinema and Theatre Patrons Association, entitled *Red Stars over Hollywood*, exposing the Communist infiltration of Hollywood, and boasting a preface by J. Edgar Hoover.

One of the most tangible effects of this sustained campaign against the dangers of Hollywood cinema was a regime of censorship in the cinema matching that directed towards the printed word. The Censorship of Films Act (1923) was one of the very first pieces of legislation passed by the new state (predating the Censorship of Publications Act by six years), and was designed to keep from exhibition films that were 'indecent, obscene or blasphemous ... or would tend to inculcate principles contrary to public morality or would be otherwise subversive of public morality'. While clearly admitting a wide range of interpretation, the first film censor, James Montgomery, made it clear where he stood when he published a retrospective reflection on the job in the Jesuit journal, *Studies*, which he entitled 'The Menace of Hollywood'. 'Every evening boys and girls from our educational institutions crowded the Picture Houses,' he announced. 'Could any people for long preserve a distinct national character in face of such a bombardment?'[67] Doing his best to man the ramparts against this bombardment, Montgomery banned 1,750 films in the years between 1924 and his retirement in 1940 – a substantial proportion of the 2,500 films banned in the Act's history.[68]

Censorship, however, was only half of the project outlined in *Vigilanti Cura*: the counterpart to the suppression of 'immoral' films was the creation of a 'moral', educational cinema, and this led to a search for a model of a national cinema other than that of Hollywood. For instance, John Grierson (the founder of the National Film Board of Canada, and the person credited with coining the word 'documentary') can be found contributing to *Studies* in 1948, with his proposals for 'A Film Policy for Ireland'. 'Like all small countries,' he observed, 'I imagine that Ireland is finding it difficult to face up to the full implications of the use of film for national purposes.' 'I am thoroughly convinced', Richard Devane wrote in 1943, 'that, apart from our commercial exploitation by cosmopolitan adventurers, nothing will ever be done as regards Irish film production proper unless we bestir ourselves and set up a system of national film-control;

---

[67] James Montgomery, 'The Menace of Hollywood', *Studies* 31 (December, 1942), 420.
[68] Another 10,000 were cut. Kevin Rockett, 'Protecting the Family and the Nation: Official Censorship of American Cinema in Ireland, 1923–1954', *Historical Journal of Film, Radio and Television* 20:9 (August 2000), 283–300, 286. See also Rockett's more extensive research on film censorship, written with Emer Rockett: *Irish Film Censorship: A Cultural Journey from Silent Cinema to Internet Pornography* (Dublin, 2004).

nor will the films be employed in nation-building until we follow the example of other States and establish a State-aided Irish Film Institute'[69] – perhaps thinking of the British Film Institute, which he knew well. However, as the qualms of the Department of Finance during the establishment of 2RN twenty years earlier had shown, an Irish government was unlikely to be either willing or able to provide a full system of state subsidy for film production. As John Grierson astutely observed: 'I have no doubt that Ireland is too divided as to whether or not it will develop the film on a governmental or a commercial basis.'[70]

Hence, any Irish film industry was going to have to be, to a large extent, commercially self-supporting. And there lay the problem. 'A very good Irish production, getting a magnificent reception, would hardly earn £10,000 in the domestic market', wrote T.J.M. Sheehy in the *Irish Monthly Magazine* in 1948. 'With careful budgeting, and excluding publicity and distribution costs, a good feature film might be produced in Ireland for £50,000.'[71] As a consequence, the Irish film industry throughout the 1930s and 1940s limped along in a series of false starts. In the 1930s, there were only thirteen films made in Ireland that were anything like feature length, often produced on minimal budgets. For instance, when Denis Johnston's film, *Guests of the Nation*, opened in 1935, it was lavishly praised for finding a cinematic idiom for the unsentimental realism of the Frank O'Connor short story on which it was based. However, whatever its merits as a film, it had been filmed on a shoestring budget in a back garden in Dublin,[72] and did not provide the basis for a film industry. In the 1940s, with resources constrained even further by the austerities of war, only two feature films were made in Ireland. 'Fifty years after the invention of cinematography we still find Ireland theorizing about Irish films,' wrote Liam O'Laoghaire at the end of the decade in *Cinema Quarterly* (published by *The Irish Catholic*), 'with amazingly little achievement and certainly no continuous flow of native films.'[73]

The problems with establishing an Irish film industry were not simply economic. In newspapers, film journals and magazines from *The Bell* to *Studies* and *The Furrow*, there is a sustained debate about the basis for an Irish film industry: what would an Irish film look like? For those Catholic polemicists for whom Hollywood was 'the mirror of our age reflecting …

[69] R.S. Devane, 'The Film in National Life', *Irish Cinema Handbook*, 13.
[70] John Grierson, 'A Film Policy for Ireland', *Studies* 37:147 (September, 1948), 283–91.
[71] T.J.M. Sheehy, 'Towards an Irish Film Industry', *Irish Monthly Magazine* (September, 1948), 418.
[72] Kevin Rockett, *The Irish Filmography: Fiction Films 1896–1996* (Dublin, 1996), 13.
[73] Liam O'Laoghaire, 'Initiation', *Cinema Quarterly* 3 (n.d.), 8.

the mechanical wonders and the moral collapse',[74] the search for an alternative form of cinema led to an interest in documentary, evident in the invitation to Grierson to contribute to *Studies* in 1948. In this regard, Robert Flaherty's *Man of Aran* is perhaps the key Irish film of the 1930s, even though its director was American, and the funding was provided through an English company, Gainsborough Pictures. Indeed, Gainsborough provided Flaherty with a budget bigger than that spent on any Irish-produced fiction film until the late 1950s – 'a bitter testimony to the history of film production Ireland', as film historian Kevin Rockett later commented.[75] Armed with the latest lightweight cameras, a selection of long lenses,[76] and a concept of the primitive life on the Aran Islands informed by reading J.M. Synge's *The Aran Islands* (1907), the film Flaherty produced has since been much criticised for presenting as ethnographic documentary something in which key scenes had to be staged to fit his mythic sense of landscape. However, on its release, *Man of Aran* received a gala premiere attended by Eamon de Valera, and was met with a sense of excitement that can perhaps be understood in terms of what it provided: an image of Ireland that looked like tradition, but was produced with the most modern media technology.

In films like *Guests of the Nation* or *Man of Aran*, almost all of the important attempts to create a distinctive Irish cinema in the middle decades of the century showed an inability to conceive of Irish cinema other than as an image of the past. This situation only began to change in the final years of the 1950s, when Emmet Dalton and Louis Elliman (who had extensive cinema and theatre holdings throughout Ireland) formed Dublin Film and Television Productions Ltd. They then used the promise of a series of films based on popular Abbey Theatre plays to fund the building of what was effectively Ireland's first film studio, Ardmore Studios, in Bray, just outside Dublin. Even though it had to bring in most of its technical crew from England, Ardmore turned out a series of films based on recent Abbey plays, including *Professor Tim* (1957), *The Big Birthday, Home is the Hero* and *This Other Eden* (all 1959). Although based on Irish plays, these were not the classic repertoire of Synge and O'Casey, but plays of contemporary Irish life. On one hand, films such as *Home is the Hero* and *This Other Eden* were so intimately engaged with the cultural

[74] 'Hollywood: Land of Make-Believe', *Irish Monthly Magazine* (September, 1939), 640.
[75] Kevin Rockett, in *Cinema and Ireland*, by Kevin Rockett, Luke Gibbons and John Hill (Syracuse, NY, 1988), 71.
[76] Harvey O'Brien, *The Real Ireland: The Evolution of Ireland in Documentary Film* (Manchester, 2004), 45.

legacy of post-independence Ireland that they were unlikely to be of interest (or even fully understood) by audiences outside of Ireland; on the other hand, in cinematic terms, there was little to distinguish them from the comedies or dramas of the English studios of the time. Caught between these two poles, the Ardmore films turned out to be a lively dead-end in Irish film history.

Of course, this was not immediately apparent at the time. If anything, this sudden flowering of an Irish film industry seemed to be very much part of a larger transformation in Irish culture. *Sally's Irish Rogue*, the first Ardmore film to be released in the United States, was first screened at the Cork Film Festival on November 28, 1958, just seven months after Aer Lingus began its first regularly scheduled trans-Atlantic flights, and just a few weeks before a senior civil servant, T.K. Whitaker, published one of the key documents in twentieth-century Irish history. That report, entitled *Industrial Development*, was to underpin Irish economic policy for the next half century by emphasising the need for overseas trade and inward investment. While Whitaker's argument was made in economic terms, it had a cultural dimension as well, and it is no coincidence that the first Dublin Theatre Festival, for instance, took place in 1957, as the Industrial Development Act was being drafted. Up until that point, Ireland's relationship with a increasingly multi-national media had been adversarial. The official task had been to resist the many-headed hydra of 'internationalism' – whether through censorship, tariffs or through attempting to create the alternatives of an Irish radio service, an Irish film industry, or an Irish-language print industry. At the same time, the actual lives of many Irish people were already oriented outwards. For instance, a poll of Dublin listeners conducted on behalf of Radio Luxembourg in 1953 showed that only 27 per cent listened to Radio Éireann, the same percentage who listened to the BBC, and less than the 33 per cent who regularly tuned in to Radio Luxembourg.[77] With Irish people listening to Radio Luxembourg, watching American Westerns and reading the *News of the World*, it was not surprising, therefore, that when official policy began to change, it was not so much as if a set of floodgates had been opened; it was more like a recognition that they had actually been open for many years.

---

[77] Curran, 'What the Listener Wants II', 314.

Media Event 5:
Helpless before the camera's eye:
October 5, 1968

From one point of view, what happened on the streets of Derry on October 5, 1968, was not a big event. One of the organisers, Eamonn McCann, later claimed that the civil-rights march was, 'perhaps four hundred strong – and a hundred of those were students from Belfast. Most of the rest were teenagers from the Bogside and Creggan.'[1] The *Sunday Independent* put the number at 500, *The Times* said 600 to 800, the local *Derry Journal* estimated 1,000, while the *Cameron Report*, which later investigated the whole affair, put the figure at 2,000.[2] Given what was to ensue, it was never going to be easy to count heads. The group assembled at the Waterside railway station, on the east bank of the River Foyle, where the morning train had brought a deputation that included Northern Ireland Labour MP, Gerry Fitt, and three English Labour MPs, who joined local organisers and a cluster of reporters. The plan was to proceed down Duke Street to the Craigavon Bridge, and across to the Diamond, the main square inside the old city walls.

Just after 3:45 p.m., the procession left the railway station, singing 'We Shall Overcome'. Marchers in the front row carried a large blue banner emblazoned with the words 'Civil Rights March', while those behind carried placards: 'Police State Here'; 'The Proper Place for Politics is in the Street'; 'A Dhia Saor Éire'.[3] Avoiding police barricades that had been

---

[1] Eamonn McCann, *War and an Irish Town*, 2nd edn (London, 1993), 83.
[2] *Cameron Report – Disturbances in Northern Ireland* (Belfast, 1969), 4:45.
[3] Bob Purdie, *Politics in the Streets: The Origins of the Civil Rights Movement in Northern Ireland* (Belfast, 1990), 140.

set up in the smaller laneways of Distillery Brae and Simpson's Brae, the main body of the march cut directly into the main thoroughfare of Duke Street. The police from Distillery Brae quickly fell back to block off the bridge end of Duke Street, where two large tenders were parked across the road. At the same time, in a flanking motion, the RUC contingent from Simpson's Brae cut off the route back to the railway station, leaving the protestors trapped by 130 police in a 100-metre section of Duke Street. As the people at the back pushed to get away from the police line forming behind them, those at the bridge end found themselves being pushed forward into the main police line.

Among those being pushed forward was Labour MP Gerry Fitt. 'I did not see or hear any order being given', he later told reporters. 'Suddenly this young policeman hit me with a baton. As I sank to my knees he decided to make certain and hit me a second time.'[4] A girl in a mini-skirt, carrying the socialist Plough and Stars flag, was grabbed by a policeman, and hauled off, while from both ends of the streets the police began wielding their batons, pulling down the banner and tearing it into pieces. Within a few minutes the centre of the street was cleared. At about 4:00 p.m. there was then a strange lull, and civil-rights leader Betty Sinclair arrived and attempted to speak to the crowd, as did other organisers. 'We are met by police with batons in their hands', declared Michael Farrell of the Young Socialist Alliance. 'Is that democracy?' However, the RUC had earlier confiscated the public-address system, and the speeches had little effect. In growing confusion, the marchers trapped in Duke Street milled back and forth. A policeman's hat was knocked off.

Then, at some point around 4:45 p.m., the police waded in with their batons and little restraint. Labour MP John Ryan claimed to have seen 'one woman who he would say was over 60, who had her spectacles removed by a policeman and hit on the head by a baton'. Others claimed to have seen men being hit in the testicles. A rumour spread through the streets that a girl had been killed.[5] 'I saw a man completely defenceless being clubbed about the head by four policemen', claimed a letter-writer to the *Belfast Telegraph*. 'But worst of all I saw a gloating hatred in some of the faces of these policemen.'[6] As the marchers fled, some making it to the bridge, the police turned on the twin-hose water cannon, crumpling

[4] 'Derry's Black Sunday', *Irish News* (October 7, 1968).
[5] Niall O Dochartaigh, *From Civil Rights to Armalites: Derry and the Birth of the Irish Troubles*, 2nd edn (London, 2005), 19.
[6] 'Letters', *Belfast Telegraph* (October 8, 1968).

people in doorways, flattening them as they ran to the bridge and smashing out first-floor windows. 'For a quarter of an hour on Saturday afternoon,' wrote *Irish Times* reporter Fergus Pyle, who was standing just behind the police lines, 'police in a Derry street punched, batoned and pursued Civil Rights demonstrators in a brutal and sickening display of what can only be called concerted violence.'[7] By 5:00 p.m., all that was left in Duke Street was a litter of sodden placards.

The afterlife of the October 5 march, however, was only just beginning. There were three television camera-crews on the scene; the BBC was there, as was Ulster Television and RTÉ. UTV cameraman Kenneth Orbinson had been given a perch by the march organisers in a first-floor flat overlooking Duke Street, and had filmed the early part of the march, but when the water cannons were turned on, he was caught in the deluge, which put a halt to his filming. The BBC crew, who were behind police lines, filmed the early scuffles, and were ideally placed to catch protestors being dragged into police vans for arrest. However, closest to the action were cameraman Gay O'Brien and soundman Eamon Hayes of RTÉ, who managed to stay with the protestors near the front of the march without being hit or too badly soaked (see illustration 10).

When the water cannon was finally turned off, Orbinson dashed back to Belfast with his salvaged film, as did the BBC crew. Orbinson's footage of scuffles, arrests and water-cannon blasts made it to the Saturday evening news on UTV, and became the lead item on the ITV network throughout the UK. ITV repeated the film on Sunday, and Ulster Television put together a extended half-hour special for broadcast on Monday evening. The BBC film was also broadcast throughout the UK that weekend. Meanwhile, word spread that Gay O'Brien of RTÉ had even better film, capturing the chaos and the fury of the baton charge close up. By Monday, the BBC had acquired his film for broadcast. As those images appeared in people's homes all over Britain, the anomaly that was the lived experience of so many people in Northern Ireland suddenly acquired an image that could be seized by viewers in England, and beyond. 'This IS happening in Britain you know,' Geoffrey Gilbert, UTV's Controller of Programmes later told an interviewer. 'We are not a foreign country. Imagine the coverage if this sort of situation was happening in an area of similar population in England, like Kent.'[8]

---

[7] Fergus Pyle, 'An Old City Faces a New Sorrow', *Irish Times* (October 7, 1968), 1.
[8] Malcolm Stuart, 'Riot through the Eyes of the TV Men in No-Man's Land', *TV Times* (1968); reprint in Linenhall Library, P1126, n.p.

Illustration 10. 'Worst of all was the gloating hatred in some of the faces of these policemen.' Television footage of the civil-rights march in Derry on October 5, 1968, shot by RTÉ's Gay O'Brien, which brought the reality of police violence into homes outside of Ulster, is seen by many as a turning point in the Northern Ireland conflict.

From that point onwards, the traumatic event for all but the people on the march was not the experience of the march itself, nor even the experience of seeing it on television – the event was increasingly the perception that others had seen it.[9] 'Millions See Derry Riots on Television', proclaimed the headline in the *Belfast Newsletter* on Monday, October 7. 'Americans See the New Derry "Siege"', announced the nationalist *Irish News* that same day, while praising UTV's coverage as 'first-rate television journalism'. The next day, the *News* picked up the same theme,

---

[9] This is not to say that there was not extensive coverage of the events themselves. The *Irish Times* devoted several pages to Fergus Pyle's vivid eye-witness reports, and published almost a full page of photographs. The *Sunday Independent* printed a photo of police battling protestors under the headline: 'Derry: City of Batons, Blood and Bonfires'. In the UK, Mary Holland published an influential account in the *Guardian*, with a photo of the injured Gerry Fitt, while *The Times* tended to support a view that the police had been attacked.

under two linked headlines: 'The World Is Watching and Waiting' and 'World Focus on Undemocratic Behavior of Unionist Government'. 'The Cameras Cannot Lie', it editorialised. What is interesting here is the widespread perception that the footage seen across Ireland and Great Britain was also being watched in the United States. In fact, NBC and ABC did not pick up the story; only the CBS Evening News covered the story on October 7, but even then Walter Cronkite only gave it a twenty-second mention. The events in Derry did, however, get attention in the American print media. The story made the front page of the *Los Angeles Times* under the headline 'Police Employ Water Hose in N. Ireland Riot'. The *Chicago Tribune* covered the story under the headline 'Irish Rights Clash Injures Hundreds', and the *Washington Post* led with 'Violence Continues in Londonderry'. 'All in all, Northern Ireland is getting a very bad press in the United States', lamented the *Irish News*.[10] What was arguably more important than the actual American coverage, however, was the perception in Ireland that America was watching the same images as Irish television viewers.

At that point, the idea that the world had seen what had happened on October 5 had become an accepted truth in its own right, even if it was not, strictly speaking, true. A Cabinet meeting held in Stormont Castle on October 8, chaired by Northern Ireland Prime Minister Terence O'Neill, was extremely concerned that 'rightly or wrongly, the media of communication – whatever their political complexion – had been wholly adverse, and as a result Northern Ireland's standing and reputation had been most seriously damaged'.[11] In the House of Commons at Westminster, Labour MP Kevin McNamara requested a special debate on Northern Ireland, 'in view of the brutalities which we witnessed on television in Londonderry a week last Saturday'; he was ruled out of order, but the point was made.[12] Five months later, O'Neill appointed a Commission 'to hold an enquiry into and to report upon the course of events leading to, and the immediate causes and nature of the violence and civil disturbance in Northern Ireland on and since 5th October 1968'. When its findings were published in 1969, the *Cameron Report* concluded that 'one of the consequences of the break up of the demonstration in Duke Street was that press and

[10] 'Northern Ireland Making the News in the United States', *Irish News* (October 18, 1968).
[11] 'Disturbances in Londonderry', PRONI MIC/686/CAB/4/1405 (October 8, 1968), 4–5.
[12] *Parliamentary Debates (Hansard) House of Commons: Session 1967–8*. Fifth Series. Vol. 770 (London, 1968), 880:43.

television reports ensured that some very damaging pictures of police violence were seen throughout the United Kingdom and abroad."[13]

What happened in Duke Street on October 5, 1968, was not particularly out of keeping with the history of Northern Ireland to that point. What was different was that the antagonism that had been part of the fabric of life for many people in Northern Ireland was now visible, and acquired a new set of meanings under the gaze of an international audience who were perceived to be watching. And, of course, such perceptions have a way of becoming self-fulfilling. Prior to October 5, St Patrick's Day had been the last time in 1968 that Ireland had been mentioned in any context on the evening news broadcasts of any of the three big American networks. In the twelve months after October 5, Northern Ireland would be featured more than ninety times on the American news broadcasts;[14] in the UK, between them, Granada and Thames Television would produce no fewer than nine news specials on the Province in the same period. From that point, everything that happened in Northern Ireland was shaped, to some extent, by an awareness of being watched by an audience – particularly in the United States and England – sitting in silent judgement.

---

[13] *Cameron Report,* 4:55.
[14] Vanderbilt Television News Archive; http://tvnews.vanderbilt.edu. Accessed March 20, 2008.

CHAPTER 6

Windows on the world: 1961–1990

PICTURES IN THE SNOW

On New Year's Eve, 1961, Telefís Éireann went on the air for the first time; however, that was by no means the first time an Irish audience had seen a television. That moment had occurred on a Wednesday evening in February of 1927, when an audience in Dublin's Theatre Royal peered with fascination at a series of short films and magic-lantern slides of what the man presenting himself as the inventor of television,[1] John Logie Baird, described as 'Seeing by Wireless'. 'Mr. Baird's ingenuity has brought near the day when beside the loud speaker in every home will stand a frame in which figures will be seen performing', enthused the *Irish Times*.[2] However, when Baird offered to speak on Irish radio about the prospect of television, Seamus Clandillon, the Director of 2RN, dismissed the whole business as 'nonsense', and only under duress agreed to let Baird give a talk – after the station had finished broadcasting for the night. Understandably, Baird declined the offer.[3]

Although in hindsight Clandillon might have been overly hasty in writing off television in 1927, he had experience on his side; after all, he had spent the previous year trying to keep a radio station ticking over with only the most begrudging support from a government never fully convinced of its usefulness. In that context, the possibility of funding some harebrained wireless cinema must have seemed remote. And, in a sense, he was right. In comparison to radio, television would take a long time to make the transition from technological possibility to mass medium. Baird

---

[1] It is worth noting, however, that the basis of television – electronic scanning and the use of the cathode tube – were developed earlier in the century, and had roots in the 1880s. See Herbert Stephen, *A History of Early Television*, 3 vols. (London, 2004).

[2] 'Television', *Irish Times* (February 7, 1927), 4.

[3] Paddy Clark, '*Dublin Calling*': *2RN and the Birth of Irish Radio* (Dublin, 1986), 52.

THE OFFICIAL ORGAN OF THE WIRELESS SOCIETY OF IRELAND

The IRISH
Radio *and* **Musical**
Review
A Journal of Radio and Musical Progress

PRICE 3D MID MONTHLY

Vol. 2. [Annual Subscription 4/- Post Free] MID-OCTOBER, 1926 No. 1

Special Contents

THE DUBLIN
WIRELESS
EXHIBITION.

OUR CROSS-WORD
PUZZLE.

BROAD TUNING.

OUR DX LOG.

CHARGING FROM THE
MAINS.

A NEW
GRAMOPHONE.

MUSIC NOTES.

WIRELESS SOCIETY
NEWS.

The " *Knock-Out* " *Receiver*
(The Set that heard the Dempsey-Tunney Fight right through)

THE BAIRD "TELEVISOR."
Our photograph shows Mr. J. L. Baird, the Inventor of Television, explaining his receiving "Televisor" to a group of ladies, who are evidently much interested in his description. The person in front of the transmitting "Televisor" is seen in the round glass pointed out by Mr. Baird in the photograph.
(See inside.)

Illustration 11. In the mid-1920s, Ireland had a number of magazines dedicated to the new medium of radio. However, radio had barely become a reality when new media technologies beckoned. This 1926 edition of the *Irish Radio and Musical Review* reports on John Logie Baird's latest invention, the 'televisor'.

had first transmitted moving images in 1926; a year after his Dublin lecture, he would transmit the first colour images, and there were Baird 'televisors' on sale in Britain when the BBC began making experimental broadcasts in 1929. However, it would not be until 1936 that the BBC began its first regular broadcasts, and it would be 1939 before the first American television station went on the air – at which point World War II put an effective end to television broadcasts in Europe, and slowed development in the United States.

Consequently, television only really became a mass medium in the post-war years. In the United States, as Paul Starr notes, the institutional shape taken by the new medium showed a 'remarkable continuity in institutional structure with radio', where regulatory decisions and market forces had inexorably herded the original plethora of small radio stations into the network oligopoly of NBC, CBS and ABC.[4] In England, there were similar continuities with radio, and television developed under the auspices of the BBC, with its Reithian mission of entertaining and informing, and its regulatory monopoly more or less intact. As had happened with radio in the 1920s, television grew faster in the wide open markets of the United States, with the number of television sets rising from 178,000 in 1947 to over 20 million in 1952; in Britain, the number of television licences in the same period grew from 14,560 to just over a million, but would reach 5 million by 1956.[5]

In the run-up to what was arguably the biggest British television event of those early years – the Coronation of Elizabeth II in June of 1952 – television broadcasting arrived on the island of Ireland. In preparation for the big event, the BBC began broadcasting from Belfast in May of 1952, initially relaying programmes from London. However, on Tuesday, May 27, the first Irish-produced television programme, 'Pattern of Ulster', was broadcast. Introduced by the Northern Ireland Prime Minister, Lord Brookeborough, it hearkened back to the earliest cinema, showing 'the daily routine at various points in Northern Ireland … with cleaners leaving the City Hall and crowds walking along the footpaths to work'.[6]

From the very beginning, viewers in the border counties of the Republic were watching BBC Northern Ireland, Dubliners were picking up BBC broadcasts from the Holme Moss transmitter in the north of England, and viewers in Cork and Wexford could pick up the Glamorgan signal. 'A rush order of 125 television masts left Cardiff Airport for Dublin yesterday', reported the *Irish Times* on May 27, 1952. 'All of them, it is understood, are to be erected in time for the Coronation.'[7] By May of 1954, the same newspaper was publishing BBC television listings, and by 1955, when the Belfast transmitter was upgraded so that its signal carried further, it was estimated that there were 4,000 television sets in the Irish Republic, with 150 new sets being sold every week. 'It has been suddenly

---

[4] Paul Starr, *The Creation of the Media: Political Origins of Modern Communications* (New York, 2004), 384.

[5] Asa Briggs and Peter Burke, *A Social History of the Media: From Gutenberg to the Internet* (London, 2002), 234–5.

[6] 'North's First T.V. Show', *Irish Times* (May 22, 1952), 1.

[7] 'Rush Order for T.V. Masts', *Irish Times* (May 27, 1952), 9.

realised', commented the *Observer*, 'that here is a medium that can jump across frontiers and laugh at censorship.'[8]

At that point, the role of television in the society of Northern Ireland diverged from that of the Republic. With relatively little fuss, by 1952, Northern Ireland, already part of the territory of BBC radio, came within the ambit of what was arguably the world's leading public-service television broadcaster. Then, to make matters even more interesting, on October 31, 1959, Ulster Television (UTV) went on the air as part of the commercial ITV network, which had been brought into being by the Television Act (1954). In other words, while politicians in the Republic were still debating the viability of television in any form, in Northern Ireland there was already in existence a television culture in which commercial and public-service broadcasters worked in parallel.

The effect of this in Northern Ireland would pull in two opposite directions. On one hand, as the Coronation broadcast had shown, television was an ideal medium for giving people living in Northern Ireland the sense that they were part of a wider United Kingdom community. To watch the Coronation in Downpatrick was to participate in it as fully as a viewer in Manchester or Birmingham, in the knowledge that the same was not true in Galway, for instance. At the same time, as the Belfast studios of both the BBC and UTV began to produce more of their own programming, the sense of a regional Ulster identity – already fostered through print and radio – was given a new audio-visual form. Later, as news and current affairs reporting on television began to reach beyond the decorum that held sway on radio for so long, it would become a medium that would make visible the fissures and inequalities in Northern Irish society.

Meanwhile in the Irish Republic, there was a sense of déjà vu, for it was as if the battles that had been fought over radio in the 1920s were being restaged. The Minister for Finance for much of the period, Sean Lemass, worried about the cost of a state-subsidised service at a time of continuing high unemployment and mass emigration, and favoured granting licences to private broadcasters, along the lines of the big US networks (or, at the very least, along the lines of UTV). 'No Television in Republic until Financial Problem Is Eased', declared a headline in the *Irish Times* in 1955. At the same time, there were powerful lobby groups in favour of state-sponsored television, not least among Irish-language activists, and

---

[8] *Observer* (November 27, 1955); cited in Robert J. Savage, *Irish Television: The Political and Social Origins* (Cork, 1996), 40.

Catholics who took their guidance on the new medium from *Vigilanti Cura*, the Papal Encyclical which had advocated the need for an educational cinema. Both of these groups had proven themselves adept at influencing government policy; they were less sure of their ability to shape the policy of a commercial broadcaster. This debate ebbed and flowed through various governmental committees in the late 1950s. In the end, no one event changed the view of the government. Instead, there was a incremental spread of the perception that accompanies any new medium once it reaches a certain critical mass; that it is inevitable, and to be denied it is, in some way, to be denied a basic inalienable right. So, after a decade of impasse, the decision to fund an Irish television service was made at a Cabinet meeting on July 31, 1959, in which Sean Lemass, who was by then Taoiseach and had all along favoured a private commercial television station, found an accommodation with Cabinet colleagues who wanted a public-service broadcaster.[9] In the end, the mixed model that was adopted for Irish television was essentially a continuation of the one that had been in use since 1926 in relation to radio.

In the process of establishing a television service, the Lemass government drafted an Act that was to form the basis for all subsequent legislation in the area. The Broadcasting Authority Act (1960) created a body, the Radio Éireann Authority, to 'establish and maintain a national television and sound broadcasting service'. The Act gave the Authority control over transmission, the right to 'originate programmes and procure programmes from any source', to make links with other broadcasting authorities, and to collect television and radio licence fees, although it could also sell advertising, albeit within limits set by the government.[10] The Act also showed traces of earlier cultural debates, particularly in Article 17, which stated: 'In performing its functions, the Authority shall bear constantly in mind the national aims of restoring the Irish language and preserving and developing the national culture.' In some respects, the Act only consolidated what had effectively been the practice since 1953, when the Minister had created a council which more or less ran Radio Éireann with little interference. However, the overall effect of the 1960 Act was to give legal definition to the place of public-service broadcasting in Ireland, partly funded by the state but with a legislatively defined independence from the elected government of the day.

---

[9] Savage, *Irish Television*, 208; John Horgan, *Irish Media: A Critical History since 1922* (London, 2001), 82.
[10] Broadcasting Authority Act (1960): 10 Sect. 21.

Given that so much ink had been spilt in previous decades in debates over literary censorship, the 1960 Act marks a clear shift in the Irish media environment. Admittedly, Section 31 of the Act – which would become increasingly contentious in the 1970s and 1980s – did permit the Minster for Posts and Telegraphs to 'direct the Authority in writing to refrain from broadcasting any particular matter or matter of any particular class, and the Authority shall comply with the direction'; if they failed to comply, the Minister could dismiss them. However, as media historian John Horgan would later note, 'these were guns that could each be fired only once'.[11] Moreover, this power was offset by the onus on the Authority under Section 18 to 'secure that, when it broadcasts any information, news or feature which relates to matters of public controversy or is the subject of current public debate, the information, news or feature is presented objectively and impartially' – which was effectively a licence to broadcast views contrary to those of the government, the Catholic Church or any other lobby group; in short, it was a licence to question authority.

So, when Telefís Éireann finally went on the air officially on New Year's Eve, 1961, broadcasting live from the Gresham Hotel in Dublin's O'Connell Street, there was a sense that more than a television station was being launched. There was a giddy feeling of staging a transition to a new kind of modernity, in which Ireland would be connected as never before to the rest of the world. Lemass told Telefís Éireann's first viewers:

The Irish people are citizens of the world as well as of Ireland ... The reasonable needs of the Irish people ... would not be satisfied by programmes of local origins. Nowadays there is a general understanding that events in all parts of the world and new ideas and developments everywhere – including such things as sporting events and new trends in fashion – can be of direct and immediate interest to our own people.

He was followed by Edward Roth, the broadcaster's new Director General, who warmly welcomed the involvement of the BBC, NBC and the European Broadcasting Union for their practical help in setting up the station. The Chairman of the new Authority, Eamonn Andrews, jokingly dismissed fears that the dreams of Ireland as Cathleen ni Houlihan would be transformed into a nation transfixed by 'Cathode ni Houlihan'.

[11] Horgan, *Irish Media*, 84–5.

Illustration 12. 'I must admit that sometimes when I think of television and radio, and their immense power, I feel somewhat afraid.' President of Ireland, Eamon de Valera, on the opening broadcast of Telefís Éireann, December 31, 1961.

Then, later in the evening, the elderly Eamon de Valera peered myopically into the camera (illustration 12), and amid all the champagne and marching bands, introduced a sombre note of warning in words resonant with the tones of *Vigilanti Cura*:

I must admit that sometimes when I think of television and radio, and their immense power, I feel somewhat afraid. Like atomic energy it can be used for incalculable good, but it can also do irreparable harm. Never before was there in the hand of man an instrument so powerful to influence the thoughts and actions of the multitude. A persistent policy pursued over radio and television, in addition to imparting knowledge, can build up the character of a whole people, inducing sturdiness and vigour and confidence. On the other hand, it can lead, through demoralisation, to decadence and dissolution.

De Valera, in turn, was followed by John Cardinal d'Alton, Archbishop of Armagh and Primate of All Ireland, who warned parents not 'to allow their children to become addicts to TV ... no matter how meritorious the programme'.[12] In this moment we see in a split screen, as it were, showing two Irelands. In one, we might see a modernising, new Ireland relishing its porous boundaries; in the other, an older, conservative Ireland of fixed and knowable values, bounded and preserved within the island of Ireland. However, it might be more accurate to say that what was on display that night were two forms of Irish modernity, one established and one just coming into being; either way, it was clear that the medium through which these differences were being staged clearly belonged to the new.

The ethos of the modernising Ireland that would very quickly come to dominate the new station was shaped by a small but influential, cohort of Irish people, many of whom who had previously worked for the BBC. This group included the writer Denis Johnston (who was a pioneering television producer for the BBC in the late 1930s), and Maurice Gorham, who had been Director of Television in the BBC in 1946, and was later Director General of Radio Éireann during the term of the Inter-Party government of John A. Costello in the early 1950s. In his 1949 book, *Television: Medium of the Future*, Gorham conjured up a utopian vision of a world connected by television – admittedly, a vision whose 'international views' would no doubt have alarmed a previous generation of Irish politicians. 'When a viewer in Birmingham, Bruges or Boston can sit at home and see what is happening in the fields and factories, the theatres and marketplaces of countries that he has never visited, then television will at last be providing what it has so long promised – a window on the world.'[13]

In everything from the typography of its annual reports (from which the *fada* over the 'E' in 'Éireann' disappeared for a few years), to the architectural design of its new headquarters, the national broadcaster became iconic of the quickstep modernisation and impatience with the past that characterised so much of Irish society in the 1960s. Where the original radio studio had been located in the symbolically rich surroundings of the General Post Office, resonant of the 1916 Rising, the new radio and television centre, built on a greenfield site in Montrose in what was then the outskirts of Dublin, was a defiantly modernist compound of steel and glass. At the same time, the broadcaster's staff increased from a handful to more than 350 people by the end of 1962. Some were experienced veterans from other media. The Head of Current Affairs, for

---

[12] 'President Opens Irish TV Service', *Irish Times* (January 1, 1962), 3.
[13] Maurice Gorham, *Television: Medium of the Future* (London, 1949), 123.

instance, Jack White, had been a journalist and editor with the *Irish Times*. James Plunkett, a prominent trade unionist, also transferred from radio, where he had been working in the Drama and Variety Department, as had broadcaster Seán Mac Reamoinn, who had been working in radio since 1947. But others were fresh young faces, broadcasters such as Gay Byrne, John Bowman and Christopher Fitz-Simon; most were well-educated, young and often impatient with the old pieties. And as a team came together in those early years, there was an invigorating feeling of adventure. 'Newspapers ran features and photos with learned explanations of electronic mysteries. Enthusiasms were geared to prodigies. Prodigies gave free rein to enthusiasms, miracles and muddles. ... Gardeners became vision-mixers. A Coca-Cola bottlewasher became a sound operator. A motor car salesman became a cameraman. A ship's wireless operator became an electronic technician.'[14]

By the end of 1962, there were 221,874 licenced television sets in the Republic, which the Authority estimated were being watched by some 1,228,000 people, out of a population of 2,818,341 (all the more remarkable when we keep in mind that in 1961 reception was still only available in 39 per cent of the country). Half of these televisions, it was estimated, could receive not only Telefís Éireann, as the service was originally called,[15] but could also pick up the BBC and Ulster Television.

HAVE GUN, WILL TRAVEL

Even those viewers who could not convince their aerials to find the BBC or UTV, however, were not going to find themselves immersed in a fully Irish televisual world, and in this respect television as a medium would be very different from radio. Almost everything on radio was home-produced; the occasional special broadcast would be relayed from the BBC, or acquired from other European broadcasters; and, of course, much of the recorded music came from outside Ireland. However, the programmes almost all originated in the Radio Éireann studios, and the vast majority were broadcast live. With television, it was a different story, for two reasons. Television programmes were more expensive to produce than radio programmes, and the development of magnetic videotape

[14] Jack Dowling, Lelia Doolan and Bob Quinn, *Sit Down and Be Counted: The Cultural Evolution of a Television Station* (Dublin, 1969), 21.

[15] Telefís Éireann, sometimes abbreviated as TÉ, was the television service of Radio Éireann (RÉ); in March, 1966, the entire organisation was renamed Radio Telefís Éireann (RTÉ).

(first introduced by Ampex in the US in 1956) meant that it was no longer necessary to broadcast everything live, so that a recorded programme could be shown over and over again, around the world, making money every time it was transmitted.

Whereas the BBC showed relatively little American programming, throughout the 1960s the US networks accounted for roughly half of everything broadcast by Telefís Éireann, a ratio that would remain more or less constant over the coming decades. The reason for this was simple economics: according to one estimate from the time, the average cost of producing an hour of programming at the BBC was £2,500; Telefís Éireann was budgeting for £214 per hour; and the average cost of screening an American series was £20 per hour. There was no way that an Irish programme produced at one-tenth of the cost could compete with a British programme; however, an American programme, bought for 1 per cent of that cost, could. To put it simply, without American television, there would have been no Irish television.

The impact of this intimate immersion in American popular culture, in an Ireland already fond of Westerns and jazz dancing, was complex. On one hand, particularly for those viewers for whom the BBC was only the turn of a dial away, it emphasised the difference between not only Ireland and England, but between the Republic of Ireland and Northern Ireland. The Irish national broadcaster was more Americanised, so to be from the Republic was, in a sense, to be more Americanised, to be more a part of the world of *Dragnet* and *The Lucy Show* than of *Z Cars* and *Coronation Street*. At the same time, the Irish relationship to American television would always be marked by a time lag. For instance, in its first week of broadcasting, Telefís Éireann aired two series in that most American of genres, the Western: *The Restless Gun* and *Have Gun, Will Travel*, featuring Richard Boone as 'the most erudite sharp-shooter on TV'.[16] Westerns would continue to be popular, so much so that up until the late 1960s, there would be more television hours devoted to Westerns than to Irish sport on Telefís Éireann. At the same time, neither of the Westerns Irish viewers saw that first week was entirely new. *The Restless Gun*, for instance, had been cancelled by NBC in 1959, and while *Have Gun, Will Travel* was still playing on CBS in the United States, Irish viewers were shown episodes from a series several years old.

Consequently, American programmes introduced into Irish life a kind of belated modernity, putting Irish people within sight of a shiny new

---

[16] 'Listings', *RTV Guide* (January 6, 1962), 8.

world that was already slightly out of date. Telefís Éireann in its first year would broadcast Jackie Gleason's *The Honeymooners*, and the children's series *Rin Tin Tin*, both of which had finished runs on CBS and ABC, respectively, in 1957. The biggest single category of programming in that first year were American detective and adventure series, which took up more broadcast hours than news. Viewers saw *The Silent Service*, a short-lived US submarine drama from 1957, the detective series *Dragnet*, which had finished its run in 1959, and the first episodes of Rod Sterling's supernatural serial, *The Twilight Zone*, also from 1959. Over time, as Irish television worked through the American networks' back catalogue, the time-lag narrowed but never quite closed. By 1966, for instance, RTÉ was showing season three of the ninety-minute Western series, *The Virginian*, as well as the spy spoof *Get Smart*, and ABC's *The Long Hot Summer*, both of which had premièred the previous season on the American networks – and all of which were consistently among RTÉ's most highly rated programmes during their runs.

As Irish families sat down night after night to gunslingers and detectives, and as substantial numbers continued to watch BBC and UTV, their expectations of television drama were shaped somewhere between *Bonanza* and *Dixon of Dock Green*. For Irish producers, on the other hand, the challenge was to find forms for the new medium that were, in some respects, distinctively Irish. Initially, Irish television hired theatre people – Hilton Edwards, Carolyn Swift and Shelagh Richards – in the hope that Ireland's strong theatrical legacy could be transferred to the new medium. For a time, this meant that Irish television drama became synonymous with studio-bound versions of stage plays, often with a minimal or stylised set. In this regard, the very first home-produced drama broadcast by the station, a 1962 production of J.M. Synge's *Well of the Saints*,[17] was a sign of what was to come. The timing of this broadcast is also significant; it went on the air at 9:30 on a Sunday evening, just after the Sunday play, a fixture on Irish radio. 'On Sunday night at 8 o'clock', recalled one avid theatre-goer from the period, 'everything stopped and everybody listened to the play.'[18] It thus made a certain amount of sense that television would follow radio in catering to this theatre audience, and the list of plays produced for television in the 1960s was impressive, including work by Samuel Beckett, Brian Friel,

---

[17] J. M. Synge, *Well of the Saints*, tx. TÉ (January 7, 1962).
[18] John Devitt, in conversation with Nicholas Grene and Chris Morash, *Shifting Scenes: Irish Theatre Going 1955–1985* (Dublin, 2008), 9.

Denis Johnston and Eugene McCabe. By the end of RTÉ's first decade, roughly half of the 136 plays produced for Irish television had originated on the stage, 81 of which were by living Irish writers.

At the same time, by the mid-1960s RTÉ recognised that it needed to develop Irish television dramas that looked more like the English and American programmes that its viewers liked so much. So, for instance, from 1964 until 1968, one of the most highly rated programmes on Irish television was *Tolka Row*. Initially based on a stage play of the same name by Maura Laverty, with its inter-connected cast of working-class characters living in Dublin, it bore more than a passing resemblance to Granada Television's *Coronation Street*, which had premièred in 1960. In some respects, the most distinctive Irish television drama of the 1960s was its rural serial, *The Riordans*, which consistently topped the weekly ratings throughout its long run from 1965 to 1979. In a decade in which much of the population of Dublin had been born in rural Ireland, *The Riordans* created a virtual rural Irish community, the fictional Leestown. RTÉ did everything possible to make Leestown real: it published maps of the town in its weekly *RTÉ Guide*, created a fictional local newspaper and reported on the lives of characters such as Benjy Riordan as if they were real people. Perhaps most importantly, however, the series was filmed on location, using a real church, a real pub and a real farm. Although the original reasons for doing so were primarily economic, this was an innovation that attracted the attention of television producers from other countries (something of which RTÉ would become extremely proud). '*The Riordans*,' argued two RTÉ producers who would later be critical of the station's first decade, Lelia Doolan and Jack Dowling, 'with all its faults, its didacticisms, its essentially up-lifting and optimistic tone, the lack of development in the characters, is more truly dramatic in television terms than *The Playboy of the Western World*. ... It is fictionalised reality.'[19]

AN ARGUMENT EVERY NIGHT

'One of the most heartening and encouraging aspects of Telefís,' noted the *Daily Mail*'s television critic, Ken Gray, early in 1962, 'has been its willingness at least to tip-toe in where for long Radio Éireann has feared to tread.'[20] While it may have taken a few years before a drama series such as *The Riordans* found its idiom, factual genres established themselves

[19] Dowling, Doolan and Quinn, *Sit Down and Be Counted*, 282.
[20] Ken Gray, 'Candid Look at T. E.'s Performance', *RTV Guide* 1:14 (March 2, 1962), 4.

more quickly, partly because they were cheaper to produce, but also because the appeal of imported news was limited. 'We like to have an argument every night, a conflict, where people can be brought into opposition in their viewpoints', claimed P.P. O'Reilly, the presenter of *Broadsheet*, an early nightly news broadcast.[21] Whereas the prepared talk, not the debate, had been the default format in Irish radio, it was clear that a government minister talking to a camera was not going to hold viewers' attention – particularly if *Bonanza* was blazing away on UTV. Current affairs thus became firmly part of the mission of Irish television, through programmes such as *Division, The Hurler on the Ditch* and *Seven Days*. Gently at first, and with increasing vigour by the end of the decade, the producers of many of these shows saw their role as provoking debate, and challenging established views. Indeed, one of leading current-affairs producers in RTÉ in those years, Jack Dowling, once claimed that a good current-affairs television programme was one that annoyed 90 per cent of the Irish people.[22]

If the argumentative tone of news and current affairs were the most visible signs of a different kind of public sphere emerging in Ireland in the 1960s, the fact that controversy could spring up in more unlikely television genres is perhaps indicative that this was part of a much wider change taking place in Irish society of the time. For instance, where the Irish media had never been less than deferential to the Catholic Church since the foundation of the state, the RÉ Authority made it clear from the outset that while they would provide a level of religious programming commensurate with their public-service remit, they did not intend to become an unofficial outlet of Vatican radio. The first sign of this muscle-flexing came when they chose not to appoint as the station's religious advisor a young priest named Fr. Joe Dunn, who was the nominee of the powerful Archbishop of Dublin, John Charles McQuaid. A furious McQuaid responded by funding Dunn to make his own programmes, thus effectively establishing Ireland's first independent television production company, Radharc. However, this did not have quite the effect that the conservative McQuaid might have intended, for while some Radharc documentaries dealt with pilgrimages and religious vocations, others opened up social issues in ways that had not been seen before on Irish television, in films such as 'Down and Out in Dublin'

[21] 'Broadsheet', *RTV Guide* 1:11 (February 9, 1962), 22.
[22] John Horgan, *Broadcasting and Public Life: RTÉ News and Current Affairs 1926–1997* (Dublin, 2004), 47.

(1964), 'Smuggling and Smugglers' (1965) and 'Open Port' (1968), which dealt with prostitution in Cork. In later decades – Radharc would continue to make films until 1997 – crews went to countries such as Chile and El Salvador to make films dealing with development and human-rights issues, thus creating a new kind of oppositional voice for the Catholic Church in Irish public life.

It was not always the more overtly serious genres that were most controversial, however. In July of 1962, a late-night talk show modelled on NBC's *Tonight Show* went on the air: *The Late Late Show*. Initially, attention focused on the novelty of a television programme with a live studio audience that continued running after the unearthly hour of 11:00 p.m. 'Had the invisible clappers and laughers no homes to go to?' marvelled one television critic.[23] However, it quickly became apparent that its host, a young broadcaster named Gay Byrne who had experience of British television, had a finely honed, almost instinctive sense of the potential of live television. Television's power, Hilton Edwards observed later that same year, 'is that of catching people, as it were, on the wrong foot, letting us glimpse how they are, not how they wish us to believe them; the Minister of State in an unguarded moment, or, even if on guard, defenceless before the camera's eye'.[24] Always the professional's professional, Byrne was in many ways the perfect embodiment of the period. While there were others in RTÉ at the time who had strongly held ideological beliefs, Byrne seldom appeared to have an axe to grind; instead, he had the ability to let his guests speak, 'defenceless before the camera's eye'. In the end, it was not Byrne who shocked Irish people; it was Irish people who shocked themselves.

One Saturday evening, on February 12, 1966, Byrne was playing a game with some audience members, where, among other things, he asked a husband to name the colour of his wife's nightgown on their wedding night. The husband guessed that it had been transparent; the wife then responded that she had not worn anything at all, provoking protests from, among others, the Bishop of Clonfert. 'The country is going to hell', editorialised the *Irish Times*, tongue firmly in cheek, 'but the bishops are on to it.'[25] A few weeks later, a guest on the programme referred to the Bishop of Galway as a 'moron'; when an audience member protested that

[23] G. A. Olden, 'Time Out of Joint', *Irish Times* (July 12, 1962), 8.
[24] Hilton Edwards, 'The Problems and Possibilities of Television Drama', *RTV Guide* (January 26, 1962), 4.
[25] 'The Bishop and the Nightie', *Irish Times* (February 14, 1966), 10.

Byrne should not be bringing on speakers 'to slag the clergy,' Byrne replied that he had done no such thing, as he could not control what someone in the audience might say. And so the row spilled over into newspapers, and beyond the media into ordinary conversation. 'In Enniscorthy when I was a lad,' recalled the writer Colm Tóibín, 'nobody ever turned the *Late Late Show* off. The show was too unpredictable: you just never knew what you might miss.'[26]

INTO ORBIT

Somewhere between that first broadcast in the snow on New Year's Eve, 1961, and the Bishop of Galway being called a moron in February 1966, a tectonic plate shifted in the Irish public sphere. Later, in October of 1966, a heated debate erupted about the national broadcaster's freedom from government intervention, when the Minister for Agriculture, Charles Haughey, told RTÉ to remove from the nightly news broadcast a statement by the National Farmers' Association at which Haughey had taken umbrage. In its editorial comment, the *Irish Times* was unambiguous: 'Direct intervention by a Minister when other means of rectification are open to him is to be deprecated.'[27] Like the spats with the Hierarchy earlier in the year, there was a clear public consensus that the right to information was superior to the authority of office – whether of church or of state. Indeed, there was a tacit legal recognition given to this principle the following year, when the Censorship of Publications Act was reformed, automatically removing the restrictions imposed on any publication banned after twelve years.[28] At a stroke, dozens of books that had never been seen openly on Irish bookshelves suddenly materialised, and a piece of legislation that had defined Irish culture since the 1920s was defanged.

If there is a single quality that characterises Irish media culture in this period, it is expansion, along more than one axis. As taboos were lifted, the understanding as to what constituted the job of the journalist changed, and newspapers such as the *Irish Times* and *Irish Independent* began to devote more space to investigative articles. Media historian John Horgan has argued, for instance, that new ground was broken by the

---

[26] Colm Tóibín, *The Trial of the Generals: Selected Journalism 1980–1990* (Dublin, 1990), 87.
[27] 'Reviewing the News', *Irish Times* (October 3, 1966), 7.
[28] Censorship of Publications Act, 1967 (No. 15/1967).

lengthy pieces – some of which ran over a number of issues – by journalist Michael Viney in the *Irish Times*, on issues such as divorce, children born out of wedlock and adoption.[29] Physically, as well, daily newspapers had grown, with the morning papers averaging between thirty and forty pages (and the Sunday papers longer again), giving more room for comment and for longer investigative articles.

In other ways too, the perceptual world of Ireland expanded in the 1960s. In 1962, the same year that Telefís Éireann went on the air, Radio Éireann carried the voice of astronaut John Glenn, beamed live from the *Mercury 6* spacecraft in orbit above the Earth. 'It was, perhaps, sound radio's greatest day,' proclaimed Station Manager Denis Meehan.[30] The Telstar satellite was launched later that year, eventually making it possible to relay live television signals across the Atlantic. In 1966, RTÉ broadcast its first overseas sporting event live, when Irish viewers watched games from the Football World Cup from London. By 1967, the Irish evening news regularly carried film from around Europe, relayed via the Eurovision network, and in 1968 RTÉ used the Early Bird satellite to show live daily coverage of the Olympic Games in Mexico City. The following year, there were experimental Irish transmissions of colour television, and Irish viewers watched their first colour satellite broadcast in June of 1971, when a football match was beamed live from Mexico City. In that same year, RTÉ made its own first colour broadcast, of a hurling match. Meanwhile the number of televisions in Ireland continued to increase steadily, from the Television Commission's estimate of 20,000 in 1958, to 150,000 licensed sets by March of 1963, climbing steadily to 433,000 in 1971 – and that was only those with licences. In 1971, colour televisions accounted for only one in thirty of the licensed sets in the country; by 1974, that would more than double to one in twelve. Radios also became more ubiquitous, particularly in cars, and hence their numbers are more difficult to estimate with accuracy. However, assuming everyone who purchased a combined radio and television licence had both, radio ownership in the Republic was at least 500,000, but in reality probably far higher.

Admittedly, there were still some gaps in this rush to the future. As late as 1971, RTÉ television coverage still only extended to 88 per cent of urban areas, and 62 per cent of rural areas, although some of those would have been reached by the Northern Ireland broadcasts of BBC or UTV. Still,

---

[29] John Horgan, *Irish Media*, 93.
[30] Denis Meehan, 'This Was Radio's Greatest Day', *RTV Guide* 1:14 (March 2, 1962), 4.

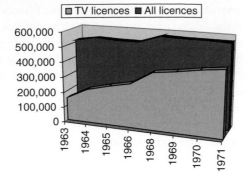

Fig 4. Television and radio licences in the Irish Republic, 1963–71.

by the early 1970s, the envelope of the electronic media was steadily extending over all of Ireland; by 1979, it was estimated that 90 per cent of all Irish homes had television.

As the flow of information increased in the late 1960s and early 1970s, a number of things happened, more or less simultaneously. Irish men and women increasingly lived in a world with multiple viewpoints: watching and listening to the BBC, UTV and RTÉ with its richly disjunctive mix of home-produced debate and American drama; reading the *Irish Times,* reading the *Daily Mail;* listening to the Rolling Stones, and listening to Tommy Makem. In the midst of such a multiplicity of media, the authority of any single piece of information was open to question in a way that had not been true in preceding decades. It is entirely possible that if the Irish economy had continued to grow in the 1970s at a rate that was in some way commensurate with the expansion of the media, the mediated world would have mapped more closely on to the world of lived experience. But it did not. By the early 1970s the Irish economy had become increasingly integrated into world markets, and when those markets began to falter, aggravated by a crisis in world oil prices, the fragile Irish economy went into a tailspin; economic growth slowed, unemployment rose, and as the conflict in Northern Ireland deepened, a patina of unending crisis descended. With it came a sense of dislocation. In the early 1960s, RTÉ television had seemed the perfect embodiment of the shiny new modern Ireland. 'The energy, enthusiasm, and genuine team spirit generated by the pressure to have "our own" television service carried right through until about 1965', one early producer later recalled. 'Then came the inevitable solidifying of the planet.'[31]

The first real rumblings of dissent from within the organisation came in when a producer named Bob Quinn tendered his resignation. For Quinn, those aspects of Irish culture that for many liberal commentators represented a stultifying conservative traditionalism – particularly the Irish language – were, in fact, its most radical elements, providing the perspective from which a global media culture could be, if not resisted, at least understood critically. So, protesting, among other things, at 'the Americanism of the service's output, both sound and television', Quinn abruptly quit in May of 1969, followed shortly after by two senior producers, Lelia Doolan and Jack Dowling. Quinn moved to the West of Ireland where he began making films in the Irish language, most notably *Poitín* (1978). Indeed, in the decade that followed, when Irish feature-film production became practically non-existent, Quinn, a self-styled maverick, would become one of the very few film-makers active in the country.

With the expansion of television, it was not simply the case that Irish culture was more porous, more open to what was now a global media culture than at any time in its history. Many of the images, the sounds, the words that poured in during the late 1960s and early 1970s were of dissent: students barricading the streets of Paris, anti-Vietnam War protestors on the streets of Washington, civil-rights marches in Alabama, and behind it all, music that created a soundtrack for dissent. Moreover, these events, however geographically distant, had a context after 1968, as the civil-rights movement in Northern Ireland gave way to rioting, and the arrival of British troops on the streets of the province by August 1969. The following year, the Provisional IRA came into being, and the first British soldier was killed in 1971. Then, on January 30, 1972, the British Army killed thirteen civilians in a civil-rights march in Derry, in what became known as Bloody Sunday. At that point, a complex, intimate and increasingly vicious civil war took shape, with a plethora of Unionist paramilitary groups, the Royal Irish Constabulary, the British Army, the IRA (Official and Provisional, followed by a later Republican splinter group, the INLA), and the Irish Army and police all locked in what seemed by the mid-1970s to be an intractable struggle. Ireland, neutral in World War II, had been absent from the world's media for decades; suddenly, it was back in the news. Indeed, at times it sometimes seemed

---

[31] Bunny Carr, 'A Long, Tedious Pregnancy', *Irish Times* (November 2, 1978), 16.

that there was too much news from Northern Ireland. As Brum Henderson, the long-serving Director of Ulster Television noted in an article in the *TV Times* in 1969: 'Above all we want to prevent the Saturday afternoon Ulster riot from becoming a replacement for *World of Sport.*'[32]

Consequently, in spite of the unprecedented expansion of the Irish media in the period, there was often a sense that the mainstream media was not quite adequate to the task at hand, and there was a search for alternatives. For instance, writing in the Belfast-based magazine, *Fortnight*, Ian Hill noticed in November of 1970 that with 'the coming of the photo and-or offset litho printing machine', it was possible for just about anyone to begin printing their own periodical. 'The counter of my newsagent is almost awash with political news sheets of many persuasions', wrote Hill, leafing through the Cork-based *Communist Comment*, the Belfast-based *Northern Radical*, the Republican *Voice of the North*, and the Rev. Ian Paisley's *Protestant Telegraph*, which would go on to become a fully fledged weekly with a reasonable circulation.[33]

Similarly, when the Dublin Corporation (like many municipal governments of the time) moved residents from inner city slums to tower blocks on the outskirts of the city in the late 1960s, 'it concentrated and compounded all the possible problems of working-class life and of housing estate life in Dublin.'[34] A group of unemployed residents in the new community of Ballymun responded by creating *Ballymun News*, which provided an alternative view of the area, frequently satirising the municipal government through mock interviews with imaginary bureaucrats such as Percy Horation Stuffem, the Corporation's Peasant Control Officer, or Aloysius Socrates Slapem, the area's Director of Education. As Ian Hill had observed in relation to Northern Ireland: 'By litho, out of crisis, came the pamphlet.'

Indeed, Northern Ireland had not been short of newspapers before the advent of the new do-it-yourself technology. The politically driven proliferation of local newspapers that had taken place throughout the island in the late nineteenth and early twentieth centuries had settled down somewhat in the Irish Free State after 1922, and even the animosities of the Civil War usually managed to find some point of reconciliation in the local press, although there were exceptions. In Northern Ireland, on

[32] Malcolm Stuart, 'Riot through the Eyes of the TV Men in No-Man's Land', *TV Times* (1968); reprint in Linenhall Library, P1126.
[33] Ian J. Hill, 'Pamphlets Galore', *Fortnight* (November 20, 1970), 13.
[34] Brian Trench, 'Ballymun: Inside Looking Out', *Hibernia* (September 13, 1974), 10.

the other hand, a politically divided print culture persisted, so that by the 1970s most communities had at least two local newspapers, one nationalist, and one unionist, 'an uneasy and unharmonic duet'[35] as one commentator put it. As a result, in 1970 there were no fewer than forty-five newspapers outside of Belfast, or roughly one newspaper per every 20,000 of the population (compared to one for every 35,000 people in the rest of the British Isles). In Belfast, the venerable *Belfast Telegraph* was read by sections of both communities; however, the Unionist *Belfast Newsletter* had circulation figures of 70,000 in 1970 among a readership that was 87 per cent Protestant, while the *Irish News* sold about 50,000 to a readership that was 93 per cent Catholic.[36] 'Anyone who consistently reads and compares the two main morning newspapers published in Belfast learns something of their special contribution to the siege-mentality problem of the Province,' argued another contributor to *Fortnight* in 1971. 'It must surely accelerate the polarisation it mirrors.'[37] Indeed, *Fortnight* itself, launched in October of 1970, was intended to provide a bridge between the communities, its innocuous name (it is published fortnightly) chosen in an attempt to find a word that could not possibly suggest any political affiliation whatsoever.

This is not to suggest, however, that the mainstream newspapers were losing readers in the Republic: quite the contrary. While Dublin's *Evening Herald* dropped from 140,000 readers in 1970 to 117,000 in 1978, other daily newspapers increased their circulation. The *Evening Press* went from 146,000 to 161,000 in the same period; the *Irish Independent* from 168,000 to 174,000, the *Cork Examiner* from 59,000 to 66,000, and the *Irish Times* developed its small, but influential base, from 56,000 in 1970 to 66,000 in 1978, for a 12 per cent share of the market. At the same time, 61 per cent of the population read a provincial paper along with the national dailies, and 49 per cent of the population read two provincial papers per week. In 1973, a new Sunday paper entered the market, the *Sunday World*, modelled to some extent on the English tabloids (its marketing slogan was 'We Go All the Way'); it joined the *Sunday Independent* and the *Sunday Press*. All told, 88 per cent of the adult population in Ireland read a Sunday newspaper.[38]

[35] Ian J. Hill, 'Profile: The Local Press', *Fortnight* (October 23, 1970), 9.
[36] Richard Rose, *Governing without Consensus: An Irish Perspective* (London, 1971), 353–5.
[37] Gay Firth, 'Polar Press', *Fortnight* (May 14, 1971), 15.
[38] Irish Marketing Surveys, *Joint National Media Research* (Dublin, 1980).

HIGH TIMES

While most of the small newspapers and magazines that rolled out of the litho machines in the early 1970s were aligned to political groups or local communities, the short-lived *High Times* was only interested in rock and roll. For the readers of *High Times*, RTÉ radio, which broadcast only a few hours of pop music every day, existed in another, not very interesting, world. Of course, tuning in to John Peel on the BBC was one option; but equally important were the offshore pirate radio stations, particularly Radio Caroline. Founded by Irishman Ronan O'Rahilly, Caroline began broadcasting from a ship in the North Sea in 1964, and, along with Radio Luxembourg, for a whole generation of Irish radio listeners it opened up a world of the Rolling Stones, Pink Floyd and Led Zeppelin. At the same time, where in the 1950s recorded music was still sold largely in music stores along with pianos and violin strings, by the 1970s it was being sold in record shops, and there was vastly more available, increasingly on new formats such as the 8-track and, later, cassette tapes.

When radio had first appeared in the 1920s, there had been predictions that it would lead to a new internationalism, with the *Irish Radio Journal* speculating in 1925 that broadcasts in the international language, Esperanto, would bring the world 'a step nearer that state of existence that people have been seeking since the confusion of tongues'.[39] It would not be Esperanto, however, that would become the international language of the airwaves: it would be rock and pop music. Listening to Radio Caroline broadcasting from a ship moored in international waters in the North Sea was not simply a means of hearing music that the national broadcaster was not playing; it was connecting to an extraterritorial community, one whose very existence was a repudiation of a national identity fostered by a national broadcaster.

In this extraterritorial community, there was space to be an Irish musician in a way that laid claim to multiple heritages, not all (or indeed, any) of them recognisably Irish. Blues guitarist Rory Gallagher, for instance, may have grown up in Cork; but he played and sang as if he had spent his formative years on Muddy Waters' front porch in Mississippi. With his plaid shirt and battered Stratocaster, he was, in many respects, the embodiment of a certain kind of musical authenticity, but not an authenticity that owed anything to existing definitions of Irish tradition. The same was true of Thin Lizzy, a band with members from

[39] 'International Radio Language', *Irish Radio Journal* 2:3 (January 1, 1925), 635.

Dublin and Belfast, fronted by the charismatic Phil Lynott, who grew up in a working-class estate in Crumlin, on Dublin's south side, listening, by his own account, to 'The Yardbirds, The Who, The Animals', and watching Westerns at the local cinemas. And, again, other than their surprise hit 'Whiskey in the Jar', their music was squarely in the mainstream of rock, a common language from Detroit to Dresden. 'If the harsh violent sounds of hard rock were a culture shock to the Irish,' Fintan O'Toole later wrote, 'Thin Lizzy narrowed the gap and nationalised the music.'[40] Further along the spectrum, bands such as Planxty and Moving Hearts were combining the instrumentation of rock music with the forms and instruments of Irish traditional music. Indeed, in their mix of bass, drums, guitar and uilleann pipes, Moving Hearts carried out a furious act of translation. All were embraced as Irish, part of a new mediated community linked by the Esperanto of the air that, like a more powerful radio signal, simply drowned out older definitions of Irish culture whose energies had been focused on reviving an imagined past and defending its boundaries.

'Because we were so interested in Radio Caroline, we had to have our own station', recalled one of the founders of Radio Melinda, who found themselves in court in February 1973 for running a radio station from a cellar in Dublin's north inner city. In their defence, they claimed that they were playing pop music, and thus not competing with RTÉ. The £2 fines received by the operators of Radio Melinda were no deterrent, and over the following decade a succession of small pirate-radio stations burst on to the air and faded like so many fireworks. Concentrated in, but by no means confined to Dublin, in the early 1970s most were sending out signals from small transmitters in back bedrooms. From the smallest to the largest, however, none had licences, for the simple reason that there was no way to apply for a licence. Undeterred by its illegality, however, in 1978 Radio Dublin – run from a house in Inchicore – claimed to have 30 per cent of the radio audience in the Dublin area, 80 per cent of whom were aged 16 to 30, and 'were not interested in discussions, news or current affairs'. When the station was temporarily closed by a police raid later that year, an appeal from a hastily rigged transmitter brought 10,000 people on to Dublin's O'Connell Street in protest.[41]

[40] Fintan O'Toole, 'Don't Believe a Word: The Life and Death of Phil Lynott', *Magill* 9:5 (January, 1986), 40.
[41] 'The Pirates Rule the Airwaves: But for How Long?' *Magill* 1:8 (May, 1978), 10. See also Peter Mulryan, *Radio Radio: The Story of Independent, Local, Community and Pirate Radio in Ireland* (Dublin, 1988).

With this kind of listenership for a station that did not even legally exist, RTÉ was naturally concerned. The broadcaster had had a foretaste of what taking on the pirate stations might mean when on March 28, 1970, one group of Irish-language activists, unhappy with the amount of Irish-language broadcasting provided by RTÉ, set up their own pirate radio station, Saor-Raidió Chonamara (Radio Free Connemara). It was duly raided, and put off the air. However, given that Saor-Raidió Chonamara's aims were only those that had been patriotically proclaimed by successive Irish governments ever since Douglas Hyde first took to the airwaves in 1926, the state had little room for prevarication. Work began on a new studio in Casla, County Galway, and the state-sponsored Raidió na Gaeltachta was able to make its first broadcast on April 2, 1972.

Ultimately, the Saor-Raidió Chonamara episode would help set the agenda for the response to pirates more interested in Bowie than the bhodhrán. As pirate stations roamed with impunity over the airwaves, pillaging listeners from RTÉ, it became clear to the broadcaster that it needed its own pop and rock music station. 'There seems to be no argument about the existence of the market for popular music programmes', noted the *Irish Times*' radio critic, Mary Leland, when RTE's Radio 2 began broadcasting on May 31, 1979. 'There is no doubt either that RTE's hand has been pushed in this matter.'[42] Indeed, the *Irish Independent* greeted the arrival of the new station with a banner headline: 'Pirates to Walk the Plank'[43] – prematurely, as it turned out, for in 1979 there were twenty-five pirate stations operating in Dublin alone. 'The Minister may well be bolting the gate after the horse has fled when he introduces legislation to control broadcasting', commented the news magazine *Hibernia* in 1978. 'Pirate stations have proven in most cases that they have the support of large sections of the population. The battle of the airwaves which has been raging for only one year now, seems to have swung in favour of the pirates, and the belated Montrose reaction has a lot of ground to cover.'[44] Eager to make up that ground, Radio 2 showed its intention to go head-to-head with its outlaw rivals, even going so far as to poach one of pirate radio's cult DJs, Dave Fanning, on whose late-night pirate-radio show, as John Waters later recalled, 'you might as easily tune into four hours of Tom Waits as an all-Irish rock night'.[45]

---

[42] Mary Leland, 'The New Radio Channel', *Irish Times* (May 30, 1979), 12.
[43] Jim Farrelly, 'Pirates to Walk the Plank', *Irish Independent* 87:259 (November 2, 1978), 1.
[44] Darach MacDonald, 'Pirate Radios Get Set for Showdown', *Hibernia* (September 7, 1978), 9.
[45] John Waters, *Race of Angels: Ireland and the Genesis of U2* (Belfast, 1994), 101.

Meanwhile, even as Radio 2 was establishing itself, pirate radio was in the process of growing well beyond its enthusiastic amateur roots. In 1980, Chris Carey and Robbie Robertson, both of whom had been associated with Radio Caroline in the 1960s, arrived in Dublin to start the first of the 'super-pirates', Sunshine Radio. They soon parted ways, and Robertson continued with Sunshine, while Carey started Radio Nova, both of which effectively operated as professional radio stations, with advertising departments and full-time employees who made income-tax returns.

THE LANDSCAPE OF FACT

The introduction of Radio 2 was part of a larger expansion plan within RTÉ, that included the introduction of a new television station, RTÉ2, which went on the air on November 2, 1978 – 'the most important development since the arrival of television itself', according to the hyperbolic assessment of RTÉ's Director General, Vincent Finn.[46] In fact, if the celebrations that had greeted the launch of Telefís Éireann twenty-seven years earlier had been emblematic of an optimistic embrace of modernity and generational change that was in many ways characteristic of Irish society in the early 1960s, the more muted reception that met the launch of RTÉ2 was equally of its time. On the day the new station opened, Ken Gray, writing in the *Irish Times* noted: 'There may be exciting times ahead. On the other hand, there may be, once the first novelty has worn thin, merely twice as much boredom.' He went on, however, to suggest that in the battle for viewers a new channel would further raise the temperature in the already heated cultural wars. This prediction seemed like it would be borne out, as Vincent Finn announced plans to broadcast the BBC series, *Caligula*, with its orgy scenes, and Dennis Potter's *Pennies from Heaven*, in which 'Dublin-born actress Gemma Craven appears naked to the waist' – a sight, Gray predicted, certain to shock 'the Irish Mrs. Grundies'.[47]

In some respects, the comparative lack of fanfare with which RTÉ2 simply appeared demonstrated once again the nagging sense that the media provided by the state could not cope with the new forms of Irish culture. In the year before RTÉ2 was launched, statistics showed that 50 per cent of the Irish population were under 26, and 41 per cent were under 19. In that same year, Niall Stokes launched a new magazine, *Hot Press*. 'Not the most healthy climate in which to launch a newspaper?' he asked in his first issue:

---

[46] Vincent Finn, 'RTE 2', *Irish Times* (November 2, 1978), 16.
[47] Ken Gray, 'A New Freedom of Choice', *Irish Times* (November 2, 1978), 16.

And yet there *is* hope of sorts. … in this last week before a general election dominated by the same boring old faces that have been popping up on posters since any of us can remember – because this is the general election where Rock n' Roll fans move towards a majority … a mighty 400,000 of them have never voted – that's enough to obliterate the old order, if it only had something decent to vote for.[48]

In that same year, journalist Vincent Browne started a monthly news magazine, *Magill,* which published vigorous investigative writing by journalists such as Bruce Arnold, Gene Kerrigan and Mary Holland. *Magill* in turn picked up from *Hibernia,* a robustly critical fortnightly news and arts magazine that had flourished in the 1970s, and which in some respects set the agenda for the magazines that would follow it in the 1980s. The editors of *Hibernia* had a particularly intense fascination with the Irish media itself, and its ability – or inability – to analyse a confluence of political, cultural and economic circumstances that often seemed to elude understanding in the daily rounds of news reporting. This self-reflection would be taken a step further in 1983, with the launch of the satirical magazine, *The Phoenix.* Modelled to some extent on the English *Private Eye,* with its parodies of newspapers and gossip about the inner workings of RTÉ (and, indeed, of government), *The Phoenix* would be all but unintelligible to a reader who did not live on a rich, intense diet of news and current affairs. If nothing else, its early circulation figures of 20,000, and its continued survival in the volatile magazine market, are a reminder that a small, but nonetheless sizeable, percentage of the Irish population live in an intensely media-saturated environment. Throughout the 1980s *Hot Press, Magill* and *The Phoenix* shared newsstands with *In Dublin. In Dublin* had begun as a listings guide in 1976 (publishing, among other things, the schedules of pirate stations), but it was soon publishing articles by young writers who had come of age in the new mediated Ireland, including Colm Tóibín, Roddy Doyle, Michael Dwyer and Fintan O'Toole, who would later become editor of *Magill* in the mid-1980s. 'The connection between *Hot Press, In Dublin* and the current affairs magazine *Magill* was less to do with content or objectives than with attitude and style', claimed one of *In Dublin's* early contributors, John Waters. 'Together they amounted to an Irish counterculture.'[49]

The Irish media's simmering dissatisfaction with itself in those years had many targets: spiralling unemployment, the almost routine atrocity in

---

[48] 'The Whole Hog', *Hot Press* 1:1 (June 9, 1977), 3.
[49] Waters, *Race of Angels,* 102.

Northern Ireland, politicians caught up in internal power struggles, and the general sense that Ireland had become, to use a phrase current at the time, a 'banana republic'. For many in the Republic, this discontent found a focus in Section 31 of the Broadcasting Act. The original Act had given the Minister the power to 'direct the Authority in writing to refrain from broadcasting any particular matter', but this power was not really exercised until after there came to be a real fear in the Irish Republic that the conflict in Northern Ireland would spill over the border. In 1971, the relevant minister, Gerard Collins, specifically directed RTÉ not to broadcast anything that might be construed to promote any organisation involved in political violence. A year later, on November 19, 1972, RTÉ broadcast an interview with a senior IRA leader; the minister demanded an explanation, and was told it was an internal RTÉ matter – whereupon he dismissed the entire RTÉ Authority. Collins' successor, the Labour Minister for Posts and Telegraphs, Conor Cruise O'Brien, set out to ensure that there would be no further ambiguity, extending the directive in 1976 to direct RTÉ to 'refrain from broadcasting any matter which is an interview, or report of an interview, with a spokesman' for any one of a number of named organisations, including the IRA, Provisional Sinn Fein or several of the Unionist paramilitary organisations; furthermore, the ban extended to any spokesperson for 'any organisation which in Northern Ireland is proscribed within the meaning of Section 28 of the Act of the British Parliament entitled the Northern Ireland (Emergency Provisions) Act, 1973'.

The effect of this legislation was, in some respects, comparable to that of the Censorship of Publications Act in the first half of the century, in that it seemed to sum up a wider malaise: an inability to reconcile the state's founding ideals with its current condition, even if that inability was explicable in terms of those founding ideals. 'If I were to choose the single most destructive imposition on RTÉ in its history,' broadcaster and film-maker Bob Quinn later wrote, 'I would opt for the directive under Section 31 of the Broadcasting Act of October 1971.'[50] The very existence of the Irish Republic was predicated on the idea that Ireland had a right to be an independent state, and this was, of course, the *raison d'être* of Sinn Fein. And yet, in order to prevent Sinn Fein from entering into the public sphere, the 1976 Broadcasting Act linked Irish law to what some saw as a repressive piece of British legislation. To make matters worse, there was no comparable censorship legislation in Northern Ireland itself, in spite of

[50] Bob Quinn, *Maverick: A Dissident View of Broadcasting Today* (Dingle, 2001), 66.

the existence of other draconian curtailments of civil liberties in the province, including at one period the introduction of internment. In some quarters in England, this stirred up indignant outrage, and in 1981 a motion was introduced in the House of Lords arguing that 'BBC news items seemed oriented towards the IRA rather than their victims.' In the Republic, the contrast between the investigative journalism produced by the BBC, and that which RTÉ felt it could attempt under Section 31 was equally a source of humiliation. 'Can it be that RTE staff do not have the courage of their British counterparts,' asked Peter Sheridan in *Hot Press*, 'who frequently report stories that are an embarrassment to the government which writes their pay cheques?'[51] 'A climate of near hysteria was developing,' wrote Michael Farrell in 1986, 'in which any criticism of the government's security policies was branded as support for the IRA.'[52] And, indeed, while the National Union of Journalists in Ireland did try to challenge the legislation, and Section 31 was widely debated in the press, it is indicative of the doublethink of Irish political culture in those years that the legislation was renewed annually by the Dáil until 1994, with no serious attempt within the legislature to overturn it.

Not least of the ironies of the situation was that the organisation at whom Section 31 was primarily directed, Sinn Fein, used its own public-relations machine to interpret the restrictions as the predictable product of a political culture in need of a good dose of republican socialism. Just as pirate radio and magazines such as *Hot Press* and *In Dublin* set up alternative media channels, Sinn Fein went a step further, and set up its own press centre. Throughout the 1970s, it published two newspapers, *Republican News* in Belfast, and *An Phoblacht* in Dublin, which merged in 1979 to become *An Phoblacht / Republican News*, based in the party's offices on the Falls Road in Belfast. The Republican Press Centre published books and pamphlets, as well as the weekly newspaper, which was distributed directly by volunteers, who often hawked copies in sympathetic pubs. For Sinn Fein, there was no ambiguity as to what was taking place in Northern Ireland: it was a war, and so *An Phoblacht* printed a weekly column of 'War News', reports of new IRA weaponry, military operations and political strategy. As John Horgan later recalled, *An Phoblacht*, 'was avidly read by politicians, senior public servants and administrators in Dublin, Belfast and London concerned with ongoing attempts to resolve the Northern Ireland crisis', because it reported on

[51] Peter Sheridan, 'The Muzzle on RTE', *Hot Press* 1:1 (June 9, 1977), 8.
[52] Michael Farrell, *The Apparatus of Repression* (Derry, 1986), 19.

'issues and events which media lack of interest or (in the case of radio and television) censorship had kept below the political horizon'.[53]

The Republican Press Centre also used an earlier piece of technology to release material directly to international news agencies: the telex machine. The telex, which had been developed in Germany in the 1930s, was a development of the telegraph, using the telephone network to send point-to-point typed messages, which could be printed or read on a screen. Although it had been used by news agencies for many years, it would undergo a revival in the early 1980s, and for Sinn Fein it became a vital piece of equipment. Indeed, so much so that *An Phoblacht* reported on a number of raids on the Press Centre in which 'the primary objective of the RUC men engaged in searching the premises was to establish a direct connection between the telex machine, its operator, and the IRA whose supplied statements, including claims for military operations, are regularly issued through the telex machine.' During one such raid, it was gleefully reported, an over-eager soldier threw the offending machine through an upstairs window, later to discover that it was property of the Post Office, and had to be replaced.[54]

AN EXPANSIVE RECESSION

In a sense, the telex in the Republican Press Office was like the pirate radio stations: both can stand as images of attempts to find technologies that would make the media match the shifting landscape of the real. As the playwright Brian Friel, quoting the theorist George Steiner, put it in his 1979 play, *Translations*: 'It can happen that a civilization can be imprisoned in a linguistic contour which no longer matches the landscape of ... fact.'[55] Ireland in 1961, with its shiny new television station, had seemed like a country in which an expanding, outward-looking economy was matched by a suitably modern media. By the early 1980s, the opposite seemed to be true, and reality seemed to have outgrown the capacity of the mainstream media to reflect – much less direct – what was happening in Irish society or in the Irish economy. Indeed, the Irish media of the period even coined an acronym to sum up this sense of dislocation. When in 1982 a wanted murderer inexplicably turned up in the house of the Attorney General, the Taoiseach of the day, Charles Haughey, pronounced the

53 Horgan, *Irish Media*, 149.
54 Seamus Boyle, 'RUC Attack Press Centre', *An Phoblacht / Republican News* 4:2 (January 14, 1982), 5.
55 Brian Friel, *Translations*, in *Selected Plays of Brian Friel* (London, 1984), 419.

affair to be 'grotesque, *u*nbelievable, *b*izarre, *u*nprecedented' – and the word 'gubu' entered the vocabulary. Moreover, there would be plenty of opportunity to use it. By 1986, the Republic of Ireland had the second-slowest rate of economic growth in Europe; its unemployment rate was growing faster than anywhere in Europe, apart from Italy, standing at 17.7 per cent in January; at 19.9 per cent, the unemployment rate in Northern Ireland was even worse. 'Growth has stopped,' editorialised *The Economist* in November of that year, 'investment has crashed, unemployment is surging, interest rates are over the moon. The rising generation, fresh out of the expensively refurbished education system, is seeking its fortune abroad. The Irish are fed up.'[56]

One of the paradoxes of Ireland in the 1980s is that while the economy contracted in recession, the media world grew. The introduction of Radio 2 and RTÉ2 in the late 1970s was in some respects a foretaste of what would happen in the decade ahead. For instance, it had been feared that more television would mean less reading or radio listening. And yet, by the early 1980s, newspaper readership in Ireland had become the highest in Europe, with 95 per cent of the population reading a newspaper at least once a week. When a new Sunday paper, *The Sunday Tribune*, was initially launched in 1980 (and relaunched with Vincent Browne as editor in 1983), it stepped into an expanding market, and barely made a dent in the sales of existing titles, such as the *Sunday Independent*. Among the daily papers, after some shifts in personnel and a few years of declining sales, by 1983 the *Irish Times* was boasting the highest circulation figures in its history.

Meanwhile, radio listenership was also increasing, as the largest of the pirate stations had become fully professional organisations: Sunshine Radio at that point had fifty-three full-time employees, and more listeners than Radio 2. 'Within the next decade', predicted *The Phoenix* in 1983, 'there will be a virtual revolution in the use of cable and satellite broadcasting while the new government's response to the existing pirate radios and the potential TV operators will have the most profound effect on the whole future of RTÉ.'[57] This prediction would prove correct in 1988, when Ray Burke, the Minister for Communications, put forward Acts that would transform the broadcasting environment. The Broadcasting and Wireless Telegraphy Act 1988 (19/1988) shut down the pirates by making it an offence to advertise on an unlicenced station, meaning that the state

---

[56] 'Another Soft Day', *The Economist* (November 1, 1986), 14.
[57] 'Pillars of Society', *The Phoenix* 1:1 (January 9, 1983), 8.

could pursue advertisers as well as broadcasters. At the same time, he put forward the Radio and Television Act 1988 (20/1988), which opened up the market for commercial broadcasting licences – including television licences – under the auspices of a new body, the Independent Radio and Television Commission (IRTC),[58] thereby preparing the ground for the broadcasting environment of the next decade, which would increasingly include commercial broadcasters.

In 1986, the same year that Ireland's economy almost touched the bottom of the European recession, there were 315,000 video recorders in the country (where there had been almost none five years earlier), and video-rental shops were becoming common sights in most Irish towns and villages, transforming the way in which people watched films. Moreover, there were beginning to be Irish films to watch. One of the more astounding features of the strange mixture of economic stagnation and media growth that marks the 1980s is that after three decades in which only a handful of Irish feature films had been made, beginning in 1981 an Irish film industry began once again to flicker to life.

To a large extent, this was triggered by the establishment of An Bord Scannán na hÉireann [The Irish Film Board] by an Act of the Dáil in 1980. The first production funded by the new body in some ways set the agenda for the next decade. Neil Jordan's *Angel* (1982; released in the US as *Danny Boy*), received £100,000 from the Film Board, supplemented by an additional £400,000 from Channel 4 in the UK,[59] thus making it technically an Irish-British co-production. A stylised (and stylish) film about an unwilling gunman in the Northern Ireland conflict, *Angel* was very much an *auteur* film, the work of a film-maker with a distinctive aesthetic. In this regard, it would set the pattern for Irish film-making throughout the 1980s, as Irish film located itself closer to an *auteur*ist European model of cinema. At the same time, its cultural points of reference were more frequently American, as in the case of Peter Ormrod's *Eat the Peach* (1986), about a group of characters who build a 'wall of death' after watching an Elvis film, *Roustabout*. Films of those years, such as Pat Murphy's *Anne Devlin* (1984) or Bob Quinn's *Budawanny* (1987) were all received, in their various ways, as works of major cultural significance, although by the end of the decade a crime film such as *The Courier* (1987) marked a move to a more commercial kind of film-making. Even so, there remained a firm conviction that Irish film

[58] Horgan, *Irish Media*, 151.
[59] Lance Pettitt, *Screening Ireland: Film and Television Representation* (Manchester, 2000), 106.

was a fragile plant in an international market, in need of government support to survive. Reviewing *Eat the Peach* in 1986, film critic Ray Comiskey argued that 'it offers timely proof that the skills for an Irish film industry are here now. Let's hope that Government indifference to the plight of Irish film-makers does not allow those skills to wither away.'[60]

Television had arrived in Ireland in 1961 to a media environment whose primary goal had been the cultivation of an indigenous, largely autonomous culture, and in some respects the films of the 1980s drew on that ethos in their determined focus on an Irish audience. In this respect, Irish cinema of the 1980s could almost be seen as fighting a rearguard action in a media culture that was becoming increasingly globalised. Indeed, as early as 1978, when RTÉ2 went on the air, the *Irish Times* would admonish its readers: 'We should not cod ourselves into thinking that we are intellectually superior to the other nations of Western Europe who depend largely, too, on that universal currency of soap-opera and fantasy, so much of which emanates from America.'[61] By the end of the 1980s, the world of the Irish media would thus be more open than at any point in the past, and it was clear that the new legislative environment taking shape would make it even more so. What was only perhaps apparent to the most wide-eyed futurologist at that point, however, was that there were already new media technologies taking shape that would not only further open the pores of an already porous media culture, but would eventually absorb all earlier media into a completely different kind of informational order.

---

[60] Ray Comiskey, 'Uneasy Rider on the Wall of Death', *Irish Times* (March 14, 1986), 10.
[61] 'RTE: For the Saintly and the Learned?' *Irish Times* (November 3, 1978), 11.

Media Event 6:
With satellite television you can go anywhere:
July 13, 1985

'We're an Irish band, we come from Dublin city, Ireland,' announced Bono from the stage at Wembley Stadium on July 13, 1985. Behind him the metronomic opening of 'Bad' faded in, and Bono started off not with the song's lyrics, but with a vocal riff from Lou Reed's 'Satellite of Love'. U2 had already played 'Sunday, Bloody Sunday', and were supposed to play 'Bad', and 'Pride' as well, but somewhere in the middle of 'Bad', Bono disappeared from the view of the rest of the band. 'The band were on stage feeling a little lost because they didn't know where he'd gone', manager Paul McGuinness later recalled. 'He was down at the front treating it for what it was, a TV show, and in some kind of inspired way he understood that.'[1] As Bono clambered over speakers and finally jumped down from the stage to pull a woman out of the audience, he was directly visible to only perhaps a couple of hundred fans packed into the front of the crowd – and, of course, to the cameras, which meant that he was also seen not only on screens on either side of the stage, but also by more than a billion people around the world. And in that curious moment of imbalance, when Bono was lost to the sight of his band, but visible around the planet, we have an iconic image of the curious new alignments and asymmetries of a world connected by satellite.

The possibility of a simultaneous global event had been realised almost twenty years earlier, when the Mexico City Olympics had been broadcast live by satellite to audiences in Europe and the Americas in 1968. The

[1] Neil McCormack and U2, *U2 by U2* (London, 2006), 162.

197

technology was thus not new that made it possible to transmit the Live Aid concerts from London and Philadelphia, and to broadcast them simultaneously on radio and television to more than 100 countries around the world. What made Live Aid different, and what made it in some respects the culmination of a particular phase of media globalisation was its own consciousness of itself as a global event. 'Go back twenty years', organiser Bob Geldof reminded an interviewer in 2004. 'Mobile phones: only the extremely rich had them. Faxes were unknown. ... The common form of international communication was telex. There was no global television. ... Live Aid proved that we were all connected.'[2]

Live Aid was not simply about global television; it was a product of television, triggered by the news broadcasts of BBC correspondent Michael Buerk. Indeed, it is possible to narrow down the few seconds of broadcasting that produced Live Aid. It began with a simple panning shot that opened a 1984 report, filmed against the rising sun, across a field of starving Ethiopian refugees, their skeletal arms and legs protruding from flowing robes the colour of the parched earth on which they lay dying, framed by Buerk's voice-over: 'Dawn, and as the sun breaks through the piercing chill of night on the plain outside Korem, it lights up a biblical famine, now, in the twentieth century.' In a retrospective documentary, *Ethiopia: A Journey Back*, broadcast by the BBC in 2004, Buerk saw what followed in these terms: 'This is a story ... of how three million iron age families were saved by the power of television.'[3] The story is, of course, well known; how Dublin-born singer Bob Geldof saw Buerk's broadcast, called in his friend Midge Ure from the band Ultravox, organised the charity single 'Do They Know It's Christmas', and then went on, against the odds, to organise the Live Aid concerts, which were broadcast to a global audience of more than 1 billion, and were ultimately to raise more than $US150 million.

One of the organisers of the American concert, Michael Mitchell, who had worked on the Los Angeles Olympics the previous year, told the *Irish Times*: 'We had years to plan the Olympics. We've got weeks to do this one.'[4] With press coverage such as this, the production values of the event became part of the event, the focus often less on the music than on the logistics of organising concerts on two continents, of flying some of the musicians by Concorde from London to Philadelphia so they could play

[2] David Fricke, 'Geldof Rings in Christmas', *Rolling Stone* (December, 2004).
[3] *This World: Ethiopia – A Journey with Michael Buerk*, BBC (tx. January 11, 2004).
[4] 'Channelling the Vitality of Rock to Feed the Hungry', *Irish Times* (July 13, 1985), 4.

on both stages, of hundreds of individual telethons collecting money that, at one point, was pouring in at a rate of GB£300 per second. In short, the apparatus of Live Aid's production – and particularly its global dimension – effectively made a spectacle of the event itself. 'I'm told', comedian Billy Connolly announced to the audience at one point, 'that ninety-five per cent of the televisions in the world are tuned to us.' While Connolly might not be the most reliable source of statistics, accuracy was beside the point. What defined Live Aid was the perception that viewers around the world had come together via satellite as part of a collective global television audience; and they had come together because the eye of television had turned, momentarily, to Ethiopia; and it had all been organised by an Irishman.

The experience of Live Aid was thus one of a vertiginous asymmetry of the watchers and the watched; of being part of more than a billion watchers, looking at an Irish singer, or at a lone unnamed Ethiopian child.[5] In this new asymmetrical mediated world, the place of Ireland took a sudden shift over the course of the sixteen hours of broadcasting. In the 1970s and early 1980s, Ireland had been dogged by a feeling of belatedness, whether it was Irish listeners tuning into Radio Caroline to catch music that simply was not played on RTÉ, or viewers tuning into documentaries dealing with Northern Ireland on BBC that highlighted the restrictions placed on Irish broadcasters by Section 31 of the Broadcasting Act. The Ireland into which Live Aid was broadcast had a generally ailing Irish economy, a barely surviving film industry and a telephone system best summed up by a cheeky classified advertisement placed by a travel agent in May, 1984. Addressed to the head of Bord Telecom, it read: 'If you can guarantee that our phones will work for at least one week, you or anyone else you care to nominate will be given a holiday in Crete this weekend.'[6]

Live Aid staged the radical asymmetry of a globally mediated world in a way that would demonstrate the potential of the new media technologies to reverse this feeling of Irish peripherality. On July 13, 1985, the Irish media seemed to have little doubt that Live Aid was, somehow, funda-mentally an Irish event. Central to this perception was the figure of Geldof himself, whose Irishness was mentioned by media commentators everywhere, his energy, profanity and scruffiness fitting neatly into an opposition with Prince Charles and Princess Diana, with whom he

---

[5] Twenty years later, the girl, Birhan Woldu, would appear on stage with Geldof at the Live8 concert in 2005.
[6] 'To Mr Byrnes of Bord Telecom', *Irish Times* (May 16, 1984), 22.

appeared at the beginning of the concert. Equally, the sense of Live Aid as an Irish event was underlined by the performance of U2, particularly by Bono's foray into the crowd, where his selection of one from among the many captured, instinctively and in a purely televisual way, the event's central asymmetry in a way unmatched throughout the rest of the broadcast. And, of course, all of this took place within the context of Irish radio and newspaper commentators pointing out similarities between images of the Ethiopian famine, and images of the Irish Famine of the 1840s. So, it came as little surprise to many when the *Sunday Independent*, on the day after the event, led with a story that 'the big-hearted Irish today lead the world in famine concern contributing almost £2 million to Live Aid in Africa or ten times more per head than joint concert hosts, our cross-channel neighbours'. Perhaps, the *Independent* speculated, this 'showed the nation still bore the scars of famine in its folk memory'.[7] This idea would percolate through Irish public debate well into the 1990s, connecting an image of the past with imagery that was the product of a globalised media.

In the years that followed, it would become increasingly common for Irish people to understand Ireland's place in the world in terms of the altered geography that emerged that July afternoon. Whether it was in Bono's or in Geldof's increasing prominence as campaigners on behalf of the developing world, or in the international advocacy of Irish President Mary Robinson (elected in 1990), there was a perception that Ireland, as what cultural critic Luke Gibbons memorably called 'a first world country with a third world memory,' had a global ethical force that was disproportionate to geography or size. In 1985, there were already people who were predicting that technology would accelerate the same radical asymmetry staged by Live Aid over the next two decades. However, few indeed would have predicted that, in the case of Ireland, this asymmetry would move from the realm of the ethical into the economic. In the course of a summer's day, Live Aid staged the recognition that geography could be made not to matter; in a globalised world linked by satellite, the centre became a shifting point, defined by the camera's eye. With the centre gone, there was no longer a periphery, and so the place of Ireland in the world shifted once again.

[7] Alan O'Keefe, Tony O'Brien and Charles Mallon, 'Big-Hearted Irish Lead World Aid', *Sunday Independent* (July 14, 1985), 1.

CHAPTER 7

Since 1990: digitised

MOORE'S LAW AND THE HYPERSONIC ROCKET PLANE

Standing on the banks of the Grand Canal, in Robertstown, County Kildare on an August afternoon in 1967, Erskine Childers, then Minister for Transport, Power, Posts and Telegraphs, had a vision of the future. 'The changes in telecommunications will be immense', he told his audience:

The average household will be linked by multiple cable or by radio with an immense variety of services, bringing people closer together all over the world. There will be a multiple of TV services available from all over the world by dialling. With the use of a large screen, people will have television discussions by telephone as a family party. The home newspaper, printed by magnetic characters, made available by dialling different numbers might emerge.

Warming to his theme of a world connected by code, the minister predicted the advent of '15,000 mph hypersonic rocket planes bringing Sydney within an hour of Dublin'. Then, perhaps frightened by the boldness of his own vision, he ended on a note of warning. An Ireland so thoroughly immersed in a global culture, he warned, could be faced with a loss 'of character, of integrity, of individuality, of thought'.[1]

The opening section of Childers' speech re-appeared in a 1996 report for the government-sponsored development agency, Forbairt, entitled: *Ireland: The Digital Age, the Internet.* By 1996, in media terms, 1967 seemed like a very long time ago. 'The Digital Age poses a threat to Ireland', begins the report's author, Gerry McGovern. 'It also presents a major opportunity.' This in many ways sums up the mixture of anxiety and anticipation with which the advent of what was starting to be called an 'information society' was greeted in the Ireland of the mid-1990s.

---

[1] Cited in Gerry McGovern, *Ireland: The Digital Age, the Internet* (Dublin, 1996), 1; also, 'Childers Looks at the Future of Transport', *Irish Times* (August 7, 1967), 9.

On one hand, Childers' fears were never far away, although not always voiced: would Ireland's immersion in a globalised information society so profoundly transform Irish culture that it would become all but impossible to speak of Irish culture at all? On the other hand, in the 1990s there was a new sense of opportunity, of being given the chance for a clean start. 'In the Industrial Age we are now leaving,' continued McGovern, 'those who prospered generally had access to physical raw materials, such as coal and iron, in which Ireland was relatively poor. The raw materials of the Digital Age are in the imagination – which Irish people have in abundance.'[2] If most of Ireland (with some notable exceptions along the east coast), had missed out on the first Industrial Revolution, the argument went, there was a chance – a brief window of opportunity – to be part of the next Industrial Revolution, the Information Revolution.

Back in 1967, Childers had imagined moving images, dialogue and print flashed by code in an instantaneous field all over the world; he had also imagined hypersonic rocket planes. By 1996, the 'multiple of TV services available from all over the world' and newspapers 'printed by magnetic characters' had arrived; but people were still waiting in the jetport for the hypersonic rocket plane. Looking at the reasons why this was so provides us with a perspective on the velocity of change – both its speed and its direction – in the media of the early 1990s.

One place to begin is with Moore's Law. Gordon Moore, an engineer and later co-founder of microprocessor manufacturer Intel, published a series of articles in the mid-1960s in which he argued that the number of transistors on a microprocessor (and hence its processing power) would double roughly every two years; in the same period, the cost of a microprocessor would be cut in half – a trajectory that has since become known as 'Moore's Law'. The result, he argued, was that affordable processing power would increase exponentially until well into the twenty-first century, at which point miniaturisation would start to hit physical limits.[3] What makes Moore's Law so important is that it was accurate enough to become a self-fulfilling gospel in the microprocessor industry. So, where Moore was looking at circuits with fifty transistors in 1965, the company he helped to found, Intel, would introduce a processor with 3.1 million transistors in 1993, at a fraction of the price of the 1965 processor.[4]

---

[2] McGovern, *The Digital Age*, iii.

[3] Gordon E. Moore, 'Cramming More Components onto Integrated Circuits', *Electronics* 38:8 (April 19, 1965).

[4] In 2008, processors with 2 billion transistors were being announced.

However, if the principles of Moore's Law had worked in the same way with air travel (as an Intel publicity document vividly puts it), a commercial flight between New York and Paris that in 1978 cost around US$900 and took seven hours 'would now cost about a penny and take less than one second'.[5]

In an age of print, the speed at which information travelled was directly linked to geographical space, and could only travel as fast as roads, railroads, canals and sea lanes could carry the printed word. In such a world, Ireland's position was peripheral, a colonised marginal economy off the coast of Europe. The telegraph, and later the telephone, changed that to some extent, if only through geographical accident that placed Ireland at the hub of the trans-Atlantic cable networks. In the early years of the twentieth century, the phonograph and the cinema had transformed the kind of information that could be transported, but they could still only travel as fast as the vehicle that carried them, and in that sense belonged to an earlier informational order. The early years of radio gave Irish listeners a sense of what a deterritorialised world might be like, as signals flooded in from all over the world, and this sense would continue with the offshore pirate stations such as Radio Caroline. Irish radio and television did bring sounds and images from around the world, but always framed within an Irish context. However, the development of relatively cheap, powerful microprocessors was to lead, in the 1990s, to a media culture that was deterritorialised to an extent far beyond anything that had ever preceded it.

At about the same time Childers was talking by the Grand Canal, a group of computer scientists in UCLA were working on a research project that would allow computers to send packets of information to one another, and in October of 1969 what was effectively the first email was sent from UCLA to Stanford University in California. The number of connected computers grew quickly, creating a network called ARPANET, initially within the continental United States, but connecting with Hawaii by satellite 1973, and with Europe by 1974 – the year in which the word 'internet' was first used. However, even by the early 1980s, for anyone who was not a computer enthusiast, there was only a dim sense of something forming just beyond the edge of vision. In October of 1983, for instance, the *Irish Times* ran a front-page story on four California teenagers who had tapped into ARPANET. By the mid-1980s, the paper had a regular

---

[5] Moore's Law in Perspective, http://download.intel.com/museum/Moores_Law/Printed_Materials/Moores_Law_Perspective.pdf.

computing column, written by journalist Dick Ahlstrom, who used the
word 'internet' in the newspaper for the first time in an article published
in August of 1985. In those same years, the pursuit of Moore's Law in the
microprocessor industry finally reached a tipping point of sorts, so that
computers that once required whole rooms and their own air-condition-
ing systems now fitted on a desktop, and were affordable for home users.
US manufacturer Commodore introduced its Commodore 64 in 1982,
Apple first marketed its Macintosh in 1984, and Amstrad's PC-1512 was for
sale in Ireland in 1986, followed by a portable version with a built-in
modem in 1987. By 1986, then, the conditions were in place for the
fundamental change in the nature of information that would take place
over the next decade.

The pivotal moment of change came in 1990, when a group of
researchers based in Geneva at CERN (Conseil européen pour la recherche
nucléaire), led by Tim Berners-Lee and Robert Cailliau, working on the
problem of data-sharing, turned to the work of an earlier online pioneer,
Ted Nelson. Nelson's ecstatic, utopian 1974 pamphlet, *Computer Lib/
Dream Machines* had heralded a new way of thinking made possible by
computers, using associative, non-sequential linkages of ideas within
documents in something he called 'hypertext'. By the end of 1990,
Berners-Lee and his team had written a language, Hypertext Mark-up
Language (HTML), that would fundamentally change not only the look
of digital documents, but the ways in which they organised information.
Hypertext linkages, which connected one piece of information to another
by content, made it possible to search for a piece of information based not
on where it was located, but on what it was.

In the spirit of Nelson and other early online advocates, Berners-Lee
made what he called the 'World Wide Web' freely available through the
internet on August 6, 1991. In 1992, Marc Andreessen, a student working
in the National Centre for Supercomputer Applications at the University
of Illinois, 'bored off his ass', decided to take a crack at giving the Web the
graphical, media-rich face that it lacked, and developed a web browser
called Mosaic, which he made available on the internet in 1993.[6] In that
same year, Intel released its Pentium processor, which dramatically
increased computing power. 'Point-and-click methods promise to make
the Internet more accessible than ever before',[7] the *Irish Times* told its
readers in September of 1994, and three months later Netscape Navigator

---

[6] Cited in Manuel Castells, *The Rise of the Network Society*, 2nd edn (Oxford, 2000), 51.
[7] Fiachra Ó Marcaigh, 'Caught in a Web', *Irish Times* (September 12, 1994), 19.

(in whose development Andreessen was also involved) was launched, quickly defining the way in which most people used their computers as part of a network. The following year, 1995, Microsoft – whose software dominated the personal computer market – released the latest version of its Windows operating system, Windows 95, which incorporated a web browser. That same year, one of the earliest online retailers, Amazon.com, began selling books over the internet. By the beginning of 1996, the internet was mainstream.

The distinction between content and location was the crucial distinction between the World Wide Web and its predecessors, the most complete sundering of the link between geography and information since the advent of the telegraph. Radio and television had always been broadcast *from* somewhere, and books had always displayed their place of publication prominently. For the vast majority of web users, images, words and sounds simply appeared on their screens, their points of origin irrelevant or invisible. New maps began appearing of what would be called 'cyberspace', often looking like elaborate star constellations, or (unsurprisingly) shining spider webs, their lack of centre or of direction rendering quaintly obsolete the idea of 'the information superhighway', an inadequately linear, spatial metaphor for the internet that enjoyed a brief currency in the early 1990s.

'The potential "death of distance" has the result that the relative geographical periphery of places like Ireland will be considerably reduced', reported the Information Society Steering Committee, an Irish government advisory group, in 1996. However, 'potential' was very much the operative word in the Ireland of the mid-1990s. By the middle of the decade, only 20 per cent of Irish adults had a computer, and nationally only 5 per cent used the internet (a figure that dropped below 2 per cent in Ulster and Connaught).[8] And yet, in spite of the fact that more Irish people were reading about the Web in newspapers in 1996 than were actually using it, there was a strong sense that Ireland was part of the Information Revolution.

Beginning in the late 1980s, the Irish government had begun aggressively to encourage inward investment by giving tax incentives to foreign companies – particularly American companies looking for a European base. To a certain extent, the kinds of industry that were most actively encouraged were dictated by the historical narrative that saw Ireland as

---

[8] Information Society for Ireland, *Strategy for Action: Report on Ireland's Information Society Steering Committee* (Dublin, 1996), 5, 30.

having missed out on the first Industrial Revolution. 'Ireland was disad-
vantaged in the Industrial era by its lack of resources and capital', wrote
the author of a report commissioned by the European Movement in 1996.
'By contrast, an early entry by Ireland to the successor of the Industrial
Society, the Information Society, may realize some special advantages.'[9]
In one particularly prescient move, as far back as 1983 the Irish government made a substantial investment in a new digital telephone network,
with a view to enabling computer data transfer long before most of the
population realised just what this entailed. As a result, the Irish telecommunications infrastructure changed 'as much in five years as ... in the
preceding 80 years'.[10] Shortly afterwards, in 1985, Microsoft (who would
launch the first version of Windows that year), established an office in
Ireland. In 1990, Intel, the world's leading microprocessor manufacturer,
set up a major manufacturing facility in County Kildare; the following
year, Iona Technologies, a small start-up company based in Trinity
College, Dublin, began what would become a global computer network
business. Visiting Ireland's first cybercafé in the summer of 1995, the
Minister for Arts, Culture and the Gaeltacht, Michael D. Higgins, told
reporters, that 'down at the Department of Finance these days, the talk is
all of cyberspace, gophers and turbogophers'.[11] He was only partly joking.

INFORMATION WANTS TO BE FREE

In the same years in which digital media were emerging in Ireland like
some mercurial leviathan, the older media in Ireland were, for the most
part, trying to consolidate, and shake off some of the ramshackleness of
their histories. To a certain extent, the trajectories of radio, television and
cinema in the Irish Republic in the 1990s would be determined by
legislation that was passed in 1988: in the case of radio and television,
the Broadcasting and Wireless Telegraphy Act, and the Sound Broadcasting Act (both 1988); and in the case of cinema, Section 35 of the 1987
Finance Bill (and its successor, Section 481), which contained an incentive
for companies to invest in Irish film production.

  The effect of the 1988 legislation was most dramatic – and perhaps most
predictable – in relation to radio. The airwaves of the 1980s had been a
legal no-man's land, where the signals of pirates operating with varying

---

[9] Liam Breslin, *The Information Society: Irish Feast or Irish Famine?* (Dublin, 1996), 17.
[10] 'A New Phone System', *Irish Times* (July 20, 1983), 15.
[11] Michael O'Kelly, 'Higgins Surfs the Net at Dublin's First Cyber Café', *Irish Times* (July 26, 1995), 2.

degrees of professionalism drifted in and out of reception, while a government aware of their popularity contrived not to hear them. The new legislation finally shut down the pirate radio stations, and at the same time established the basis for commercial radio and community-based radio stations under the control of a new body, the Independent Radio and Television Commission (IRTC), established in 1988. The IRTC were also charged with establishing a new commercial television station, although this would take longer. The first of the new commercial radio stations went on the air on July 20, 1989, broadcasting from Dublin as Capital Radio (later FM104); four days later, the first station outside of Dublin, MWR FM in County Mayo started up. By the summer of 1990, the IRTC had issued twenty-four radio licences for commercial stations, and this number would remain more or less stable throughout the decade. These regional stations all fed the same appetite for the fine details of the local hurling match, or the latest planning dispute, that could never be adequately catered for by the national media. For its part, RTÉ continued to base its main programming schedule around personalities, promoting broadcasters such as Gay Byrne, Pat Kenny, Marian Finucane and later Ryan Tubridy as national stars. The national broadcaster would be particularly influential not only in news and current affairs, but in using the phone-in format (most notably in the afternoon programme, Live Line) to shape national debates, and, on more than one occasion, change the direction of public policy. In spite of this, as early as 1994, local stations collectively accounted for half of all radio listeners in Ireland, and sixteen of the twenty local stations in operation at the time were ahead of RTÉ in their local areas.[12] By 1999, RTÉ would be reduced to 27 per cent of the national audience – although by that point it too had diversified, launching a national classical music station, Lyric FM, on May 1, 1999.

One way to understand the speed with which local radio became part of the Irish media landscape is to think of these broadcasters as analogous to the local newspaper industry (not least because owners of regional papers were frequently involved in local radio as well). Historically, while newspapers had been published in the larger towns and cities outside Dublin and Belfast since the eighteenth century, the regional press had mushroomed in the nineteenth century, as each political or sectarian faction in a community felt the need for its own weekly mouthpiece. As the political climate cooled (at least, outside of Ulster), so too had the number of regional papers fallen in the Irish Republic after 1922, with forty-one titles

[12] *IRTC Review 1994* (Dublin, 1994), 16.

surviving in the South in 1969 (although the more heated political climate in Northern Ireland continued to nurture forty-five titles outside of Belfast). By 1993, however, there were fifty-three regional newspapers in the Republic (and forty in Northern Ireland), and, as John Horgan notes, as they prospered 'they became increasingly attractive prospects for both domestic as well as foreign predators'.[13] For instance, the *Cork Examiner* (founded in 1841), bought the Mayo-based *Western People* (founded in 1883) in 1995; the following year the Cork paper swapped 'Cork' for 'Irish', and in 2000 rebranded itself as a national newspaper, *The Irish Examiner*. And, of course, the importance of local radio and newsprint makes perfect sense for a country in which Gaelic Games produce fiercely passionate attachments to local teams at parish and county level, and in which local issues set national political agendas to an extraordinary degree. Indeed, a recognition of the strength of local attachments may even help to explain why a national culture in Ireland has had to state and restate its claims so frequently and so forcefully: it is constantly struggling against the appeal of the local. In this regard, the tug of war between Radio Kerry and RTÉ1, or between the *Donegal Democrat* and the *Irish Independent* both produce, and reflect, one of the central dynamics in Irish culture.

As local and commercial radio settled into a secure regulatory environment in the early 1990s, it eased one aspect of the disjunction between media and society that had been felt so strongly in the previous two decades. However, in other areas this disjointedness continued, erupting most forcefully in the unlikely area of two competing cable television technologies. Since the late 1960s, cable television had been available in most urban areas of the country through Cablelink, a subsidiary of RTÉ. However, not only was it not feasible to run cable in many rural areas, there were still a few remote areas that could not pick up any terrestrial television signal. This meant that in order to watch BBC or Channel 4 (and, in some few cases, to watch RTÉ), many rural viewers needed some form of wireless cable. In response to this situation, in 1989 the Minister for Communications, Ray Burke, issued a number of licences for what were known as MMDS franchises, which used microwaves to broadcast television signals. Meanwhile, however, local entrepreneurs had run across a cheaper technology in the form of aerials known as 'deflectors', which could transmit signals to remote areas at a significantly lower cost. Technically, these were operated illegally; however, as had been the case

---

[13] John Horgan, *Irish Media: A Critical History since 1922* (London, 2001), 174.

with pirate radio in the 1980s, they were popular and provided a necessary service, so the local gardai tended to turn a blind eye to their operation.

By 1994, businesses that had invested in MMDS started crying foul, while on the other hand the deflector operators argued that the people of rural Ireland should be able to choose their cable supplier. As early as September of 1992, there was a protest march when police shut down an illegal deflector in Cork, and by the time of the 1997 election a number of independent candidates along the western seaboard were preparing to stand on the single issue of the inalienable right to multi-channel television. 'For too long we have been forgotten and ignored', one activist said in 1997; 'and now its time for people in Mayo and Donegal to stand up for themselves.'[14] By that point, the controversy was about more than profits or convenience; it was about uneven development, about the fear of being left out of the new media world.

One way to think about the battle over deflectors and MMDS in the early 1990s is to remember that these were precisely the same years in which the internet was becoming part of public consciousness. Writing in the *Irish Times* on January 17, 1994, columnist Nuala O'Faolain told readers how she had encountered the internet for the first time after being told that one of her articles had sparked a lively online debate – a concept that was completely new to her (and, indeed, to most *Irish Times* readers at the time). She recounted meeting a group of young computer scientists in Trinity College, Dublin, who showed her the internet for the first time, and helped her to send her first emails. These young men, she wrote, possessed something new, 'a sense of light and dark sweeping around the globe – an intuitive awareness of time-zones – rather than distances'. 'Most appropriately,' she wrote, 'I saw the thing in action on the day Section 31 was lifted. Because one of the most striking implications of this technological advance is that it subverts any kind of censorship ... "Information wants to be free" is how my young tutors in Trinity put it.'[15]

Throughout the 1970s and 1980s, Section 31 of the Broadcasting Act, which had forbidden interviews with members of organisations involved in political violence, including Sinn Fein, had been the suppuration point of Irish media debate, proof of the old adage that truth is the first victim of war. Some would go so far as to claim that its existence was evidence

---

[14] Uinsionn Mac Dubhghaill, 'TV, Water Charges Candidates Likely to Contest Election', *Irish Times* (March 11, 1997), 7.
[15] Nuala O'Faolain, 'Reshaping the World through Contemporary Communications', *Irish Times* (January 17, 1994), 12.

that the Irish Republic was a police state. After so much fury, when the government minister Michael D. Higgins announced that he would not be renewing it in January of 1994, in the wake of an IRA ceasefire in 1993, the effect was curiously anti-climactic, more embarrassed relief than triumphant jubilation. At the same moment, in some parts of the country the suggestion that illegal deflectors would be pulled down was being met with street protests. In a sense, both the quiet acknowledgement of the end of censorship, and the fierce indignation stirred up by the deflector dispute were two faces of the same growing sense that access to ever-increasing amounts of information was something akin to a basic civil right.

THE POWERS THAT BE

'It's not fair what the powers that be are doing to rural Ireland',[16] one aggrieved campaigner for the illegal deflectors told a journalist in 1997. When the dust cleared from the 1997 General Election, however, some journalists found themselves asking who 'the powers that be' actually were. On the eve of the election, in a demonstration of the continuing power of newsprint, the largest-circulation broadsheet daily newspaper, the *Irish Independent*, published an editorial in which it urged voters to replace the existing coalition government with a new government led by the Fianna Fáil party – which duly happened. It later emerged that there had been talks regarding the deflector debate between members of Fianna Fáil and the parent company who owned the *Independent*, Independent News and Media, who had also invested heavily in MMDS transmitters, and wanted their illegal competition shut down. The *Irish Times* published accounts of allegations that the paper had done a deal with Fianna Fáil, an allegation the *Independent* strenuously denied.[17] After the heat had waned from the issue, it became clear that regardless of what had actually happened, the very possibility that influence in one medium might have been used to shape policy in another medium brought with it the realisation that Ireland had moved into a period in which large vertically and horizontally integrated media conglomerates would have increasing power.

Throughout the history of the state, considerable energy had been directed towards protecting indigenous Irish media. It is not surprising, therefore, that in the rumbling grassroots demand for more media in the early 1990s, there was a vague assumption that more media in Ireland

---

[16] Joan Tobin, 'Black-out Viewers May Channel Their Anger', *Irish Times* (March 17, 1997), 2.
[17] Horgan, *Irish Media*, 170–1.

would mean more Irish-owned media. However, by that point the very idea of an indigenous media had become problematic. It was not simply the case, for instance, that a newspaper or a radio station would be either Irish-owned, or part of a foreign multi-national. Increasingly, it was possible to be both, as the early 1990s saw the emergence of home-grown Irish multi-nationals, with two in particular dominating the landscape. Denis O'Brien's Communicorp was founded in 1989 from roots in pirate radio, and soon grew from owning 98FM in Dublin, to ownership of a radio station in the Czech Republic, and to eventual ownership of forty-two radio stations in eight countries, many operating a variation of the same 'classic hits' broadcasting formula used with the Irish stations. O'Brien would later branch out into mobile telephones, and would be part of the private consortium that would launch a bid for commercial digital terrestrial television in 2008. Meanwhile, when Tony O'Reilly had gained control of Independent Newspapers back in 1973, and announced that he planned to develop the business into 'an international communications group', expanding into 'fields of advertising, publicity and commercial radio and television',[18] the response from the Irish media had been more incredulous than anything else. However, by the mid-1990s Independent News and Media had indeed become a multi-national conglomerate, controlling national newspapers and magazines in Ireland, the UK, South Africa, Australia and New Zealand, with interests in Hong Kong and Portugal. It would eventually have worldwide ownership of more than 130 radio stations, more than 200 print periodical titles and more than 100 websites, as well as internet service providers and cable television companies.

The flip side of these Irish-owned companies expanding outwards was the investment into Ireland of non-Irish based conglomerates, with Scottish Radio Holdings becoming a particularly big player in the Irish market in the late 1990s. Similarly, when a commercial Irish television station – TV3 – finally went on the air in September of 1998 (a decade after the legislation that made it possible was introduced), one of the largest shareholders was a Canadian conglomerate, CanWest, who owned networks in Canada and Australia, and would later buy Scottish Radio Holdings' share of UTV. For their part, SRH would at various points own substantial shares in Belfast's Downtown Radio, and important regional newspapers, including the *Kilkenny People* and the Clonmel-based *Nationalist* (founded in 1893 and 1890, respectively).

---

[18] 'Monopolising the Media?', *Hibernia* (February 1, 1974), 7.

The speed with which a media industry with multi-national tentacles – both inward and outward – was acquiring interests in everything from TV3 to the venerable *Kilkenny People* was sometimes disorienting in those years. It also produced a number of curious ironies, not least of which was the danger of success; whenever any media enterprise became profitable, it was liable to be taken over. After decades of operating on shoestrings and non-existent profit margins, there was the swirl of banknotes. By 1993, only four years after the first commercial station went on the air, advertising revenue for commercial radio stations in Ireland amounted to IR£18.1 million annually. It would rise steeply throughout the decade, exceeding IR£39 million by 1999. In the same period, newspaper advertising was also on the rise, going from IR£91.9 million in 1995 to IR£181.3 million in 1999, with sales of daily papers growing by 93,000 in the same period.[19] Much of this increase was accounted for by British newspapers, many of which had long-established readerships in Ireland, and who were increasingly keen to take advantage of new computerised printing technologies that made localisation of papers easier and cheaper. In particular, the *Irish Sun*, the Irish version of the British tabloid, made significant inroads into the daily market, as did the *Irish Daily Star*, which was partly owned by the Independent group. Meanwhile, the *Irish Press*, founded by Eamon de Valera in 1931 as a patriotic endeavour funded by subscription, went bankrupt in 1995.[20]

Perhaps even more indicative of the way in which economics had superseded politics would be the takeover of the Unionist *Belfast Telegraph* in 2000 by the Independent Group, whose own Irish titles had always been firmly nationalist. The Independent installed the chair of the Unionist Party, Lord Rogan, as head of the new board, and loudly declared a hands-off editorial policy: this, the new owners made clear, was purely business. 'Generally, I regret independent newspapers falling into the hands of big-time proprietors,' the Democratic Unionist leader, the Rev. Ian Paisley commented, 'whether big-time Irish entrepreneurs or big-time Australian entrepreneurs.'[21] The *Telegraph* would continue to be a Unionist newspaper, just as the main Irish title in the Independent Group, the *Irish Independent*, would continue to be broadly nationalist; however, both were equally now subsumed within a larger context of what Paisley called 'big-time entrepreneurs'. In some ways, the juxtaposition of

---

[19] Horgan, *Irish Media*, 164.
[20] See Ray Burke, *Press Delete: The Decline and Fall of* The Irish Press (Dublin, 2005).
[21] Gerry Moriarty, 'UUP and DUP Differ on Newspaper Takeover', *Irish Times* (July 18, 2000), 15.

these three events: the *Sun*'s growth, the *Telegraph*'s takeover by Independent News and Media, and the *Irish Press*'s implosion makes a good snapshot of what was happening to the Irish media in the 1990s. It was a world away from the *Irish Press*'s first editorial in 1931, which proclaimed: 'Henceforth other nations will have a means of knowing that Irish opinion is not merely an indistinct echo of the opinions of a section of the British press.'

THE LEAKY VESSEL OF POLITICAL AUTONOMY

In 1995, the Minister for Arts, Culture and the Gaeltacht, Michael D. Higgins, published a Green Paper that spelled out the situation of the Irish media in the 1990s with remarkable clarity. 'The process of globalization which information flows facilitate means that complex networks of power reside less and less in a unified territorial site or bloc and increasingly in decentalised global companies and institutions', the *Green Paper on Broadcasting* began. 'National sovereignty is becoming a leaky vessel for political autonomy.' The *Green Paper* went on to note that 'with the centrality of mediated experience for contemporary living, the meaning of "local" and "national" is not so clear any more as social relations in any one place are increasingly affected by distant events'.[22]

In many ways, this went to the nub of the issue. Published in the same year that Windows 95 and Netscape effectively consolidated the place of the web in Irish culture, the *Green Paper* responded to the repercussions of technological changes that had combined with legislative changes in the late 1980s to transform the Irish mediascape. The response of RTÉ to the *Green Paper* was to re-affirm the value of public-service broadcasting. 'If we Irish – at home and abroad – are to debate our past, present, and future, if we are to give public expression to our values, then we will need indigenous broadcasting on radio and television to express this community's dialogue with itself and with the rest of the world.'[23] However, just how this was to be achieved was far from obvious.

With commercial broadcasting already a reality in radio, and commercial television on the horizon, the definition of public-service broadcasting was suddenly up for debate. When Telefís Éireann had begun broadcasting in the early 1960s, effectively anything it broadcast was considered a public service, from political debates to *The Twilight Zone*; the simple fact

---

[22] *Active or Passive? Broadcasting in the Future Tense.* Green Paper on Broadcasting (Dublin, 1995), 129.
[23] *RTÉ Response to the Green Paper on Broadcasting* (Dublin, [1996]), 10.

of being a national broadcaster was a public service in its own right. However, unlike the BBC, for instance, RTÉ was a public-service broadcaster that also sold advertising, in a compromise that went back to the *White Paper on Wireless Broadcasting* in 1923. When there had been no commercial broadcasters with whom to compete for advertising, this did not really matter. With the advent of Irish commercial broadcasting, it suddenly mattered very much, and as a result the content of public-service broadcasting suddenly came into crisp focus. From within the commercial sector, the definition of 'public service' tended to be narrow, effectively limited to everything other than sports that was worthy, but loss-making: current affairs, documentaries, arts and educational programming. From within RTÉ, it was pointed out that talk shows like *The Late Late Show*, satirical comedy such as *Hall's Pictorial Weekly* in the 1970s, or *Nighthawks* in the early 1990s had shaped public opinion as much as more strictly factual genres. The definition of terms such as 'home-produced' and 'public-service broadcasting' were further muddied when RTÉ set up its Independent Production Unit in 1993, which outsourced production to small independent production companies, so that increasingly the broadcaster acted more as commissioning body than as a programme producer.[24] This paralleled a process already underway in Northern Ireland, as the BBC began taking advantage of Section 35 tax incentives in the early 1990s to produce programmes in the Republic. From 1994 to 1998, for instance, BBC Northern Ireland spent £56m on film and drama production outside of Northern Ireland, but only £7.4m inside the Province.[25]

The debate over the respective merits of public-service broadcasting and commercial terrestrial broadcasting in Ireland in the mid-1990s was argued forcefully on both sides. And yet, throughout it all, there was an elephant in the room: satellite broadcasting. The most influential satellite broadcaster in an Irish context would be Sky, who began transmissions in 1989 with four channels using the Astra satellite, merging the following year with British Satellite Broadcasting to form BSkyB. In Ireland, Sky was initially something of an expensive novelty, until in 1992 it gained exclusive live television rights to the FA Premier League football matches, shocking football fans into treating it as a necessity (and prompting the installation of large televisions in pubs all over the country). Meanwhile,

---

[24] In 1993, there were 16 productions by independents; by 1996, this had increased to 122. *The Strategic Development of the Irish Film and Television Industry 2000–2010* (Dublin, 1999), 25.

[25] John Hill, *Cinema and Northern Ireland: Film, Culture and Politics* (London, 2006), 175.

Sky continued to add channels, many of which were American in origin; five in 1994, and six in 1995, including the History Channel and the Disney Channel. In those same years, there was an expansion of the network of cable companies on whom Sky depended for its transmission in Ireland, so that there were fifteen cable licences and eight MMDS licences by 1998. In that same year, a new generation of Astra satellite made digital satellite broadcasting possible, exponentially multiplying the possible number of channels. Over the next decade, the number of channels available to Irish viewers would multiply, covering every possible viewing niche, from travel to food to highly specialised forms of pornography. By the end of 1998, Ireland would have the second-highest penetration of cable television per capita in the world, slightly behind Canada, but ahead of the United States.[26]

The recognition of what was happening in Ireland only really became apparent after the fact. Sky's acquisition of the rights to the new Premier League football in 1992 was one milestone; another was Sky's launch in 1995 of Playboy TV. Although not available at the time on the Irish Sky package, the channel could still be received in Ireland by anyone eager enough to erect their own dish. This brought the startled recognition that a culture of censorship (particularly censorship of pornography), which had been one of the defining features of Irish life since the 1920s, and which had contributed so much to the sense of Irish insularity, was simply gone. The prospect of Irish viewers choosing Playboy TV out of hundreds of possible stations, commented the *Irish Times'* media correspondent Michael Foley in 1995, 'underlines the increasing difficulty the authorities will have in implementing censorship laws in the face of technological developments, whether the delivery systems are via phone lines to computers or satellite'.[27]

It took more than just technology to change the Irish media world so profoundly, and so quickly. Equally important was legislative change, not just at national level, but also increasingly at EU level. Arriving only one year after the Acts that had opened up the Irish market to internal competition, the European Council Directive on Broadcasting (1989), enshrined the principle of a Europe-wide market. 'Member States shall ensure freedom of reception and shall not restrict retransmission on their

[26] David McWilliams, *'The Bigger Picture': An Independent Economic Report Commissioned by the Film Makers Ireland on the Irish Film & Television Industry* (Dublin, 1999), 14.
[27] Michael Foley, 'Playboy TV on Way, despite Ban on Magazine', *Irish Times* (May 12, 1995), 5.

territory of television broadcasts from other Member States',[28] declared the Directive, although it did allow certain limited exceptions (which in practice would prove to be very limited indeed). Once again, the sense that Ireland could live within its own little media bubble was given another dent.

Both technology and legislation contributed to, and were part of, a wider cultural change, which can be registered in the fact that in the same year that Playboy TV became available, the Irish electorate in a referendum overturned a ban on divorce that went back to the early years of the state. By the same token, back in the 1930s and 1940s, even many of the most principled objectors to censorship supported some kind of control on pornography, and this view would seem to have been fairly widespread. However, when the ban on *Playboy* magazine (imposed with the magazine's first issue in 1959) was lifted early in 1996, it hardly merited a mention in the newspapers. Within a year, Irish sales of the magazine accounted for 45 per cent of the total sales in the UK and Ireland, in spite of the fact that Ireland in 1996 had a population of 3.6 million, as opposed to the more than 58 million in the UK.[29]

For some commentators, the eagerness with which so many Irish people in the 1990s rushed through the breaches in the crumbling ramparts of cultural integrity waving copies of *Playboy* could be understood, at least partly, as the product of a long mistrust of official versions of what constituted a national culture. Writing in response to the *Green Paper* (and to the arrival of satellite television more generally), journalist Vincent Browne declared. 'Not all of us think that these transnational cultural forms are bad and not all of us care more than a jot about our cultural identity … In fact we dislike it so much that our dislike forms part of our personal identity.'[30] While Browne was not above playing devil's advocate on occasion, his comments here hit upon one of the threads that runs through the often contradictory cultural debate of the 1990s. Irish culture had been for so long haunted by the notion of its own insularity, provinciality and a certain kind of prudishness, that even though the sudden immersion in a new kind of instantaneous global culture felt

---

[28] Council Directive 89/552/EEC of 3 October 1989 on the coordination of certain provisions laid down by Law, Regulation or Administrative Action in Member States concerning the pursuit of television broadcasting activities, II:2:2.

[29] '*Playboy* Magazine Celebrates One-Year Anniversary in Republic of Ireland: A Business Success Story', *Business Wire* (January 13, 1997).

[30] Vincent Browne, 'The State of Culture versus the Culture of the State', *Irish Times* (August 16, 1995), 12.

threatening – culturally and economically – it also carried with it an invigorating sense of liberation. It also became normal startlingly fast, carrying with it a strange cultural amnesia. 'Does anyone remember visiting the weird, "RTÉ only" twilight-world that was a cousin's house down in the country, where deprivation from "Top of the Pops" was the norm?' asked one writer in 1999. 'That was only the 1980s.'[31]

Just what this new form of selective cultural amnesia could mean in practice became apparent on October 31, 1996, when Telefís na Gaeilge went on the air. Douglas Hyde's speech inaugurating 2RN seventy years earlier had proclaimed that it was 'a sign to the world that times have changed when we can take our own place amongst other nations, and use the wireless in our own language'.[32] In the debates leading up to the establishment of Telefís Éireann in 1960, the Irish-language lobby group, Comhdhail Naisiunta na Gaelige, had declared that 'the interest of the Irish language very strongly reinforced the powerful reasons for establishing a national television service without delay'.[33] In spite of these good intentions, however, in the intervening decades the promise of an Irish-language television station waxed and waned with almost seasonal regularity. So, when the money for the station was finally allocated in 1995 (initially IR£4 million, with a promise of IR£10 million annually), for some it seemed like a step back into an earlier, more dogmatic, cultural ethos. 'The predictable hostility to the establishment of the Irish-language channel was soon apparent', Cathal Goan, the station's first director (and later Director General of RTÉ), later recalled. 'Phone-in radio programs specialized in contrasting the dire needs of a health service in crisis with the sinful extravagance of establishing a television channel in a "dead" language.'[34]

However, Telefís na Gaeilge (later rebranded as Telefís Gaeilge 4, or TG4 in autumn, 1999), soon proved to be anything but the tediously worthy museum of folk culture that its critics had feared. Partly because it would have been impossible, given the station's grant, to produce enough quality Irish-language programming to fill a full broadcasting schedule, from the outset much of the airtime was given over to imported programmes (sometimes dubbed into Irish or subtitled), as well as to a mixture of home-produced dramas in familiar television genres, including

[31] McWilliams, 'The Bigger Picture', 12.
[32] *Irish Independent* (January 2, 1926).
[33] 'TV Service Urged as Aid to Language', *Irish Times* (January 16, 1956), 7.
[34] Cathal Goan, 'Telefís na Gaeilge: Ten Years A-Growing,' *New Hibernia Review* 11:2 (Summer, 2006), 109, 110.

a soap opera, *Ros na Rún.* It was as if, as Irish media culture became more multiple, Irish-language culture was free to become just one option among many, rather than the tabernacle of Irish nationality. The result was an Irish-language broadcasting ethos that could accommodate both *sean-nós* singing and Spongebob Squarepants *as gaelige.*

One explanation for this new form of cultural forgetting – whether it was seen as liberation or simply as a loss – is as a recognition of the way in which economic arguments supplanted ideological, cultural or political arguments as the ground of debate over Irish media in the 1990s. Indeed, this appears perhaps most clearly with Irish film. Attempts to create an Irish national cinema had sputtered along for the first century of cinema, with bursts of indigenous film-making in the 1920s, and again in the 1950s; however, by the 1970s, with a few heroic exceptions – notably Bob Quinn and Joe Comerford – it had almost come to a halt. In the 1980s, after the creation of the Irish Film Board in 1981, the situation had improved, as ten Irish feature films were made under its auspices up until 1987. By 1989, Neil Jordan had established himself, through films such as *Angel* (1982) and *Mona Lisa* (1986), as a director who could attract actors such as Robert de Niro, Sean Penn and Demi Moore for his 1989 film, *We're No Angels.* Jim Sheridan's *My Left Foot,* based on a book by a Dublin writer, Christy Brown, was released that same year, and went on to win two Oscars (for Daniel Day-Lewis and Brenda Fricker) in 1990. As the decade began, then, for the first time since Ardmore Studios was built in the late 1950s, there began to be serious discussion not just of an Irish national cinema, but of an Irish film industry (which is not neces-sarily the same thing); however, that discussion was also tempered by the Film Board having been dismantled in 1987.

In 1993, the Board was re-established. However, it found itself operat-ing in a different environment than the first Film Board. Its new director, Lelia Doolan (who had been involved in the criticism of RTÉ for its lack of inventive indigenous production back in the late 1960s), commented: 'I think that notion that Irish filmmakers are somehow idealistic artists is just a fantasy. Everybody wants to get their films seen.'[35] This new kind of pragmatism was emphasised in the Republic by the dramatic upswing in the economy, and in Northern Ireland by the 1993 ceasefires. These fundamental shifts in Irish political culture carried with them a change in thinking about the arts, signalled in Northern Ireland by the publica-tion of John Myerscough's influential report, *The Arts and the Northern*

---

[35] Johnny Gogan, 'On the Board', *Film Ireland* 36 (August/September, 1993), 3.

Ireland Economy (1996), which emphasised the economic aspects of film as an industry, over the cultural impact of film as an artform. As a result, for the film scholar John Hill, 'culturally challenging "indigenous" films ... have all but disappeared'.[36] From within the industry, however, the opposite view often prevailed. 'Periods of cultural flowering and commercial energy, often, indeed usually, go together', declared an Irish-government-commissioned report on film and television in 1999. 'The fact that this was not the case in the early 20th century Irish cultural revival has perhaps skewed Irish perceptions in this respect.'[37]

The challenge, then, for Irish film-makers, was not simply to make Irish films; but to make Irish films that made money. From this perspective, the key film of the period is arguably Neil Jordan's *Michael Collins*, released in 1996. For an international audience, the film, which starred Liam Neeson and Julia Roberts, looked like a big-budget historical drama. Indeed, many critics noted its visual and narrative similarity to the gangster film, particularly a key sequence in which scenes of Neeson and Roberts together are cross-cut with a scenes of simultaneous executions of British secret-service agents – a sequence that was based loosely on historical fact, but which cinematically echoed a similar sequence in Francis Ford Coppola's *The Godfather*. *Michael Collins* would go on to become the largest-grossing Irish film in Irish cinema history, seen by an astonishing 1.5 million Irish cinema-goers (or just over 41 per cent of the entire population). *Michael Collins* suggested that it was possible to make a film that could both reach out to an international audience, and speak to the specificities of Irish experience. 'For good or ill,' commented Nuala O'Faolain after its première, 'the Neil Jordan film is going to constitute our first shared story of the foundation of this state.'[38]

In some respects, this tension between creating 'shared stories' and establishing an industry would define Irish media as a whole in the 1990s, and needs to be seen in the context of the increasing complexity of talking about a national media culture – much less a national industry – in a globalised media world. For instance, most accounts of Irish cinema in the period linger over Thaddeus O'Sullivan's *December Bride* (1991) based on a novel by Ulster writer Sam Hanna Bell, and set in the north of Ireland; few would dispute that it is an Irish film. However, it was a

[36] Hill, *Cinema and Northern Ireland*, 181.
[37] *The Strategic Development of Irish Film and Television*, 46.
[38] Nuala O'Faolain, 'Cinematic Revival of Classics Helps Form Community', *Irish Times* (November 25, 1996), 14.

co-production of British Screen International, Central Independent Television, Channel 4 Films and the Dublin-based Little Bird Productions, which means that, from one point of view, it is as much a British film as it is an Irish film – which may well accord with its content. However, if this is true, we need to go on to recall that Little Bird also co-produced *Enemy at the Gates* (2001) with American, British and German partners; it had a French director (Jean-Jacques Annaud), and was based on the true story of a duel between a Russian and a German sniper during the siege of Leningrad; indeed, the Russian sniper, Vassili Zaitsev, was something of a folk hero in Russia. And, yet, from an industry point of view, *Enemy at the Gates* was, at least in part, an Irish film. From the opposite side of the fence, *The Wind that Shakes the Barley* (2006) went on to win the Palme d'Or at Cannes. Like Jordan's *Michael Collins*, it deals with the Irish War of Independence and Civil War; yet it was directed by Ken Loach, who is English, and the film was an Irish, British, German, Italian, Spanish and French co-production. These two films – *Enemy at the Gates* and *The Wind that Shakes the Barley* – are, in their differing ways, both Irish (just both are also German and British). In short, as international co-production (particularly for European films) becomes the norm, trying to think about cinema in terms of an exclusive national affiliation is increasingly futile. Films may continue to be parts of national cinemas; but that nationality is better understood as multiple, rather than singular.

IRELAND IN THE WORLD

By early in the first decade of the twenty-first century, in the wake of the Good Friday Agreement in 1998 that laid the basis for a power-sharing government in Northern Ireland, it was clear that something had shifted radically in Irish culture. Just how radical that shift had been became apparent in 2004, when the journal *Foreign Policy* ranked Ireland as the most globalised society in the world for the third year in a row, ahead of more obvious contenders, such as Singapore or the United States.[39] In those years of the new century, Ireland's integration into a global culture took on a tangible form, as inward migration became a feature of

---

[39] 'Measuring Globalisation', *Foreign Policy* (March/April 2004), 54–69. 'The Index tracks and assesses changes in four components of global integration, incorporating such measures as trade and financial flows, movement of people across borders, international telephone traffic, Internet usage, and participation in international treaties and peace-keeping operations' (58).

demographic change for the first time since the seventeenth century. By the middle of the decade, for instance, there was a Chinese community in Ireland almost 100,000 strong, and a substantial Nigerian community. After the expansion of the European Union in May of 2004, the Eastern European community in Ireland – hitherto an almost non-existent group in Irish society – became a large, visible part of Irish society. Lithuanians, Estonians, Czechs, Slovaks and, most significantly, Poles, established large and growing communities (although these numbers would decline slightly with the economic downturn at the end of the decade). In many cases, these 'New Irish', as they came to be called, not only established social networks; they began to link into transnational media networks. In most cases, they turned first to print. The most significant development in this regard was the founding of *Metro Éireann* by two Nigerian immigrants in April 2000, initially as a monthly, but later becoming a weekly aimed at a range of New Irish communities. It would be joined by later newspapers, notably the weekly Dublin-published *Polska Gazeta*, founded in May, 2005, as well as by supplements in Polish published by some of the established Irish titles. At the same time, small satellite dishes began to spring up on apartment balconies and in laneways, pointed not at the Astra satellite, but at Hotbird, from which it was possible to tune in Polonia 1 from Poland. In other words, it was possible to live simultaneously in Cork and Cracow; working in Cork, reading a Polish-Irish newspaper, listening to Polskie Radio 1 on the internet, and watching Polish television every evening.

Effectively, these changes reversed what had been two of the dominant features of Irish culture since at least the end of the nineteenth century; the sense that, through a combination of geography and history, Ireland was insulated from the rest of the world, and hence from the transformative powers of modernity (or indeed post-modernity). Related to this sense of isolation was the perception that Ireland was divided between two languages, and hence two cultures: English and Irish. By the early years of the twenty-first century, neither of these perceptions could be sustained. Whatever the validity of the measures used by the editors of *Foreign Policy*, it was clear that Ireland was culturally one of the most porous nations in the world. It was equally clear that as a result Irish culture was no longer binary; it was multiple.

The recognition that Ireland was so fully immersed in a globalised media world made the existing gaps in the country's infrastructure appear all the more stark, and increasingly anomalous. For instance, when digital television became technically possible in the late 1990s, the commercial satellite broadcasters – notably Sky – were quick to grasp the potential to multiply almost indefinitely the number of stations that could be offered, and were able to do so because of the enormous economies of scale on which they operated. By the same token, the BBC also moved quickly to set a timescale for the adoption of Digitial Terrestrial Television (DTT), as well as for the related technology of Digital Audio Broadcasting (DAB) in radio. Indeed, by 2003, the BBC was offering a DAB service in Northern Ireland, which soon covered 90 per cent of the population. This offered Northern Ireland listeners not only an expanded range of services, but also the ability to alter the times at which they listened to a given programme, thereby weakening the link between radio listening and the structure of the day.

RTÉ, on the other hand, began cautiously looking into digital broadcasting technology in the late 1990s. However, it would not be until 2008 that the Minister for Energy, Communications and Natural Resources, Eamon Ryan, published a new, comprehensive Broadcasting Bill. Among other things, it enshrined in Irish law a commitment to shut off the old analogue service, a change that had been mandated by European legislation for 2012. In the spring of 2008, RTÉ shut down its AM radio service and by December of that year had introduced a digital radio DAB service. It was also announcing plans for both commercial digital and public-service terrestrial television (DTT) platforms to be rolled out the following year, in advance of the target date of 2012 for shutting down analogue transmission across the European Union. Admittedly, the tough recessionary economic conditions that took hold not long after this announcement would make that target look problematic.

However, even before the end of the first decade of the twenty-first century, digital technologies were transforming the ways in which Irish people listened to radio, and watched television. RTÉ had introduced its online service on May 24, 1996, streaming *The Late Late Show* live over the internet to mark the occasion; three years later, in 1999, it had launched its online news service, making its news-gathering resources available on the web. So, by the early years of the twenty-first century, its radio and television programmes were available on the web, not only as live streams, but, in the case of radio, as podcasts, to be downloaded and played at will, with no reference to the broadcast schedule. This in turn would increasingly change the sense of who constituted an Irish listenership, as the Irish diaspora, whether in Los Angeles or Sydney, could download the programme of an RTÉ broadcaster such as Gerry Ryan or Pat Kenny, and save it to listen to in the Antipodean morning.

Meanwhile, across the internet, on sites such as YouTube, individual men and women were archiving what would become an astonishing collection of audio-visual material, that could be accessed at any time, breaking the link not only between content and location, but between content and any kind of schedule of viewing or listening.

In some ways, it could be argued that RTÉ's slow adoption of the new broadcast technologies – even if it was not by design – created a point of apparent stability in a mediascape that was mutating rapidly. In 2004, the station re-stated its commitment to a public-service ethos, adapting it to the new multiplicity of Irish culture, pledging to 'strive to reflect fairly and equally the regional, cultural and political diversity of Ireland and its peoples'.[40] And, indeed, even as the number of available satellite channels grew almost beyond counting on the new digital platforms, RTÉ continued to hold on to its audience, as did the BBC in Northern Ireland. In March of 2008, for instance, RTÉ1 had a market share of 21.8 per cent (and RTÉ2 had a 9.6 per cent share) among households with cable or satellite; the biggest single market share of any non-Irish based station in the Republic was BBC1, with 5.9 per cent.[41] There are two ways of looking at this. One would be to say that collectively the seven Irish-based stations (RTÉ1, RTÉ2, TG4, TV3, the new commercial station Channel 6, along with UTV and BBC Northern Ireland) account for more than 55 per cent of Irish television viewing. The flip side of this is the recognition that almost half of Irish viewers were watching channels that originated outside of Ireland; in addition, roughly half of what is broadcast on RTÉ (and more in the cases of TV3 and Channel 6) continues to originate outside of the state.

In part, the ability of the established terrestrial broadcasters in Ireland to hold on to their audiences in the middle of the first decade of the twenty-first century may well have been a residual effect of the country's relatively underdeveloped communications infrastructure. In its annual report in the year 2000, the Information Society Commission noted that 'Ireland has been slow to move from high awareness to adoption of new technology.'[42] In the years that followed, this would change dramatically in the case of mobile-telephone ownership: only 23 per cent of the population used a mobile phone in 1996; by 2000 this had increased to

[40] *Public Service Broadcasting Charter* (Dublin, 2004), 2.
[41] AGB Neilsen Media Research, *Monthly Newsletter* (March 2008); www.agbneilsen.com; accessed April, 2008.
[42] *Third Report of the Information Society Commission* (Dublin, 2000), 1.2.

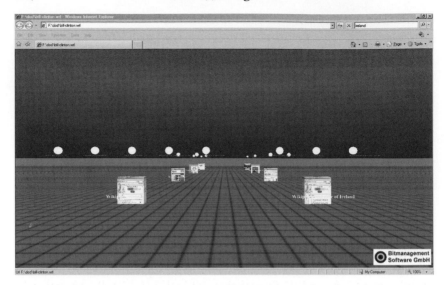

Illustration 13. This internet visualisation suggests a way of picturing the results when searching for the word 'Ireland' using the internet search engine Google. The programme that produced it allows the viewer to visualise the links from one page to the next; the balls on the horizon break down into individual pages as the viewer moves towards them.

62 per cent, and by 2008 it had exploded to 114 per cent – more than one for every man, woman and child in Ireland. Indeed, the extent to which Irish people were connecting with one another by the end of the first decade of the twenty-first century was phenomenal, with 25 million SMS (or text) messages sent every day within Ireland. Computer ownership peaked earlier; according to the 2002 Census figures, there were almost 830,000 personal computers in Ireland; by the first quarter of 2007, this had increased to just under 1 million. However, the biggest change – and one of the slowest areas to develop – was broadband access. As late as 2006, only 13 per cent of Irish households had broadband access, for a variety of reasons relating to ownership of the telecommunications market. However, this would increase to 31 per cent in 2007, and it appeared that further improvements were on the horizon (illustration 13).

In the middle decades of the twentieth century, before anyone kept league tables of globalisation, there was a sense that the Irish media muddled along somewhere in the bottom of the middle division. In relation to the broadcast media, radio and television, there was more often than not a feeling of belatedness, of joining a party that was bigger and brighter somewhere else. All of that changed in the first decade of the twenty-first century, and Ireland became an island of extremes: the most globalised, the biggest exporter of software, the most expensive and so on. Indeed, superlatives became the norm. Even when the Irish economy took a drastic downturn in 2008, responding to a large degree to recession in the United States and elsewhere, the rate of decline in Ireland was faster than in most other economies. While a different set of superlatives were needed, they remained superlatives, at least in part because Ireland's integration into a global economy remained so intense. Indeed, when the downturn in the Irish economy was first recognised as a recession in June of 2008, on a single day, the news was reported by just over 500 outlets around the world. This should remind us that while the Irish rush to immersion in a globalised media took place during a period of unprecedented economic growth in Ireland, economic growth was not purely the driver behind the media growth (nor was the opposite purely the case). Instead, it is arguable that the defining feature of Irish culture in the early twenty-first century is neither prosperity nor its opposite, but a deeply engrained, mediated connectedness between Ireland and the rest of the world. Projecting this twenty-first-century awareness backwards, we may find ourselves discarding this opposition between 'Ireland' and 'the world' (as if either were stable entities), replacing it with a concept of 'Ireland' as an idea, or a space, that, to differing extents and in differing ways, has been produced by media – from the first trickle of books of the sixteenth century, to the digital waves of the twenty-first century.

Conclusion: imagining a mediated Ireland

Ireland has been imagined in many ways: as a territory, as a state, as an economy and as a culture variously defined by language, literature or historical narrative. However, it is also possible to imagine Ireland in another way: as the confluence of information flows, as the nodal point around which books, newspapers, signals, sounds and images circulate.

To imagine Ireland in this way is to conjure up something far less stable than an island bounded by the sea, a set of political boundaries, or a culture with some kind of fixed core, however tenuously or strategically defined. By the same token, to think of Ireland in terms of media flows is not quite the same thing as saying that it is simply a market in which books or radio signals circulate, even though it is certainly true that almost all media exist within a market of some sort. Unlike cattle or soap, however, books, newspapers and radio broadcasts have content, and that content helps to formulate the ways in which it is possible to think about the state, the geography, the culture and, indeed, the economy in which that market operates. In other words, that which moulds and shapes the flow of information is created, at least in part, by that flow of information.

If the idea of Ireland as circulating media challenges the cultural notion of a 'real' Ireland, outside of (or prior to) mediation, so too does it exceed the territorial or political idea of Ireland, spilling messily over borders, whether they be drawn by statesmen or simply etched in the wet sand at the edge of the ocean. Even before books were being printed in Ireland, they were arriving in Irish ports, along with cloth and candles, primarily from England, although not exclusively so. By the time regular Irish newspapers were established in the first decade of the eighteenth century, not only were there books flowing in from outside (and, after the Copyright Act of 1709, flowing out of Ireland as well); there were also established streams of information, which were digested, written up and printed, initially in Dublin, but soon all over the island. As such, reports from Vienna, Amsterdam or Paris became part of an Irish public sphere, read, discussed and absorbed, even when they did not deal with the matter of Ireland *per se*.

For the next 150 years, information could only travel as fast as a person could carry it, whether by horse, ship or rail. Hence, geography mattered, and Ireland's location as an island on the western seaboard of Europe could often produce a sense of being the last to hear any news – of peripherality. All of that changed, however, with the telegraph. 'It is a triumph of science and energy over time and space ... pregnant with results beyond the conception of a finite mind', proclaimed Daniel Tiemann, the Mayor of New York, in one of the first telegrams sent over the first trans-Atlantic telegraph on August 23, 1858, to the Mayor of London – and duly reported in *The Nation* in Dublin, which received the text by its own telegraph service.[1] With the telegraph, Irish men and women first experienced the dizzying modern experience of distance freed from duration. That is to say, where distance was once a matter of how long it took news to travel, all points on the globe (at least, all those connected by telegraph) were now equidistant. In effect, with the telegraph, the place of Ireland in the world changed.

Calibrating that change can be a case of mapping more familiar historical narratives on to the history of the media in Ireland. For instance, the organisation that later became the Fenian movement was launched in Dublin on St Patrick's Day, 1858; less than five months later, in August 1858, the first trans-Atlantic telegraph cable was laid; later, the Fenians were at their most active on both sides of the Atlantic in 1866 and 1867, just as the first regular trans-Atlantic telegraph service came into being. To juxtapose these two sequences is not to say that the telegraph created the Fenian movement in any simple, technological-determinist, way. It is to say, however, that Irish nationalism in the 1860s would have had a different form were it not for the telegraph, which made it possible to imagine an Ireland of trans-Atlantic informational flows, woven from a simultaneous field that included New York and London as well as Dublin and Cork, no longer bounded by the geographical territory of the island.

Indeed, there is something telling in the fact that the same years at the end of the nineteenth century that saw the most concerted efforts to re-imagine Ireland – socially, politically and culturally – saw an unprecedented succession of new media technologies. In 1876, Alexander Graham Bell patented the telephone; in 1878, Thomas Edison patented the phonograph; by the early 1890s, it was possible to watch moving pictures; and in

---

[1] 'The Atlantic Telegraph', *The Nation* (August 28, 1858), 3.

1897, Marconi would patent a wireless telegraph – used for news reporting for the first time in the world the following year to relay reports of a yacht race from Kingstown (Dun Laoghaire) to Dublin. 'The present is an epoch of astounding activity in physical science', proclaimed the *Dublin Evening Mail,* reporting on Marconi's accomplishment. 'Progress is a thing of months and weeks, almost of days. The long lines of isolated ripples of past discovery seem to be blending into a mighty wave, on the crest of which one seems to discern some oncoming magnificent general-isation.'[2] None of these developments originated in Ireland; however, all would be used within Ireland, undoing and weaving yet again the media flow through which Irish people understood themselves, and their rela-tionship to others in the world. Without looking for any simple causal relationship, we need to at least acknowledge, for instance, that the Gaelic League was being formed just as the first phonographs and kinetoscopes were going on display; or that the manifesto of the Irish Literary Theatre of 1897 was written within months of the first Lumière films being shot in Ireland.

Indeed, it is at this moment in the 1890s that the limit point of thinking about Ireland in terms of media history comes most sharply into focus. This book began by acknowledging that there is an area into which a history of the media cannot venture: a parallel world of talk, of words spoken directly from one person to another (and this in turn blurs into other areas which are only partially mediated, such as manuscripts, particu-larly when they pass from hand to hand rather than being bought and sold). However, once we begin to publish or record dispatches from this unmediated Ireland, it disappears from view; the act of writing about it, or recording it effectively causes it to vanish. And yet, for reasons that may well go back to the original uses to which print was put in Ireland in the early seventeenth century, one of the most enduring ideas of Ireland would insist that the definitive form of Irish culture was to be found outside of the mediated world. This idea was particularly powerful in the 1890s, and the first decade of the twentieth century.

'Last night I went to a wide place on the Kiltartan road to listen to some Irish songs', wrote W.B. Yeats in a 1901 essay on folklore. 'The voices melted into the twilight, and were mixed into the trees, and when I thought of the words they too melted away, and were mixed with the generations of men. Now it was a phrase, now it was an attitude of mind,

---

[2] The reporter was quoting a speech by Prof. Lodge; in Michael Sexton, *Marconi: The Irish Connection* (Dublin, 2005), 45.

an emotional form, that had carried my memory to older verses, or even to forgotten mythologies.'[3] Two years later, in 1903, the piper James McAuliffe sat down to record some of the earliest wax cylinders of Irish traditional music. As his tunes were etched into the revolving cylinder, the music became detached from the two things that define the traditional: attachment to time and attachment to place. The effects of this are complex, and contradictory. In the first place, the music is preserved; however, at the same time, by making it possible for this hitherto unmediated experience of Irish culture to spread beyond 'the wide place on the Kiltartan road', a kind of dangerous excess is produced, threatening the integrity that the traditional once seemed to promise. Over time, as that which fully escapes the reach of the mediated world shrinks into smaller and smaller circles, the possibility of a pure, unmediated culture comes to seem more and more phantasmal.

In some respects, it is with radio that we see most clearly the way in which an idea of Ireland was both created and exceeded by a new medium. The Irish Free State came into being in the same years as radio. The first commercial station in the United States, KDKA, went on the air during the War of Independence; the BBC began broadcasting in 1922, just as the Civil War was beginning, and the major Irish stations – 2BE in Belfast and 2RN in Dublin – started up in 1924 and 1926, respectively. At the same time, the relationship between these two things – the establishment of an independent Irish state, partition and radio – is not simple. In the early years of radio, it was possible to tune in stations from all over the world. So, at the very moment in the early 1920s that two political states had come into being in defence of their respective integral cultures, homes all over Ireland were listening, for the first time in history, to voices from the United States, England and all over Europe. On the other hand, when public service radio was established, both in the Irish Free State and in Northern Ireland, it created two parallel imagined communities of the airwaves, as listeners from Letterkenny to Lismore could listen (at least in theory) to the same words spoken at the same moment, as could listeners from Bushmills to Banbridge. Regardless of the content of the broadcasts, these segegated experiences gave the idea of two distinct cultures a form and a reality – albeit a mediated reality. Something similar happened later in the century with television, although this time the voices from around the world were contained within the national broadcasts.

---

[3] W. B. Yeats, *The Celtic Twilight: Myth, Fantasy and Folklore* (1893; 1902; rpt Dorset, 1990), 119. [This essay is dated 1901.]

It may well be that we have only now reached the point at which we can begin to think about Ireland in terms of this kind of media history, and to begin to trace the ways in which this history maps on to other histories, political, cultural or economic. Marshall McLuhan once observed that 'each new technology creates an environment that is itself regarded as corrupt and degrading. Yet the new one turns its predecessor into an art form.'[4] If this is so, he suggests, it is only possible to see a given medium after it has been absorbed as the content of a new medium. It would now appear that one effect of the advent of digital media, which have taken all earlier forms of media as their content more rapidly and more voraciously than any previous technology, is to allow us to see those earlier media more clearly. Recordings, books, newspapers, pamphlets, films and television programmes now make up an electronic archive that is growing by the day. As all previous media thus become digital content, we can begin think about Ireland in a new way, as the nodal point of successive and overlapping forms of media, and we can begin to trace the outlines of this archival grid of overlapping media. As we do so, we need to remember that this grid, or network, does not simply exist at a given moment; it has a history, and it changes, moment by moment, in scope and coverage, throughout that history. Finally, as this historical grid comes into focus, we can also begin to see the places left empty by those things that it cannot contain, the unmediated; at that point, we can at least gesture towards that which is lost to history, but which we may still wish to claim for an imagined Ireland.

[4] Marshall McLuhan, *Understanding Media: The Extensions of Man* (New York, 1964), ix.

Bibliographic essay

The best short overview of Irish print culture is Vincent Kinane's *Brief History of Printing and Publishing in Ireland* (Dublin, 2002). For an authoritative summary of early Irish print culture, see Robert Welch's 'The Book in Ireland from the Tudor Re-conquest to the Battle of the Boyne' in *The Cambridge History of the Book in Britain*, Vol. IV: *1557–1695*, ed. John Barnard and D.F. McKenzie (Cambridge, 2002). Welch is the General Editor, along with Brian Walker, of *The Oxford History of the Irish Book*, which is projected to run to five volumes. At the time of writing, only Volume III had appeared, but it provides the foundation for any consideration of early Irish print culture: Raymond Gillespie and Andrew Hadfield (eds.) *The Oxford History of the Irish Book*, Vol. III: *The Irish Book in English 1550–1800* (Oxford, 2006). This volume builds on a long tradition of more specialised scholarship, including Mary Pollard, *Dublin's Trade in Books, 1550–1800* (Oxford, 1989), and her *Dictionary of Members of The Dublin Book Trade 1550–1800* (London, 2000). Pollard's *Dictionary* can be usefully read in conjunction with Robert Munter's *Dictionary of the Print Trade in Ireland, 1550–1775* (New York, 1988), and James W. Phillips, *Printing and Bookselling in Dublin, 1670–1800: A Bibliographic Enquiry* (Dublin, 1998). The work of Pollard, Phillips and Munter looks back in turn to the earlier foundational scholarship of E.R. McClintock Dix, particularly his *Printing in Dublin Prior to 1601* (Dublin, 1932). To move beyond the Dublin focus of much early print scholarship, see Séamus Ó Casaide, *A Typographical Gazetteer of Ireland: The Beginnings of Printing in Irish Towns* (Dublin, 1923). For the impact of print culture, the key book for the early period is Raymond Gillespie's *Reading Ireland: Print, Reading and Social Change in Early Modern Ireland* (Manchester, 2005).

For anyone interested in the books themselves, the *Early English Books Online* database contains about 100,000 of the 125,000 titles listed in

Pollard and Redgrave's *Short-Title Catalogue (1475–1640)* and Wing's *Short-Title Catalogue (1641–1700)*, as well as the Thomason Tracts (1640–1661), thus covering most of the material printed in Ireland prior to 1700. Less comprehensive but nonetheless larger is the *Eighteenth-Century Collections Online* database, which contains a further 150,000 books, pamphlets and other printed items prior to 1800. For a sense of how these books circulated, see Gerard Long (ed.), *Books beyond the Pale: Aspects of the Provincial Book Trade in Ireland before 1850* (Dublin, 1996). Few writers dealing with Ireland in the eighteenth century can resist the allure of the pamphlet culture of the period; however, for a particularly vigorous account, see: W.J. McCormack, *The Dublin Paper War of 1786–1788* (Dublin, 1993).

For the later eighteenth century and early nineteenth century, see Mary Daly and David Dickson (eds), *The Origins of Popular Literacy in Ireland* (Dublin, 1990), Niall Ó Ciosáin, *Print and Popular Culture in Ireland, 1750–1850* (Basingstoke, 1997) as well as J.R.R. Adams, *The Printed Word and the Common Man: Popular Culture in Ulster 1700–1900* (Belfast, 1987). Charles Benson carries earlier work on distribution through to the early nineteenth century in 'Printers and Booksellers in Dublin, 1800–1850', *Spreading the Word: The Distribution of Networks of Print, 1550–1850*, ed. Robin Myers and Michael Harris (Winchester, 1990). Although twentieth-century Irish book history has not attracted the same volume of research as the earlier period, a good starting point is: Clare Hutton (ed.), *The Irish Book in the Twentieth Century* (Dublin, 2004), while there is a lively history of the century's most influential book distributor, L.M. Cullen, *Eason & Son: A History* (Dublin, 1989). Given the importance of bilingualism (and more recently, multi-lingualism) in Irish culture, see also Michael Cronin, *Translating Ireland: Translation, Languages, Culture* (Cork, 1996).

A good readable overview of the Irish newspaper can be found in Hugh Oram's *The Newspaper Book: A History of Newspapers in Ireland, 1649–1983* (Dublin, 1983). The standard study of the early Irish newspaper is still Robert Munter's *The History of the Irish Newspaper: 1685–1760* (Cambridge, 1967), although it is worth supplementing this with Joad Raymond's *The Invention of the English Newspaper: English Newsbooks 1641–1649* (Oxford, 1996). It is also worth consulting a much earlier piece of scholarship, Richard Robert Madden's *History of Irish Periodical Literature* (London, 1867), which is a rich source of detail. For the early nineteenth-century newspaper culture, see Brian Inglis, *The Freedom of the Press in Ireland: 1784–1841* (London, 1954). The basis for more detailed work on the Irish press in all periods exists in the comprehensive list of Irish newspapers in the Newsplan project: James O'Toole and Sara Smyth, *Newsplan: Report of the Newsplan Project in Ireland,* 2nd edn (Dublin and London, 1998), also available as a database. For periodicals more generally, see Barbara Hayley and Enda McKay (eds), *300 Years of Irish Periodicals* (Dublin, 1987).

For a usefully detailed study of Irish newspaper culture in the nineteenth century (which includes a valuable appendix of nineteenth-century Irish provincial newspapers), see: Marie-Louise Legg, *The Irish Provincial Press, 1850–1892* (Dublin, 1999). There is no single study of twentieth-century Irish newspapers, although there have been studies of individual newspapers. Mark O'Brien has written two excellent studies of individual newspapers: *De Valera, Fianna Fáil and the 'Irish Press'* (Dublin, 2001), and *'The Irish Times': A History* (Dublin, 2008). More anecdotal, but also worth reading on the same papers are Ray Burke's *Press Delete: The Decline and Fall of 'The Irish Press'* (Blackrock, 2005), and Dermot James, *From the Margins to the Centre: A History of 'The Irish Times'* (Dublin, 2008). Irish journalists have seldom been shy about autobiographical writing, thus producing rich sources for media history. To pick only two, Andrew Dunlop's *Fifty Years of Irish Journalism* (Dublin, 1911) is rich in detail of the working life of a nineteenth-century journalist, while Conor Brady's *Up with the Times* (Dublin, 2005) provides a more recent sense of what it means to be a journalist in Ireland. However, increasingly the best source for newspaper history in Ireland are digital archives of the papers themselves. *The Irish Times* is fully searchable back to 1859, and at the time of writing the Irish Newspaper Archive database was just reaching critical mass, with about 500,000 issues of Irish papers, from the *Freeman's Journal* in 1763, to *The Nation* in the 1840s, as well as recent editions of regional and national newspapers, including the *Irish Independent.*

Although not specifically Irish in its focus, one of the best introductions to the media culture of the late nineteenth century is Paul Starr's *The Creation of the Media* (New York, 2004). More specifically Irish in focus is Edward Chandler, *Photography in Dublin During the Victorian Era* (Dublin, 1983), and Thomas F. Wall's privately published *Notes towards a History of Telecommunications in Ireland* (Dublin, 2005). In relation to cinema, Ruth Barton's *Irish National Cinema* (London, 2004) provides an insightful history, although the book that had been the standard work for many years still has much to recommend it: Kevin Rockett, Luke Gibbons and John Hill, *Cinema and Ireland* (New York, 1988). The most detailed study of the early period is Denis Condon's *Early Irish Cinema 1895–1921*

(Dublin, 2008). Barton's work is part of an upsurge in writing about Irish cinema that includes Lance Pettitt's *Screening Ireland* (Manchester, 2000), Harvey O'Brien's study of non-fiction films, *The Real Ireland: The Evolution of Ireland in Documentary Film* (Manchester, 2004), Ruth Barton and Harvey O'Brien (eds), *Keeping It Real: Irish Film and Television* (London, 2004) and John Hill, *Cinema and Northern Ireland: Film, Culture and Politics* (London, 2006). The scholarly bedrock of much of this work is Kevin Rockett's *The Irish Filmography: Fiction Films 1896–1996* (Dublin, 1996), which is being supplemented by a database project that will include non-fiction films.

Irish censorship has (perhaps ironically) developed its own extensive literature. The first major work was Michael Adams, *Censorship: The Irish Experience* (Tuscaloosa, AL, 1968), followed by Kieran Woodman's *Media Control In Ireland, 1923–1983* (Carbondale, IL, 1985), Donal Ó Drisceoil's *Censorship in Ireland, 1923–1945* (Cork, 1996) and Kevin Rockett's comprehensive *Irish Film Censorship* (Dublin, 2004), while the volume edited by Julia Carlson, *Banned in Ireland: Censorship and the Irish Writer* (London, 1990), usefully brings together a number of key texts.

For Irish media in the twentieth century more generally, particularly in terms of the politics of media, the definitive work is John Horgan's *Irish Media: A Critical History since 1922* (London and New York, 2001). There is a very detailed study of the origins of Irish radio: Richard Pine, *2RN and the Origins of Irish Radio* (Dublin, 2002), which can be supplemented with the same author's *Music and Broadcasting in Ireland* (Dublin, 2005). Also of use here is Paddy Clarke's earlier *'Dublin Calling': 2RN and the Birth of Irish Radio* (Dublin, 1986). For the technological background to the first broadcasts, see Michael Sexton, *Marconi: The Irish Connection* (Dublin, 2005). For television, there is a detailed political prehistory of Telefís Éireann in Robert J. Savage, *Irish Television: The Political and Social Origins* (Cork, 1996). For public affairs broadcasting more generally, the standard work is John Horgan, *Broadcasting and Public Life: RTÉ News and Current Affairs 1926–1997* (Dublin, 2004). Jonathan Bardon's *Beyond the Studio: A History of BBC Northern Ireland* (Belfast, 2000) provides a readable survey of the broadcasting culture that developed in Northern Ireland. However, it should be supplemented with Rex Cathcart's *The Most Contrary Region: The BBC in Northern Ireland, 1924–1984* (Belfast, 1984), and the collection edited by Martin McLoone, *Broadcasting in a Divided Community: Seventy Years of the BBC in Northern Ireland* (Belfast, 1996). Indeed, the media's role in the Northern Ireland conflict has generated a whole shelf of books; the quickest way into this debate is

Bill Rolston (ed.), *War and Words: The Northern Ireland Media Reader* (Belfast, 1996).

For Irish-language broadcasting, see Iarfhlaith Watson's *Broadcasting in Ireland: Minority Language, Radio, Television and Identity* (Dublin, 2003), while Helena Sheehan has traced Irish television drama through two volumes: *Irish Television Drama* (Dublin, 1987), and *The Continuing Story of Irish Television Drama: Tracking the Tiger* (Dublin, 2004). Also worth considering here is Martin McLoone (ed.), *Culture, Identity and Broadcasting in Ireland* (Belfast, 1991). Farrel Corcoran's *RTÉ and the Globalisation of Irish Television* (London, 2004) provides an informed insider's view of the politics of Irish television in the 1990s. The actual television and radio programmes themselves, on the other hand, are more difficult to access, although RTÉ and BBC Northern Ireland are both beginning to digitise their archives, and there is useful Irish material available on the extensive ITN digital archive. Although all of the relevant legislation on broadcasting is available through the websites of the respective governments (Irish, UK and European), particularly eloquent is *Active or Passive? Broadcasting in the Future Tense: Green Paper on Broadcasting* (Dublin, 1995). Finally, for a good overview of the internet history traced in Chapter 7, see Rob Kitchin, *Cyberspace: The World in the Wires* (London and New York, 1998); for a more recent overview of the information society debate in Ireland, see Lee Komito, *The Information Revolution and Ireland* (Dublin, 2004), while the state of play in the ongoing project of digitising Irish culture can be found in the website of the Digital Humanities Observatory, based in the Royal Irish Academy.

Index